THE NUCLEAR
POWER DEBATE

THE NUCLEAR POWER DEBATE

Issues and Choices

Scott Fenn

PRAEGER

PRAEGER SPECIAL STUDIES • PRAEGER SCIENTIFIC

Library of Congress Cataloging in Publication Data

Fenn, Scott.
  The nuclear power debate.

  1. Atomic power industry--United States.
2. Atomic power--United States--Security measures.
I. Title.
HD9698.U52F46   338.4'762148'0973   80-28065
ISBN 0-03-059074-4

Published in 1981 by Praeger Publishers
CBS Educational and Professional Publishing
A Division of CBS, Inc.
521 Fifth Avenue, New York, New York 10175 U.S.A.

© 1981 BY INVESTOR RESPONSIBILITY RESEARCH CENTER, INC.

Printed in the United States of America

Since 1974, the nuclear power industry has been beset by crippling uncertainties that severely limited its growth. Events in recent years tended to increase rather than diminish the problems afflicting the industry, and there seems to be little indication of an early reversal of a trend toward reducing the pace of nuclear expansion.

A major uncertainty plaguing the industry relates to public acceptance of nuclear power and popular concerns about the hazards of nuclear power plants. Public opposition to and concerns about nuclear power continue to grow. These concerns have brought a new temper to the debate over nuclear power by infusing discussion of technical and economic issues with questions of corporate social responsibility. It was through its interest in questions of corporate social responsibility and public policy that the Investor Responsibility Research Center (IRRC) first became involved in the study of nuclear power.

IRRC was founded in 1972 by a number of universities and foundations seeking impartial reporting on a variety of public policy and corporate social responsibility issues, particularly those issues being raised in shareholder resolutions at corporate annual meetings. The center now provides research reports to more than 150 institutional investors, including a number of banks, insurance companies and other commercial institutions, as well as to universities and foundations, on a variety of controversial issues relating to the role of business in society. In recent years, the center has prepared analytical reports on social issues ranging from energy conservation and equal employment opportunity to the labor practices of U.S. corporations in South Africa and overseas payments.

In 1974, at the request of its subscribers, IRRC undertook a major study of the issues involved in the debate over nuclear power. The study included a survey of consultant reports, government documents and hearings; interviews with a wide spectrum of proponents and opponents of nuclear power; and analysis of responses to a detailed questionnaire that IRRC sent to 82 companies involved in all phases of the nuclear industry. IRRC published its initial report and updated it extensively in 1976 to provide the basis for the first edition of *The Nuclear Power Debate* (Praeger Publishers, 1977). That edition was subsequently issued in Portuguese and Japanese language editions.

In 1979 and 1980, as events in the field of nuclear power continued to intensify debate over nuclear development, IRRC again updated *The Nuclear Power Debate*, resulting in the publication of this edition.

The Center's study was designed to provide readers with a basic understanding of the primary issues providing the substance of the debate over nuclear power. It was not meant to pass judgment on the costs and benefits of nuclear power, because both are uncertain and subject to change. The objective of the study was to identify the factors likely to affect the relative costs and benefits and to provide readers ·with a framework against which to measure the changing aspects of the debate.

ACKNOWLEDGEMENTS

The author gratefully acknowledges the unswerving support of IRRC and its executive director, Margaret Carroll, in the preparation of this book. Special thanks are also due to Desaix Myers III for providing the research and analysis that forms the foundation of this study and for inspiration and guidance; to Carolyn Mathiasen for nurturing my prose with thoughtful and precise editing; and to Shirley Carpenter, whose extensive assistance on all phases of the copy preparation of this study has truly been beyond the call of duty.

I am also grateful to a number of reviewers who were kind enough to comment on all or part of the book. I thank particularly Wayne A. Baker of Exxon Nuclear Co., Hugh D. Hexamer and Lynn R. Wallis of General Electric Co., Hugh Kendrick of the Department of Energy's Office of Nuclear Energy, Len R. Shasteen and Thomas E. Spink of the Tennessee Valley Authority, and David K. Storrs of Yale University's Investment Office for their detailed criticisms. Jan Beyea of the National Audubon Society, Charles Komanoff of Komanoff Energy Associates, R.J. McDevitt of Pacific Gas & Electric Co., A. David Rossin of Commonwealth Edison Co., Gordon Thompson of the Center for Energy and Environmental Studies at Princeton University, and Edward Walsh of Long Island Lighting Co. also provided valuable oral or written comments on a draft of the book.

Needless to say, the interpretation of the data and conclusions contained in this study are mine, as is the reponsibility for any errors.

S.F.

CONTENTS

LIST OF FIGURES AND TABLES

THE NUCLEAR POWER DEBATE

Chapter I

INTRODUCTION

Perhaps no issue will have a greater impact on the American way of life over the next several decades than the country's decisions on energy. These decisions--about the priority given to energy conservation efforts, about energy prices and about which energy sources to invest in--will have an enormous effect on the economy and our lifestyles.

As countries around the world have groped for solutions to their energy problems, development of nuclear power to generate electricity has often been touted as the best way to reduce dependence on foreign oil, as well as to ensure ultimately a limitless and economic supply of energy for the future. A growing number of countries have built nuclear plants or made plans to acquire them.

In the United States, however, nuclear power development has been stymied by economic, technical and political uncertainties. Opposition to continued nuclear power development has grown substantially in recent years, with critics questioning the need for more nuclear plants, their safety, the adequacy of plans for storing lethal nuclear wastes, the economics of nuclear-generated power, the implications of marketing nuclear technology for nuclear weapons proliferation, and the environmental and social implications of large, centralized energy systems. Increasingly, this opposition has been able to mobilize vocal popular support and interject the debate over nuclear power into political and regulatory arenas.

The issues raised by the debate over nuclear power development are of fundamental importance to investors and the nation for a number of reasons:

● Industry and government will allocate huge sums of money to energy-related projects in the years ahead. The perceptions and decisions of policy-makers and investors about the viability of alternative energy strategies will have important implications for the U.S. and world economies.

1

• The choice among competing energy sources will have a large and pervasive influence on people's lifestyles. Although many uncertainties remain concerning the social and environmental impacts associated with various energy systems, experts are increasingly able to delineate the nature of the risks each poses.

• Increased public concern about the problems associated with nuclear power has led to increased government intervention in decisions concerning its use. This trend is likely to continue and could have a significant impact on the operations, the profits and the prospects of the nuclear power industry.

• The electric utility industry is the largest single industry in the country in terms of invested capital, number of shareholders, and impact on U.S. capital markets. The financial situations of a number of utility companies are likely to be profoundly affected by decisions about nuclear power.

• Consumer and shareholder activism in this area is growing rapidly. Increasingly, questions relating to nuclear power development are being raised in political forums and at corporations' annual meetings. Individuals and institutions holding stock in companies in the nuclear industry will be called upon to make judgments about the financial and social responsibility of companies' policies.

This report examines the issues and ramifications of the debate over nuclear power development. This *Introduction* presents the historical background of the debate. *Chapter II* discusses the energy economy and nuclear power's role in it. *Chapter III* examines the economics of nuclear power in relation to alternative energy options, especially coal-fired power. *Chapter IV* discusses the U.S. government's past involvement in nuclear power development and the changing role that government institutions are playing in the nuclear power debate. *Chapter V* describes the domestic nuclear power industry and the changes it is undergoing. *Chapter VI* outlines the status of nuclear technology. *Chapter VII* examines the issue of nuclear plant safety and the risks presented by the use of nuclear power. *Chapter VIII* examines two major safeguards issues--weapons proliferation and waste disposal--associated with the use of nuclear fuel cycles. *Chapter IX* contains the author's analysis and conclusions.

HISTORICAL BACKGROUND

Initially, nuclear power's attractiveness was directly related to the recognition of electricity as perhaps the most versatile and convenient form of energy. Throughout this century, industrial and residential consumers have steadily shifted away from coal, oil and natural gas to electricity as a source of power. As demand for electricity has grown, so has interest in nuclear power. Energy consumption for the production of electricity currently accounts for 30 percent of total U.S. energy demand. By the year 2000, some energy analysts predict, electric power generation could account for 40 to 50 percent of all energy consumed in the United States.(1)

Until recently, there has been little question about the potential benefit to be derived from the development of nuclear power. Since the successful operation of the first nuclear reactor in the United States in 1959, scientists and officials of business and government have spoken optimistically of the peaceful use of the atom to create an inexhaustible source of cheap energy. Supporters of nuclear power estimated at one time that by the year 2000 the United States would have 1,000 nuclear plants, providing more than half the country's total requirements for electricity.(2)

This optimistic vision did not, however, win universal acceptance. Early nuclear critics tended to be dismissed as gadflies, but throughout the 1970s concern over nuclear power development has deepened and been taken more seriously. The concern is now shared by organized groups in both developed nuclear nations and developing countries that lack nuclear capacity. Concern has centered, however, in the United States. Proponents of nuclear power--government, industry and, to some extent, labor--have met increasingly strong opposition from a collection of interest groups, including consumer activists, environmentalists, some prominent scientists, a smattering of utility executives, some politicians, and Ralph Nader, who once suggested that "if people knew what the facts were and if they had to choose between nuclear reactors and candles, they would choose candles."(3)

As recently as the end of 1973, nuclear power appeared to be gaining a certain institutional momentum. Congress, the president and the Atomic Energy Commission (AEC), manufacturers of nuclear power plants, and many of the nation's investor-owned utilities were proceeding apace with the development of nuclear power. The momentum built as the nation recognized a critical need for fuels to serve as alternatives to oil, coal and natural gas. The imposition of the oil embargo by the Arab nations in October 1973 underscored this need.

Utilities perceived a declining availability of natural gas; with the increased price of foreign oil, the choice of what to burn in their power plants was limited to coal or nuclear fuel. Although coal is abundant, it is expensive to mine and dirty to burn. Utilities were concerned about air pollution regulations that affected their ability to use coal without substantial expenditure on devices to clean emissions. Furthermore, the nation's ability to produce coal had not improved rapidly. Several decades of debate over environmental regulations tied up vast chunks of strip-minable coal in the Western plains states.

Against this background, nuclear power was declared a critical part of the Federal Energy Administration's Project Independence, the blueprint to reduce dependence on fuels from other countries. Orders for nuclear plants grew from seven in 1969 to 41 in 1973.(4) In 1974, President Ford urged that utilities increase the number of nuclear plants from 55 in that year to 200 by 1980.

Since 1974, however, the momentum of nuclear power has

suffered from a series of technological, institutional, political and economic setbacks that have greatly reduced original projections about the share of electrical generation nuclear power can provide. In 1979, commercial nuclear reactors operating in the United States generated about 255 billion kilowatt-hours of electricity, accounting for about 11.5 percent of total U.S. electrical production.(5) While significant, this level of nuclear electric power production represented a decrease from 1978 levels and indicates that nuclear power's share of electrical generation is beginning to level off far below the 50-percent level once predicted. Current Energy Department fore-casts project that nuclear reactors will provide about 26 percent of all central-station electricity generated in the year 2000.(6)

Government officials projecting the development of nuclear power have lowered their estimates from 200 plants operating in 1980 to 197 units in 1995. Many observers consider even these projections to be overly optimistic. Since 1974, of more than 200 nuclear plants under construction or on order, 59 have been canceled outright or "removed from schedule."(7) In addition, more than 150 plants have suffered from delays of more than a year. Only four new orders for nuclear reactors were placed by utilities in 1975, three in 1976, four in 1977, two in 1978, and none in 1979 or 1980.

The decline in nuclear power development since 1974 is largely the result of a changed economic situation. Demand for electricity has been drastically affected by higher electricity prices resulting from the rise in coal, oil and uranium prices. A growing conservation ethic appears to have contributed to the moderation in electric power demand growth rates as well. Many utilities have suddenly found themselves burdened with substantial excess generating capacity or with plants under construction that may not be needed. At the same time, utilities' financing capabilities have been adversely affected by high interest rates and rapidly escalating construction costs. The result of these conditions has been an environment where utilities are reluctant to invest in any new generating capacity, but especially in new nuclear projects. A recent report by the International Con-sultative Group on Nuclear Energy emphasized the importance of these factors.

> Whereas growth of generating capacity historically led reliably to reduced average costs and increased profit-ability, for many utilities it now carries the threat of higher average costs and a lower return on investment. With its relatively high capital costs and proneness to long lead times, marginal cost increases have been particularly marked, and financially damaging, in the case of new nuclear plants. Furthermore, the combined unpredicta-bilities of demand growth, of capital costs and lead times of new plants, and of future relative prices of primary fuel inputs, have made it much more difficult to estimate, and therefore to minimize, future systems costs and avail-abilities. Confidence in investment plans has decreased as the risks and costs of making mistakes have increased.(8)

In addition to the changed economic situation, the pace of nuclear power development has been affected by changes in the political and regulatory environment. The momentum within the federal government that had initially spurred nuclear development has slowed. The Atomic Energy Commission, which had served since its inception as both promoter and regulator of nuclear power, was superseded in 1975 by two agencies with separate responsibilities--the Energy Research and Development Administration (ERDA) and the Nuclear Regulatory Commission (NRC). ERDA was subsequently incorporated into the Department of Energy where funding for nuclear projects, while still stressed, has met increasing competition from other energy sources. In Congress, the Joint Committee on Atomic Energy--which tended to be staunchly pro-nuclear--was abolished in 1977 and its duties were taken over by various other congressional committees that were as likely to question the merits of nuclear power as promote it. Finally, increasing public concern about the hazards associated with nuclear power has led to more and stricter regulation of the industry by federal, state and local authorities.

Opponents of nuclear power welcomed the slowdown in nuclear development as an opportunity to question the wisdom of the country's nuclear energy strategy. Beginning in 1975, a number of bills challenging nuclear power were introduced in state legislatures around the country. Several states enacted moratoriums on nuclear development because of concern over the waste disposal issue. In administrative hearings, in the courts, at utility stockholders' meetings, and at nuclear plant construction sites, citizen groups challenged utilities' plans to construct more nuclear plants. Opponents of nuclear power promised to make it a major political issue in the 1980 elections.

The year 1979 was a period of extreme turmoil for the domestic nuclear power industry. In January, the Nuclear Regulatory Commission publicly disavowed major portions of a reactor safety study that for years had been widely quoted by industry and government experts at plant hearings. In February, a White House interagency task force concluded that the federal government needed to step up its research and public information efforts in the area of low-level radiation and its connection to cancer. In March, a presidential special committee informed the Carter administration that the safety of high-level radioactive waste disposal could be determined only after extensive investigations at possible disposal sites--thus tacitly backing away from earlier government predictions that the waste problem could be handled with ease. On the same day, the NRC ordered five large nuclear plants to shut down because of inadequate protection against earthquakes. Although three of these plants were soon back in service, two of them were still out of service some 18 months later. Then, on March 28, while industry officials were still reacting against these earlier government moves with interviews criticizing "excessive government regulation" and "bureaucratic delays," the newly licensed Three Mile Island reactor in Pennsylvania suffered what is widely considered to be the worst nuclear power plant accident in the country's history. While the environmental and health consequences of the accident appear to be minimal, the political, economic and emotional shockwaves from the Three Mile Island incident are likely to affect the country's nuclear power program for years to come. Finally, the industry did not receive a single order from domestic utilities in 1979, although cancellations of reactors previously planned or on order continued apace.

As it entered the 1980s, the nuclear power industry in the United States faced growing public opposition, a loss of credibility, heightened concern and scrutiny from investors and financial institutions, a dearth of new business, stricter government regulation and a spate of congressional inquiries and legal proceedings. Many of the industry's critics pronounced it dead. Supporters of nuclear power, while confident that the industry would eventually recover from its setbacks, acknowledged that the industry was in serious financial trouble. One company official compared the industry to "a giant flywheel gradually slowing down when no new energy is added." He noted that "even if new orders start up again, it is going to take a while to show up for the industry."(9)

The fate of nuclear power in the United States appears to rest on how the nuclear manufacturers, utilities and government react to this new, more hostile, environment. Unless government begins to support the nuclear option more actively than it does now, the nuclear industry is likely to move slowly toward extinction. But with more active government support, the industry might regain what one industry official termed "a sense of predictability" and continue the development of nuclear power. In that case, the speed at which nuclear power will grow is dependent on a number of factors: the rate at which demand for electricity increases, the changing economics of alternative methods of energy production, the processes by which decisions affecting nuclear power development are made, and the degree to which public concerns about the safety of nuclear energy are satisfied.

CAVEATS

Four caveats to readers are in order. First, many of the elements in the debate about nuclear power involve highly technical questions, such as what constitutes an acceptable level of exposure to radiological emissions, on which scientists of apparently equal eminence take opposing positions. In these situations, the researcher and the reader alike are faced with the question of which expert to believe.

A related difficulty arises even when agreement is reached on technical questions. Then, the issue often becomes an assessment of the likelihood an event will occur, and what level of risk is acceptable. How safe is safe enough? To such questions, only subjective answers are possible.

Third, on many issues, experience with civilian nuclear power plants is too limited to allow definitive conclusions. On issues where the technology is new, the methods of analysis are recently developed, or the operating experience of plants is short, conclusions embody a significant degree of uncertainty.

Finally, no discussion about the merits of nuclear energy or any other energy source is really complete unless it makes extensive comparisons of various energy options. This report has attempted to discuss nuclear power in the context of possible alternatives. Nevertheless, the focus of this report is on nuclear power itself; on many issues discussion of both the problems and advantages of other energy options have been treated in much less depth.

Despite these difficulties, it is possible for people other than physicists or nuclear engineers to obtain a reasonable understanding of many of the issues surrounding nuclear energy. In fact, it is because of these difficulties that many people, including a growing number of scientists and technical experts, claim a decision on nuclear power should be reached only after there is time for debate in a political forum that would allow a balancing of technical judgments against less-technical social concerns.

NOTES

(1)   National Academy of Sciences, "U.S. Energy Supply Prospects to 2010," The Report of the Supply and Delivery Panel to the Committee on Nuclear and Alternative Energy Systems (Washington, D.C., National Academy of Sciences, 1979), p. 34.

(2) U.S. Atomic Energy Commission, "Nuclear Power Growth 1973-2000," Wash. 1139 (72) (Washington, D.C., U.S. Government Printing Office, Dec. 2, 1971), p. 1.

(3) Ralph Nader, testimony before the Commonwealth of Pennsylvania, Philadelphia, Aug. 14, 1973.

(4) Atomic Industrial Forum, "Nuclear Power Facts and Figures" (Washington, D.C., August 1978), p. 1.

(5) U.S. Department of Energy, "Monthly Energy Review," Energy Information Administration, June 1980, p. 66.

(6) U.S. Department of Energy, 1979 Annual Report to Congress (Washington, D.C., Energy Information Administration, 1980), Volume 3, p. 186.

(7) Atomic Industrial Forum, "Profile of U.S. Nuclear Power Development" (Washington, D.C., 1978), updated with cancellations through February 1980.

(8) Mans Lonnroth and William Walker, "The Viability of the Civil Nuclear Industry," working paper for the International Consultative Group on Nuclear Energy (New York, The Rockefeller Foundation, 1979), p. 30.

(9)   John R. Emshwiller, "Nuclear Industry Faces Bleak Future as Orders Get Increasingly Scarce," The Wall Street Journal, Feb. 8, 1979, p. 23.

Chapter II

THE ENERGY ECONOMY

The importance of nuclear power to the energy future of the United States and the world turns on two related questions: To what extent will the demand for electricity grow? And how much of any growth in demand should be met by development of nuclear power, how much of it could be stemmed by conservation, and how much of it could be met by development of alternative energy sources?

Both proponents and opponents of nuclear power tend to see some growth in electric power demand, at least in the short run. But they differ sharply on the size of the growth, on the extent to which growth could be slowed by conservation without severe detriment to the economy, and on the methods by which new growth can best be met. These questions are of critical importance in assessing the conflicting claims of the nuclear industry--that continued development of nuclear power is essential--and of many critics--that a moratorium on further nuclear power development is both feasible and desirable.

Predictions of future growth in electricity demand are important to discussion of nuclear power because it is generally acknowledged--even by opponents of nuclear power--that there are significant constraints on the amount of energy that can be supplied by fossil fuels (coal, oil and natural gas). Thus, if demand for electricity increases beyond certain limits, some of the increase will have to be met by other means, presumably including nuclear power. The smaller the growth in demand, the more flexibility there will be in the need for nuclear energy.

HOW MUCH DEMAND?

Just how much electricity the United States will need in the next few decades is a question of great controversy. In the past, steady growth in the demand for electricity has resulted from increasing population, declining electricity prices as a consequence of new and more effective technologies, and electricity's adaptability to a variety of uses. For more than a decade, until the oil embargo at the end of 1973, growth in demand had increased at a steady rate of around 7 percent annually. Future growth was easy to predict merely by extrapolation from past rates, and according to one utility finance officer, "All we needed was a good ruler."

Since the oil embargo, however, the electric utility industry has confronted a changed world. Rising oil prices, construction costs, and interest rates increased utility costs faster than revenues, forcing sharp rate increases. The higher rates and the oil embargo encouraged a "conservation ethic" which, with the aid of a prolonged recession, cut heavily into electricity sales. Instead of growing at the 7-percent rate anticipated by utilities, annual growth in electricity sales averaged only 2.3 percent from 1973 through 1976. Sales have rebounded somewhat since 1976, but not to "pre-crisis" levels. In 1977 they climbed 5.1 percent; in 1978 they rose 3.9 percent; and in 1979 they rose 2.7 percent.(1)

These sudden shifts in consumer demand introduced new problems into the already complex field of energy forecasting. Energy planners disagreed over whether the drop in demand growth should be interpreted as a temporary aberration or the beginning of a shift in long-term consumption patterns. Although differences of opinion remain on this issue, most utility executives and industry experts now agree that annual demand growth is not likely to return to the historical rate of 7 percent in the foreseeable future. Most utilities are currently predicting that annual demand increases will average about 3.5 percent for the country as a whole in the 1980s. The Department of Energy, in its 1979 annual report to Congress, forecasts that electricity sales will grow at a 3.2-percent annual rate through 1985.(2)

More important than this overall slowdown in electricity sales growth, however, has been an accompanying slowdown in peak demand growth, a major determinant of utilities' need for new generating capacity. Over the last several years, many utilities have overestimated the rate at which peak demand in their service area would grow. As a result, overall excess generating capacity for the industry as a whole climbed from 30 percent in 1977, to 34 percent in 1978 and 38 percent in 1979.

The problem of forecasting electricity demand is still largely unresolved. Past forecasts have tended to be weighted, "either consciously or unconsciously, on the basis of the prevailing conditions at the time of the forecast," according to C.A. Falcone, director of the Economic Regulatory Administration's Division of Power Supply and Reliability.(3) And although utility forecasting techniques have become more sophisticated--through use of computers to evaluate data on the economy, estimates of population growth, weather conditions, and other factors--utility officials concede that their forecasts remain highly uncertain. Ultimately, a forecast is only "as good as the assumptions that went into it"(4), notes Theodore J. Nagel, senior executive vice president of American Electric Power Co. "Forecasting in the electric utility industry has become an annual exercise in futility," laments *Electrical World,* an industry trade journal.(5)

One major element in the uncertainty surrounding utility fore-casting involves the degree to which demand is affected by price. Economists agree that recent utility rate increases will dampen the demand for electricity, but no one is sure how strong this effect will be. Studies over the last 15 years indicate a close relationship between price and demand in the long run--with long-run elasticity estimates between 0.6 and 1.3--but many analysts say that the relationship is far less important in the short run--0.1 over the next 10 years.(6) "We're in a very difficult situation," says W. Donham Crawford, chairman of Gulf States Utilities. "We don't have a handle on elasticity, the degree to which people are going to conserve."(7)

In addition to uncertainty over the degree to which higher rates will induce current electricity consumers to conserve, utility forecasters must guess about the extent to which utility-generated electricity will continue to be viewed as a preferred energy form by consumers, residential builders and industry and government planners. Electricity is an extremely versatile and convenient form of energy. In the past, these qualities--along with falling electricity prices--encouraged use of electric heating and cooling in new homes and led to a growing demand for electric power by industry. Most energy analysts expect this trend to continue. Exxon Corp., for instance, predicts that electricity use will continue to grow faster than total energy demand because of "continuing market penetration of appliances, installation of electric heating and cooking in new housing, and growing use of electricity in the commercial and industrial sectors."(8) A major study released by the National Academy of Sciences in 1979 agrees, stating that the "many advantages of electricity for the consumer--and the motivation to substitute it where practical for uncertain oil and gas supplies--are strong reasons for believing that it will continue to grow faster than total energy use for some time into the future."(9)

In recent years, however, this reasoning has been challenged by an alternative school of thought that holds that further electrification of the country's energy economy would be inefficient, uneconomic and socially divisive. These analysts, many of whom are associated with the environmental movement, argue that the United States already has enough electrical capacity to meet those needs for which this energy form is best suited--such as lighting and electric motors--into the next century. They say that electricity is a premium energy form that is inherently inefficient at tasks such as space and water heating. They also note that cogeneration of electricity and steam by industry is becoming more popular with industrial managers. Thus, these analysts contend, increased use of utility-generated electric power can only increase the amount of energy being wasted. In the words of physicist Amory Lovins, "two main policy paths for the rich countries are now rapidly diverging, and we must jump for one or the other. The first is high-energy, nuclear, centralized, electric; the second is lower-energy, fission-free, decentralized, less electrified, softer-technology based on energy income." According to Lovins, economic, technical and net-energy constraints "lead one irresistibly to conclude that the comparatively simple, low-technology, decentralized, non-electrical energy technologies make the most sense."(10)

In many respects, then, the debate over future electricity demand is part of a larger debate over alternative energy futures--the so-called "hard technology versus soft technology" debate. Energy analysts who anticipate continued high growth in energy consumption almost invariably stress the need to increase energy supplies, including making greater use of electricity to offset increasingly scarce oil and natural gas. Alternatively, those analysts who foresee lower energy growth trends tend to emphasize the role that conservation and renewable resources can play in meeting the country's energy needs. Future electricity demand--and thus the need for additional nuclear generating capacity--will be greatly affected by the outcome of the struggle between these two alternative energy paradigms for public policy dominance. Although the country is currently closer to the "high-energy, hard-technology" path, institutional support for the "low-energy, soft-technology" path appears to be growing. Consequently, long-term estimates of future electricity demand embody a high degree of uncertainty.

THE DEBATE OVER CONSERVATION

In April 1977 President Carter announced to the American people that the nation faced an energy crisis that he described as "the greatest challenge our country will face during our lifetimes," with the exception of preventing war. Unless profound changes were made to reduce oil consumption, he said, "we now believe that early in the 1980s the world will be demanding more oil than it can produce."(11) To meet this crisis, the President asked for a national effort--"the moral equivalent of war"--to bring the demand for energy into balance with available resources. Because U.S. capabilities to increase domestic production of oil appeared limited, the President's program called for the rapid development of alternative sources of energy. The "cornerstone" of his policy, however, was to be a reduction in demand through a national energy conservation program.

The Carter administration's decision to emphasize conservation--which has since been diluted by the administration's commitment to build a massive synthetic fuels industry--ran counter to the traditional American approach and has been the subject of great controversy. For years, the United States had dealt with predicted gaps between energy demand and production by developing new energy supplies, expanding current production and importing foreign oil, rather than by trying to hold down demand. Industry and business officials, among others, seemed to favor this supply-oriented approach and were concerned that an emphasis on conservation might lead to a reduction in efforts to expand production. A growing number of environmentalists and independent analysts, on the other hand, began to hail conservation as the easiest and most environmentally sound path toward energy self-sufficiency.

The administration's decision to emphasize conservation came in large part by default, because expanded production from conventional energy sources began to have economic, environmental or strategic costs that were deemed unacceptable. The Arab oil embargo of 1973 made clear the dangers of dependence on foreign oil, but recent years have seen little increase in domestic production. Domestic production of natural gas--despite growing evidence of huge untapped reserves at depths greater than 15,000 feet--continues to decline; production of coal--the one fuel that the United States indisputably has in abundance--has increased only slightly; and the development of nuclear power, plagued by economic, political and technical uncertainties, has proceeded at a pace far below earlier expectations. As a result, the United States is more dependent on imported oil today than it was at the time of the Arab oil embargo, and its increasing dependence is the cause of serious concern, among a number of nations, for economic as well as national security reasons.

Despite the apparent attractiveness of conservation under these circumstances, however, making conservation the cornerstone of national energy policy has also caused considerable concern among business officials, environmentalists and the public at large. Some economists have linked economic growth to growth in energy demand, and they argue that a drastic reduction in energy demand could lead to a recession, diminished productivity and growing unemployment. Many people in business share this view. They support limited conservation efforts but feel that expanded production is even more important. In addition, they are concerned that government efforts to encourage conservation may lead to interference with the market system and to mandatory energy efficiency standards that limit consumer product choice. Environmentalists are concerned that conservation may be interpreted only as increased reliance on abundant fuels--such as coal or uranium--that have potentially damaging environmental impacts. They also worry that in an effort to encourage conversion to these sources, government will relax environmental and safety standards. Finally, consumers are concerned that conservation could mean shortages, limits on life styles, and higher prices.

Although a great deal of controversy remains over the extent to which conservation can reduce energy demand, and over what impact such a reduction might have on standards of living, a number of recent studies support the view that conservation can reduce energy consumption significantly without undue adverse impact.

The House Government Operations Committee issued a report in April 1978 that concluded that "the United States could reduce its energy consumption by 40 percent or more, without adverse effects on industrial output or individual lifestyles and with the positive effects of increasing employment and reducing inflation and pollution."(12)

R.L. Ludman, director of the Electric Power Research Institute's planning staff, concluded in 1978 that "energy management technologies which are currently available and appear to be economic could reduce total U.S. fuel consumption by 28 to 46 percent by the year 2000, compared with an extrapolation of present usage patterns. About one-third of this savings, or 9 to 18 percent of total energy use, could be achieved by using electricity more efficiently ...."(13)

The Demand and Conservation Panel of the National Research Council's Committee on Nuclear and Alternative Energy Systems (CONAES) concluded in 1978 that "it will be technically feasible in 2010 to use roughly a total amount of energy as low as that used today and still provide a higher level of amenities, even with total population increasing 35 percent."(14)

In 1979, a six-year research study by Harvard Business School entitled *Energy Future: Report of the Energy Project at Harvard Business School* found that "further savings in energy consumption in the United States can be achieved without affecting predicted levels of economic growth. Indeed, mounting evidence strongly suggests that energy conservation is itself a form of productive investment, yielding much more rapid and substantial real changes in the energy balance of the nation than almost any given investments in energy production. Furthermore, it can actually stimulate employment, innovation and solidly based economic growth."(15)

Industry and administration officials agree that conservation can have an important impact on consumption, but they stress the limits of that impact. As James Roger, director of energy conservation at Raytheon Co., has put it, "you can lower the thermostat only so many times.... We're (Raytheon) in a situation now where we couldn't reduce our consumption any more."(16) Industry officials typically consider conservation to be a relatively minor part of an overall approach to energy and are afraid that hastily concocted government programs to promote conservation will prove costly and disruptive. They also expect energy price increases to lead to technological developments and discoveries of new sources of conventional fuels. Overall, industry officials tend to see conservation as a short-term phenomenon, with a limited impact on long-term energy consumption trends. Many are afraid that if too much reliance is placed on potentially over-optimistic claims about conservation, the risks of energy shortages will increase greatly. As A. David Rossin, system nuclear research engineer for Commonwealth Edison Co., wrote in a recent issue of *The Futurist:*

> Some studies suggest that if it can be done carefully and gradually, with conservation and introduction of energy-efficient equipment plus solar power and other alternatives, demand growth can be slowed without economic collapse. That is fine if the planners are accurate and society responds perfectly to the signals right on time. But there is no room in their scenarios for any surprises, like the OPEC embargo in 1973-74, the natural gas shortage in 1977, the coal strike of 1978, the winters of 1978 and 1979, or Iran. For when supply and demand don't stay in balance, unattractive things begin to happen.(17)

NUCLEAR POWER AND ELECTRICITY DEMAND

Energy forecasts demonstrate the interplay between the total demand for electricity and the role of nuclear power. Figure 1 shows estimates of primary energy consumption for electricity in 1985 and 2000. Nuclear power, under these projections, would increase from 2.8 quadrillion BTUs in 1979 to between 5.6 and 8.3 quadrillion BTUs in 1985. In the year 2000, as much as 31.0 quadrillion BTUs, or as little as 11.3 quadrillion, would be produced by nuclear power. If these estimates were converted to numbers of 1,000-megawatt nuclear plants, the range would be from 180 nuclear plants operating in the year 2000 under the Princeton Scenario to 494 plants operating under the Institute for Energy Analysis "high" projection.

While the plausibility of most of these forecasts with respect to nuclear power was jeopardized by events in 1979, they do serve to illustrate the connection between growth in electricity demand and growth in nuclear power. The most significant correlations in these forecasts are between growth in demand and growth in nuclear power. It is not suprising, therefore, that opponents of nuclear power tend to stress the need for energy conservation, and supporters of nuclear power typically argue that it is unrealistic to suppose that conservation can reduce demand sufficiently to avoid continued nuclear power development without severe damage to the economy.

In addition to illustrating the connection between growth in electricity demand and the role of nuclear power, the forecasts in Figure 1 indicate that government and industry planners have made significant downward revisions in recent years in their projections of electricity demand and installed nuclear capacity. It can be seen, for example, that the Princeton forecast for the year 2000--considered by most analysts to be implausibly low at the time it was made in 1976--is now much closer to the prevailing Department of Energy forecast than are the other forecasts shown. This trend toward lower demand forecasts is highlighted in Table 1, which shows Department of Energy and Edison Electric Institute forecasts from 1977 to 1980 for fuel consumption by electric power plants in the year 1985.(18)

TABLE 1

Forecasts of Total Primary Inputs for Electricity Generation in 1985

Department of Energy and Edison Electric Institute

Forecast Year	DOE	EEI
1977	-	35.9
1978	31.9	34.7
1979	31.8	33.0
1980	28.7	-

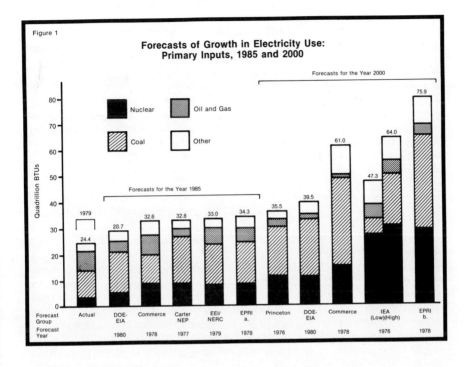

Figure 1

**Forecasts of Growth in Electricity Use:
Primary Inputs, 1985 and 2000**

Sources:

DOE-EIA: Department of Energy, Energy Information Adminis-
            tration, "Annual Report to Congress 1979," Volume 3,
            September 1979.

Commerce: U.S. Department of Commerce, "Preliminary Forecast of
            Likely U.S. Energy Consumption/Production Balances for
            1985 and 2000 by States," November 1978.

Carter NEP: Executive Office of the President, "The National Energy
            Plan," April 1977.

EPRI (a):   Electric Power Research Institute, "Supply 77," May 1978.
EPRI (b):   Electric Power Research Institute, "Research and
            Development Program Plan for 1979-1983," July 1978.

EEI/NERC: Edison Electric Institute/National Electric Reliability
            Council, "1979 Annual Electric Power Survey," April 1979.

Princeton: Frank von Hippel and Robert H. Williams, Center for
            Environmental Studies, Princeton University, testimony
            titled "Nuclear Energy Growth Projections," before the
            Nuclear Regulatory Commission Hearing Board, 1976.

IEA: Institute for Energy Analysis, "Economic and Environ-
            mental Implications of a U.S. Nuclear Moratorium
            1985-2010," September 1976.

VIEWS OF NUCLEAR POWER PROPONENTS

Supporters of expanded reliance on nuclear power make two general assertions: that growth in energy supply is essential to an improving standard of living, and that nonnuclear fuel sources are either in increasingly short supply or are for various reasons unacceptable to meet the demand for energy in the future. They predict a continuation in the shift to electricity from other forms of energy, and they see nuclear power as providing a virtually unlimited amount of energy--even as much as is assumed by higher-level projections--if regulatory and political problems can be resolved and constraints on needed material and trained manpower can be overcome.

Supply and Demand

Proponents assume, in varying degrees, steadily rising demand for energy. The demand for electricity will grow even faster, they say, because of the flexibility and attractiveness of electricity as a form of energy. Development of nuclear power, they believe, is critical to assuring an adequate supply of energy to meet that demand. And growth in energy supply, most of them assert, is an essential element in improving standards of living. Donald C. Burnham, a Westinghouse director, argues: "There is a wealth of data which substantiate the widely accepted contention that growth in energy usage and growth in the economy are inextricably linked." According to Burnham, reductions in demand could "result in substantial social upheaval, as well as economic stagnation."(19) Similarly, energy consultant Ralph E. Lapp has stated, "The fact is that GNP and GEC (Gross Energy Consumption) do march in lockstep with an association of about $17 billion (1972 dollars) per (quadrillion BTUs) of energy."(20)

Alternative Fuels

Supporters of nuclear power see no way to meet the country's growing energy demand without an expansion of nuclear power. "In the next few decades," Burnham contends, "we truly have no practical option than to shift from our present oil-gas energy economy to an electric economy based primarily on coal and nuclear."(21) Sen. J. Bennett Johnston (D-La.) agrees, flatly declaring that "if you're going to have a viable economy, you've simply got no choice but to have nuclear power."(22) They cite the decline in domestic oil and gas reserves and the rising cost of these fuels, the political and economic costs associated with oil imports, and the need to save fossil fuel for those uses for which there are no substitutes, such as the manufacturing of petrochemicals and plastics. They consider it imprudent--and potentially disastrous--to assume that new and untested technologies, such as solar-generated electricity, can be developed and commercialized on a timely basis. And although they concede that the country has abundant coal reserves, nuclear supporters believe that the economic, health and environmental costs associated with a greatly expanded use of coal make it a distinctly inferior alternative to nuclear power. A recent editorial in the *National Review* seems to sum up the sentiments of many nuclear power supporters: "The material well-being of our nation depends on the continued development of nuclear power .... We can continue then with nuclear power--or empty our pockets and dim the lights."(23)

Oil

The dependence of the United States on oil imports has increased dramatically over the last decade, and a growing portion of its oil imports has come from countries belonging to the Organization of Petroleum Exporting Countries (OPEC). In 1979, the United States imported about 46 percent of its total oil supplies; 67 percent of this imported oil came from OPEC sources, up from 48 percent at the time of the oil embargo in 1973-74.(24)

Proponents of nuclear power are concerned about this growing reliance on foreign oil and argue that by building more nuclear plants, the country could drastically reduce its dependence on imported oil. They also say that a shift to nuclear power would benefit the U.S. balance of payments situation. "In order to adequately assess the future of nuclear power," General Electric Co. told IRRC, one "must be cognizant of the fact that the heart of our energy dilemma is our growing dependence on foreign countries for almost one-half of the oil we use .... Increased use of electricity is and will continue to be the nation's best opportunity for near-term amelioration of dependency on oil imports." "The potential total savings using heat pumps and new coal and nuclear plants approaches 5 million barrels of oil per day, or an amount equal to that imported from the Mid-East," GE says.(25)

A recent Resources for the Future Study entitled *Energy in America's Future* appears to support these assertions, stating that "the importance of continued deployment of LWRS (light water reactors) is measured by the fact that even the minimum of 225,000 MW in nuclear generating capacity that is still projected for the year 2000 represents an enormous fossil fuel saving that is already being counted on--equivalent annually by then to about 80 percent of our 1978 oil imports or 90 percent of our 1978 coal production."(26)

Coal

Regarding the choice between nuclear power and coal, nuclear power is seen by its supporters as clearly the cheaper, the safer, the less damaging to the environment, and potentially the more plentiful in the long run. "In planning for the future," states Pacific Gas and Electric Co.'s 1978 annual report, "we see additional nuclear power as a proven, environmentally superior and economic way to meet growing electric demand...."(27)

Industry officials cite the dangers from mining coal--more than 100,000 coal miners have died since 1900, according to Ralph Lapp(28)--and from burning it. According to Bernard Cohen, professor of physics at the University of Pittsburgh, nuclear power is "environmentally far, far superior. The estimates of how much less harmful to health nuclear power is than coal," Cohen said, "vary from factors of a thousand or more, according to government estimates, down to factors of 10, according to the estimates given by the severest nuclear critics."(29)

Nuclear supporters note that there is a large and growing body of evidence--from sources not connected with the nuclear industry--that the routine health and environmental hazards associated with coal are greater than those of nuclear power. "The immediate health costs of nuclear power appear to be as low or lower than that of any other near-term fuel cycle," said a resolution adopted by the Governing Council of the American Public Health Association in 1978.(30) A study by William Ramsay, a Fellow in the Center for Energy Policy Research at Resources for the Future, concludes that the "the goal of preserving health--expressed in terms of routine health impacts and of the annualized health impacts from disasters that can be calculated--favors the nuclear option."(31) Ramsay adds that "for routine--that is, noncatastrophic--environmental concerns, the negative environmental impacts of coal are larger than those of nuclear."(32)

Utility managers and others also question whether sufficient amounts of coal can be made available on an assured basis. They say that the possibility of expanding coal production is limited. They point out that there has been little increase in the annual tonnage of coal mined in the last decade and that coal production has actually fallen in some years due to prolonged labor strikes. For coal to replace uranium by the year 2000, according to some observers, would require production of more than 2 billion tons a year, the equivalent of 100,000 railroad cars every day. Many people consider such growth unlikely. "For all practical purposes," says Kenneth Davis of Bechtel Corp., "the mining of coal has been essentially constant for the last 60 or more years. Coal still faces significant constraints on growth...."(33)

Perhaps the greatest impediment that utilities see to increased used of coal is more government regulation. In interviews with IRRC in 1980, utility planners were unanimous in the conviction that stricter government regulation would soon be driving up costs at coal-fired plants. "Coal plants may be about to go through the same type of heavy regulation that has hampered nuclear in recent years," a spokesman for Long Island Lighting Co. said.(34) "We expect a very real impact on the cost of coal plants from past and future regulations," a TVA representative stated. "EPA will probably have to tighten up the small particulate regulations, fly ash disposal costs could run from $10 to $100 a ton, and who knows what effect acid rain regulations might have."(35)

Renewable Resources

Nuclear power supporters tend to be extremely skeptical that any of the new electric power sources currently under development--including nuclear fusion, photovoltaic electricity, wind power, geothermal energy, and energy from temperature differences in the ocean--will be available in significant quantities before the year 2000. Moreover, they argue that such sources may prove uneconomic even when they do become available. Bernard Cohen, for instance, states that it is "very uncertain whether we'll ever use solar energy on any large scale for electric power generation. It seems almost impossible that it could ever become economically competitive with coal or nuclear energy."(36) Most nuclear power supporters do not oppose increased use of renewable energy sources. In fact, they typically argue that the United States should attempt to develop all possible energy sources. But nuclear advocates typically believe that nuclear technologies should be given priority over new technologies because the nuclear technologies are ready to use today whereas many of the new technologies will not be capable of making a significant contribution to energy supplies for several decades.

VIEWS OF NUCLEAR POWER OPPONENTS

Nuclear opponents range from those who urge a slowdown of nuclear power development to those who urge the shutdown of existing nuclear plants and a moratorium on further construction. In general, opponents assert that the country's top energy priorities should be conservation and the development of clean, renewable, nonnuclear technologies--especially solar energy.

Supply and Demand

Most critics contend that conservation--which they define as increases in energy efficiency--can reduce energy demand growth to levels that can be met without additional nuclear power development. They feel that energy growth should not be looked at as something society needs, per se, but rather as a means to certain social ends. As Amory Lovins puts it, "the basic tenet of high-energy projections is that the more energy we use, the better off we are. But how much energy we use to accomplish our social goals could instead be considered a measure less of our success than of our failure...."(37) Critics say that a reduction in demand will have tangible benefits on national productivity, inflation and unemployment. In support of this conclusion, they cite the rapidly growing number of studies--such as the CONAES and Harvard Business School projects mentioned earlier in this chapter--that endorse conservation as perhaps the country's greatest near-term energy resource.

Overdependence on Nuclear Power

Many nuclear critics assert that even if major increases in energy supplies are needed, nuclear power can never provide a substitute for fossil fuels, that it cannot be developed at the rates its proponents project, and that other technologies could more easily fill any gap between energy supplies and demand. "Nuclear power is physically unable to provide timely and significant substitution for oil," claims Lovins. "Nuclear power supplies a special and very expensive form of energy, while most needs are for much lower-quality and cheaper forms," says Lovins. "The maximum potential role for nuclear power, ignoring all constraints except those of elementary economics, is providing baseload electricity for electricity-specific applications...amounting to about 4 percent of all end-use energy and up to about 10 percent of all primary energy."[38] A recent article in *Fortune* magazine agrees, stating, "The notion that fewer reactors will mean more oil imports is a myth.... Petroleum has been too costly to burn in new generating plants since that first big OPEC price rise in 1973-74. Moreover, the government last November imposed a ban on such construction."[39]

Nuclear critics are also extremely concerned that by concentrating the bulk of its energy research and development efforts over the past two decades on nuclear power, the government has foreclosed superior energy options and given institutional momentum to a loser.

Critics also argue that projections of the rate at which nuclear power will expand have been and continue to be unduly optimistic. Many critics argue that the industry was dying even before Three Mile Island and that the accident can only hasten its demise. In the opinion of Barry Commoner, "The accident at Three Mile Island dooms nuclear power as an economically viable industry .... Nuclear power is being priced right out of the market. It makes no sense to continue it. What we've got to do is phase it out without going into blackouts, and we can do that."[40]

Alternative Fuels

Critics view the energy problem primarily as one of tiding the country over for a period of perhaps 10 to 30 years during the transition to a nonnuclear society. They believe that renewable energy sources are economic in many parts of the country today and could totally replace the energy provided by nuclear power on a national scale in the near future.

Opponents of nuclear power diverge on exactly which technologies should be used during the transition period to a solar society. Some assert that coal can fill any unmet energy needs, providing that the health and environmental costs of a coal-based energy cycle are minimized through increased attention to mine safety, reclamation of strip-mined lands and the utilization of a variety of technologies--including fluidized bed combustion and advanced emissions control systems--to minimize air pollution. Others extol the virtues of cogeneration--the simultaneous production of electricity and steam--and predict that the widespread use of industrial and commercial cogeneration systems could more than compensate for the shutdown of the country's nuclear plants. Still others believe that natural gas is the fuel that will be used in the transition. According to Commoner:

The bridging fuel, the current-non-renewable fuel that will carry us efficiently into the solar system is natural gas. Not electricity, not coal, not uranium, not oil but natural gas. If we begin to expand the use of natural gas, we can begin to introduce solar energy in a thrifty way.

Next year you could get some methane from, let's say, Ozark timber, and another year you could introduce methane into the pipeline from sugar cane residues in Louisiana. In that way you could gradually put solar methane into the natural gas pipeline....

You can get heat and electricity very easily from natural gas by putting the gas into a cogenerator.... The heat that normally gets thrown away then gets recaptured to be used for heating the house, the electricity for providing electricity.

Now you can add solar collectors to replace the heat and photovoltaic cells to replace the electricity,...cutting back on the use of methane, and meanwhile you're taking your methane from solar sources. That's a transition.(41)

NOTES

(1) U.S. Department of Energy, "Monthly Energy Review," Energy Information Administration, June 1980, p. 59.

(2) U.S. Department of Energy, *1979 Annual Report to Congress* (Washington, D.C., Energy Information Administration, 1980), Volume 3, p. 105.

(3) C.A. Falcone, "Electric Energy Technology Forecast," a paper prepared by the Energy Forecasting Group of the Institute of Electrical and Electronics Engineers, January 1975, p. 2.

(4) Georgette Jasen, "Utilities Delay, Cancel Generating Plants as Electricity Growth Continues to Slump," *The Wall Street Journal*, Feb. 7, 1979, p. 42.

(5) Quoted in Alden Meyer, "Peak Growth Collapses," *The Power Line*, Volume 5, No. 5, p. 1.

(6) Frost and Sullivan Inc., *Fossil Fuel Electric Generating Station Requirements, 1976-1985* (New York, 1976), p. 15 ff.

(7) Jasen, op. cit.

(8) Exxon Corp., "World Energy Outlook," April 1978, p. 18.

(9) National Academy of Sciences, "U.S. Energy Supply Prospects to 2010," The Report of the Supply and Delivery Panel to the Committee on Nuclear and Alternative Energy Systems (Washington, D.C., National Academy of Sciences, 1979), p. 34.

(10) Amory B. Lovins, *Non-Nuclear Futures: The Case for an Ethical Energy Strategy* (London, Friends of the Earth, 1975), p. xxvii.

(11) Text of President Carter's televised address to the nation, April 18, 1977, *Congressional Quarterly Weekly Report*, April 23, 1977, p. 753.

(12) "Nuclear Power Costs," Twenty-Third Report by the Committee on Government Operations, HR No. 95-1090 (Washington, D.C., U.S. Government Printing Office, 1978), p. 65.

(13) R.L. Rudman, "Practical Savings Achievable with Efficient Energy Use," in Craig B. Smith, ed., *Efficient Electricity Use: A Reference Book on Energy Management for Engineers, Architects, Planners and Managers* (New York, Pergamon Press, 1978), p. 3.

(14) "U.S. Energy Demand: Some Low Energy Futures," Demand and Conservation Panel of the Committee on Nuclear and Alternative Energy Systems, *Science*, Vol. 200, April 14, 1978, p. 151.

(15) Robert Stobaugh and Daniel Yergin, "After the Second Shock: Pragmatic Energy Strategies," *Foreign Affairs*, Spring 1979, p. 864.

(16) Alexander Reese, "Does Industry Really Want to Conserve Energy," *Business and Society Review*, Spring 1978, No. 25, p. 65. (For a summary of industry attitudes and practices regarding conservation, see *Energy Conservation by Industry*, Investor Responsibility Research Center, January 1979.)

(17) A. David Rossin, "The Soft Path: Where Does It Really Lead?," *The Futurist*, June 1980, p. 61.

(18) Department of Energy forecasts are "mid-case" forecasts from the Energy Information Administration's 1977, 1978 and 1979 *Annual Report to Congress*. Edison Electric Institute forecasts are from the Institute's 1977, 1978 and 1979 *Annual Electric Power Survey*.

(19) Comments of Donald C. Burnham, Energy Policy Project of the Ford Foundation, *A Time To Choose* (Cambridge, Mass., Balinger Publishing Co., 1974), p. 367.

(20) Letter dated Dec. 22, 1976, from Dr. Ralph E. Lapp to Sen. Gaylord Nelson, "Alternative Long-Range Energy Strategies," Joint Hearing before the Select Committee on Small Business and the Committee on Interior and Insular Affairs, U.S. Senate, 94-47

(Washington, D.C., U.S. Government Printing Office, Dec. 9, 1976), p. 514.

(21) Burnham, op. cit., p. 366.

(22) Walter S. Mossberg, "Harrisburg Accident Poses Threat to Future of U.S. Nuclear Power," *The Wall Street Journal*, April 2, 1979, p. 30.

(23) *National Review*, Feb. 2, 1979, p. 132.

(24) U.S. Department of Energy, "Monthly Energy Review," Energy Information Administration, June 1980, pp. 26 and 28.

(25) General Electric Co., Nuclear Energy Group, Comments to Investor Responsibility Research Center, August 1980.

(26) Sam Schurr et al., *Energy in America's Future: The Choices Before Us*, Resources for the Future (Baltimore, Md., Johns Hopkins University Press, 1979), p. 59.

(27) "Pacific Gas and Electric Co. 1978 Annual Report," p. 8.

(28) Ralph Lapp, "Nuclear Salvation or Nuclear Folly," The New York *Times Magazine*, Feb. 10, 1974, p. 73.

(29) Bernard L. Cohen, "Understanding a Trillion-Dollar Question," *National Review*, Feb. 2, 1979, p. 153.

(30) Atomic Industrial Forum, INFO press release No. 96, November 1978, p. 4.

(31) William Ramsay, *Unpaid Costs of Electrical Energy: Health and Environmental Impacts from Coal and Nuclear Power*, Resources for the Future (Baltimore, Md., Johns Hopkins University Press, 1979), p. 161.

(32) Ibid., p. 162.

(33) W. Kenneth Davis, *Hearings on Proposition 15*, Vol. II, California State Assembly, Dec. 10, 1975, p. 79.

(34) Interview with Long Island Lighting Co., August 1980.

(35) Interview with Thomas E. Spink and Len R. Shasteen, Tennessee Valley Authority, August 1980.

(36) Cohen, op. cit., p. 154.

(37) Amory B. Lovins, *Soft Energy Paths: Toward a Durable Peace* (Cambridge, Mass., Friends of the Earth, 1977), p. 4.

(38) "Environmentalists Say Nuclear Power Cannot Reduce Dependence on Petroleum," *Energy Users Report*, July 12, 1979, No. 309, p. 27.

(39) Edmund Faltermayer, "Nuclear Power After Three Mile Island," *Fortune*, May 7, 1979, p. 118.

(40) Barry Commoner, "Fueling a Third Party," *In These Times*, May 30-June 5, 1979, p. 13.

(41) Ibid., p. 12.

Chapter III

THE ECONOMICS OF NUCLEAR POWER

The continued development of nuclear power in the United States will depend largely on the extent to which nuclear-generated power is economically competitive with other electric power generation systems, particularly coal-fired power plants. Factors such as the capacity at which plants are able to operate and the cost and efficiency of equipment required to meet safety and environmental regulations will play an important role in determining the relative competitiveness of coal and nuclear power plants. Meanwhile, there is increasing evidence that, at least in some parts of the country, alternative generating sources--geothermal energy, cogeneration, low-head hydroelectric facilities and others--will soon be competing with both coal and nuclear power for a share of new generating capacity. All in all, there is widespread debate over the relative economics of nuclear, coal and other generating systems. Predicting the costs of energy generation is fraught with both technical and political uncertainties.

Supporters of nuclear power argue that it provides considerable savings to consumers. The Atomic Industrial Forum says its survey of utilities in 1978 demonstrated that nuclear power remains the lowest-cost producer of electricity. Nuclear plant operation during 1978, the forum maintains, resulted in savings of more than $3 billion and "offset consumption of the equivalent of 135 million tons of coal, or 2.9 trillion cubic feet of natural gas, or 470 million barrels of oil."(1) Customers at Baltimore Gas and Electric saved $188.1 million by having electricity generated by nuclear rather than coal and oil-fired power plants, according to the forum's figures.

Proponents concede that the economic advantage held by nuclear plants has narrowed in recent years, but they say that nuclear power will continue to hold a cost advantage over alternative fuel sources in the future. An analysis by Sargent & Lundy Engineers in February 1979, for instance, found that a 1,100-megawatt nuclear plant going into operation in 1990 would generate electricity for 13 percent less than the least expensive coal alternative.(2) Even staunch supporters of nuclear power, however, admit that if too many new government safety regulations result from the aftermath of Three Mile Island, coal could become cheaper. "Candidly, it wouldn't take very much of an increase to turn the economics of nuclear power around," says Lewis J. Perl, a vice president of National Economic Research Associates and a long-time supporter of nuclear power. "The economics of coal and nuclear are close enough that if the safety factors alone now shifted by an order of magnitude, we'd all certainly change our view that nuclear is cheaper."(3)

Critics increasingly dismiss as unfounded the claims that nuclear power is cheaper than the alternatives. They say that nuclear plants appeared to be cheaper in the past only because of huge government subsidies and because many of the true costs associated with the nuclear fuel cycle--such as the costs associated with permanent waste disposal and reactor decommissioning--never appeared on utility ledgers. Donald Cook, former chairman of American Electric Power Corp., believes that "an erroneous conception of the economics of nuclear power" sent U.S. utilities "down the wrong road." According to Cook, "the economics that were projected but never material-ized--and never will materialize--looked so good that companies couldn't resist it."(4)

Critics argue that the claims made by nuclear power enthusiasts are exaggerated or misleading. They say that many past estimates of nuclear power costs have looked only at fuel costs--where nuclear plants hold an indisputable advantage--and have failed to take into consideration the much higher capital costs of constructing nuclear plants. They also contend that many comparisons of nuclear and coal costs have been skewed in favor of the nuclear option by failure to account properly for the effects of "turnkey units"--early nuclear plants sold to utilities for less than it cost manufacturers to build them. Include these factors and remove the government subsidies, critics say, and nuclear power would no longer appear economical.

Even if nuclear power was competitive in the past, nuclear opponents contend, it will not be in the future. According to energy consultant Charles Komanoff, the effects of inflation and new regulatory requirements have had a far greater impact on nuclear plants than on coal plants over the past decade, causing the average ratio of nuclear to coal plant capital costs to increase from 1.05 in 1971 to 1.52 in 1978. "If past relationships between sector expansion and regulatory stringency continue," Komanoff concludes, "nuclear plants will cost at least 75 percent more to build (per kilowatt) than coal plants incorporating advanced pollution controls in the late 1980s."(5) Thus, the total generating cost of nuclear plants now starting construction is likely to exceed that of new coal plants by an average of 25 percent, Komanoff argues.

ELECTRIC POWER COSTS

The total cost of electricity as it leaves the power station, referred to as the busbar cost because it includes all costs incurred up to the transfer of power to the distribution system at a generating-station switch known as the busbar, is the product of several factors: (a) the construction cost of the plant, including hardware, labor, the original capital borrowed and the interest on that capital, and inflation on capital costs; (b) the cost of operating, maintaining and decommissioning the plant; (c) the cost--usually reflected under capital, operation and maintenance, or fuels costs--of meeting environmental and safety standards; and (d) the cost of the fuel itself. A recent analysis by the Department of Energy's Office of Nuclear Reactor Programs concluded that the cost of electricity from investor-owned nuclear and coal plants of similar size was about equal in 1979--with nuclear plant costs averaging 22.20 mills per kilowatt-hour versus 22.52 mills per kilowatt-hour for coal plants.(6)

The Department of Energy's Energy Information Administration estimates the per-kilowatt cost of electricity generated from nuclear, coal and oil plants in the Midwest in 1990 as shown in Figure 2.(7) As the graph shows, capital costs constitute a larger portion of total generating costs at a nuclear plant than they do at fossil fuel plants. Nuclear fuel, on the other hand, is far less costly per unit of delivered electricity than coal or oil. Thus, savings in fuel costs may enable a nuclear plant to compensate for more than its initial high capital costs, providing that the plant is able to operate efficiently as a baseload plant over an extended period of time. Frequent breakdowns, however, or extended outages for environmental or safety reasons can turn a nuclear plant into the most expensive form of electric power generation available.

In the final analysis, then, a critical determinant of busbar costs is the efficiency at which a plant is able to operate. Estimates of generating costs assume operation of a plant for a certain number of years--usually 30--at an estimated capacity level--60 to 80 percent. These assumptions, however, have been made from an extremely limited data base. The operating history of large nuclear and coal-fired plants is short. Of the 72 nuclear reactors with operating licenses in October 1980, only 12 were 1,000 megawatts or larger, and their combined operating history covered only about 50 reactor-years.(8) This small sample can be influenced strongly by the good or bad performance of just one plant. Therefore, because most of the nuclear plants currently under construction are larger than 1,000 megawatts in size, the available data must be viewed as embodying a high degree of uncertainty and may present too optimistic or too pessimistic a preview of what will occur in the future.

The following sections of this chapter outline the various component costs of power and compare the factors affecting these costs at coal and nuclear power plants. A detailed discussion of costs is limited to coal and nuclear power because the cost of generating

FIGURE 2

Electricity Cost, Midwest, 1990

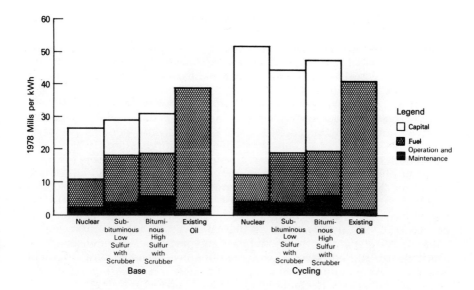

Source: Department of Energy, Energy Information Administration.

electricity by burning oil is much higher than the costs of producing energy from these two sources (and the U.S. government has prohibited construction of new baseload oil and gas-fired plants) and because cost estimates for many alternative sources remain conjectural. Limiting discussion here to a comparison of coal and nuclear power, however, is not meant to imply that alternative sources of generation will be uneconomic in the foreseeable future. In fact, the use of non-conventional energy technologies to generate electric power--both at utility central-station plants and in small, decentralized applications--is increasing. Geothermal plants in the Geysers area of northern California, small-scale hydroelectric plants in New England and many industrial cogeneration projects already provide power at a cost significantly below that of new nuclear or coal-fired capacity. While the rate at which these technologies will achieve significant market penetration is highly debatable, there is little doubt that some of them will be making major contributions by the year 2000. The Department of Energy's most recent forecast, for instance, predicts that renewable technologies alone will contribute 13 percent of total electricity generation by the year 2000--an amount of energy equal to almost twice the total output of the country's nuclear plants in 1979.(9)

CAPITAL COSTS

One official of the Atomic Industrial Forum has noted that "estimating capital costs for power plants is like shooting at a moving target." The difficulty of the task is illustrated by Figure 3. It compares various government estimates made between 1967 and 1978 of the cost of building 1,000-megawatt nuclear and coal-fired plants.

Figure 3 shows that while estimates of capital costs for both nuclear and coal plants have risen sharply since 1967, those for nuclear plants have risen somewhat faster. According to Charles Komanoff, from 1971 to 1978 the capital costs of a standard nuclear plant increased at a rate of 13.5 percent annually (in constant 1979 steam-plant dollars) compared to a 7.7-percent annual increase for coal plants.(10) It is also clear from Figure 3 that the majority of the escalation in capital costs for both nuclear and coal plants has been due to factors other than direct construction costs. According to the Department of Energy, the "increasing cost trend of nuclear units is attributable to such factors as increased design complexity, inadequate quality control in manufacturing and in field construction, shortage of skilled labor, added environmental equipment to meet newly established, more stringent environmental and safety standards, and escalating costs of equipment, materials and wages."(11)

While estimates of nuclear and coal plant capital costs have risen steadily, actual nuclear capital costs have been consistently well above these estimates. The estimates in Figure 3, for instance, predict that nuclear units beginning commercial operation in 1981 could be expected to cost about $500 per kilowatt of capacity. In actuality, nuclear units entering commercial service in the period 1977 through 1979 did so at an average cost of about $750 per kilowatt.(12) Moreover, nuclear plants entering service in 1981 can be expected to have considerably higher costs because they will be more severely affected by design changes resulting from the accident at Three Mile Island.

Both proponents and opponents of nuclear power development agree that over the last decade nuclear capital costs have risen at a faster rate than those for coal plants. A critical issue for the future of nuclear power is whether this trend will continue. Nuclear supporters and opponents tend to disagree on this question. Advocates of nuclear power say that in the past, constantly changing rules and procedures for building new nuclear plants have prevented manufacturers from relying on past experience to build plants more cheaply. They say that the technology is now attaining a maturity that could allow the future cost of nuclear power plants to fall both in real terms and in relation to coal-fired plants. The Tennessee Valley Authority, for example, told IRRC in 1980 that its most recent

Figure 3

Comparison of Cost Estimates for Nuclear and Coal-Fired Plants

(Total Investment Cost for 1000-Megawatt Units)

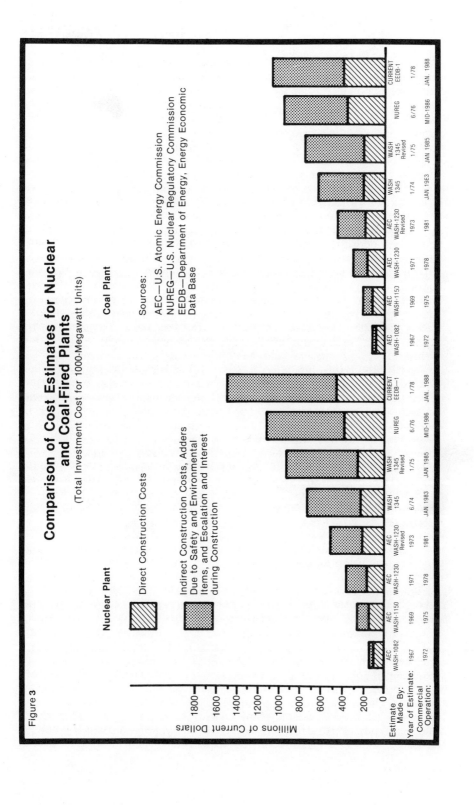

Nuclear Plant

Coal Plant

Direct Construction Costs

Indirect Construction Costs, Adders Due to Safety and Environmental Items, and Escalation and Interest during Construction

Sources:

AEC—U.S. Atomic Energy Commission
NUREG—U.S. Nuclear Regulatory Commission
EEDB—Department of Energy, Energy Economic Data Base

Millions of Current Dollars

Estimate Made By:	AEC WASH-1082	AEC WASH-1150	AEC WASH-1230	AEC WASH-1230 Revised	WASH 1345	WASH 1345 Revised	NUREG	CURRENT EEDB—1
Year of Estimate:	1967	1969	1971	1973	6/74	1/75	6/76	1/78
Commercial Operation:	1972	1975	1978	1981	JAN. 1983	JAN. 1985	MID-1986	JAN. 1988

Estimate Made By:	AEC WASH-1082	AEC WASH-1150	AEC WASH-1230	AEC WASH-1230 Revised	WASH 1345	WASH 1345 Revised	NUREG	CURRENT EEDB-1
Year of Estimate:	1967	1969	1971	1973	1/74	1/75	6/76	1/78
Commercial Operation:	1972	1975	1978	1981	JAN. 1983	JAN. 1985	MID-1986	JAN. 1988

planning estimates suggest that coal plant capital costs will average 80 to 90 percent of nuclear plant capital costs in the years ahead.(13) Nuclear opponents dispute these assumptions. They agree that changes in plant design have greatly increased nuclear capital costs, but they insist that these changes have been necessary to protect the public and nuclear workers from the hazards of an inherently dangerous technology. And they argue that the rate of capital cost escalation for nuclear plants is likely to accelerate because of design changes resulting from the Three Mile Island accident.

The importance of future trends in nuclear and coal capital costs is dramatically illustrated by comparing recent cost estimates made by National Economic Research Associates (NERA), the Department of Energy (DOE) and Komanoff Energy Associates (KEA). NERA, an economic consulting firm that does work for the electric utility industry, published an econometric study in 1978 which predicts that in 1990 nuclear plant capital costs will be about 34 percent higher than coal plant capital costs--a ratio that the NERA study says would allow nuclear power to remain cheaper than coal in many areas of the country.(14) The NERA estimates factor in nuclear and coal plant cost trends through 1977, but do not extrapolate these trends into the future. The Department of Energy, in its most recent capital cost estimates, takes nuclear and coal plant cost data through 1977 and adjusts it to determine capital costs for a single unit power plant located at a hypothetical standard plant site. Using this model, DOE predicts that for 1,000-megawatt plants entering service in 1988, nuclear capital costs will exceed coal capital costs by about 43 percent.(15) The DOE study does not make any estimates of total generating costs but states that "it is apparent that it may be years before the total comparative economics of conversion of oil to coal, new coal plants, and nuclear plants are fully determined."(16) Finally, Komanoff Energy Associates, in an econometric study issued in August 1980 which uses sector size as a variable for explaining increases in capital costs, projects that nuclear capital costs will exceed coal capital costs by 73 percent for plants entering service in 1988.(17) This model, which extends historical cost trends through 1978 out to the year 1988, concludes that nuclear plants started today will be uneconomic in all areas of the country.

Although Komanoff is seen by nuclear supporters as having an anti-nuclear bias--just as the NERA estimates are seen by critics as having a pro-nuclear slant--there is increasing support for the proposition that nuclear capital costs will continue to rise. Rand Corp. econometrician William E. Mooz, for instance, did an econometric study of the variables affecting the capital costs of light water reactors and projected that "the costs of LWRs on which construction begins in 1980 are on the order of $2,000 per kilowatt in 1976 dollars."(18) Although the Mooz study does not examine coal plant costs, it clearly supports the contention that government and utility estimates of future nuclear plant costs continue to be too low. Mooz also contends that for nuclear plants on which construction began after 1980, capital costs could be expected to continue upward at a rate of about $140 per kilowatt per year in constant dollars. Moreover, although a great deal of uncertainty remains about the accuracy of any predictions about future capital costs, nuclear analysts agree that the accident at the Three Mile Island plant in 1979 strengthened the case of those arguing that nuclear capital costs will continue to outpace those of coal plants. Finally, it has been noted that even if the capital costs for new coal plants rose at a pace equal to that of nuclear plants, the longer lead times needed to build nuclear plants would tend to favor the coal option. A recent study by Resources for the Future made this point, noting that "if the costs of building and equipping all power plants happened to rise more rapidly than the general price level, this would tend to favor coal plants over nuclear facilities."(19)

One change that could affect the competitive position of nuclear power would be a shortening of the time required to license and construct a nuclear plant. For a nuclear plant started today, more than half the projected costs of the plant can be attributed to interest during construction and to escalation. Any reduction in the time between initiating plans for a plant and putting it into operation would cut these costs dramatically, as can been seen in Table 2. Both industry and government officials hoped to reduce this period from the usual 12 years required today through standardizing plant design and a speed-up in the licensing process.

TABLE 2

Licensing & Construction Durations (years)	Total Cost (millions)	Interest & Escalation (millions)	Percent of Total
6	$ 235	$ 70	30%
7	340	120	35
8	495	185	37
9	715	285	40
10	1,135	600	53

Source: *Nuclear Industry*, April 1978

Although industry officials concede that the accident at Three Mile Island has lessened the chances for quick governmental action on licensing reform, they remain optimistic. Exxon Nuclear Co. wrote to IRRC that although the accident "undoubtedly delayed an increasing focus on regulatory reform, we feel this result will abate in view of positive reforms instituted by the nuclear industry and still anticipate significant regulatory reform in the longer term."(20) But while industry officials remain optimistic about the chances for regulatory reform, other observers say that the chances for a speed-up of the regulatory and licensing process have practically vanished in the wake of Three Mile Island. In the opinion of Nuclear Regulatory Commissioner Richard T. Kennedy:

> Until March 28, when one talked about legislation and regulation, the focus was primarily on regulatory reform and, specifically, for those of you in industry, on measures that might be enacted to speed up the licensing process. The hopes of those who sought such a speed-up are clearly a great deal dimmer today. There is little likelihood, I believe, that Congress will, in the light of TMI, move in that direction in the foreseeable future . . . .
>
> No, I suspect that what will occur, instead of any licensing speed-up, is quite the opposite. Our regulatory staff itself will, I expect, contribute to this. More intensive deliberation on its part is an inevitable and necessary consequence of the unforeseen events at TMI which called into question previously cherished ideas and beliefs about nuclear safety.(21)

The competitive position of coal plants, however, continues to be adversely affected by the costs of meeting government air pollution and waste management regulations. The new stationary source performance standards announced by the Environmental Protection Agency in May 1979 will require stack-gas scrubbing equipment on all new coal-fired power plants. This equipment, which is designed to reduce sulfur dioxide emissions by up to 90 percent, represents a major portion of the capital costs of a new coal plant. Recent estimates suggest that installation of the most up-to-date scrubbing equipment will represent from 15 to 30 percent of coal plant capital costs. Other recent regulatory changes for coal plants include stricter rules on water use effects, off-site noise levels, ground water effects, sludge and waste disposal, trace element emissions and redundant scrubber systems. As a recent Energy Department study notes, "Standards for air-quality and waste management for coal-fired plants are still proliferating. Growth of standards for coal-fired plants will continue for at least several more years before leveling off . . . . Coal plant costs may thus continue to grow after nuclear plant costs stabilize."(22)

OPERATION, MAINTENANCE AND
DECOMMISSIONING COSTS

Federal Power Commission figures for 1977 show that nuclear plants were slightly more expensive than fossil fuel plants to operate and maintain. Operation and maintenance costs averaged 2.67 mills per kilowatt hour for nuclear plants, 1.85 for fossil fuel plants.(23) (Because the FPC data does not distinguish between coal-fired plants and oil-fired plants, however, it is probable that operation and maintenance costs for nuclear and coal plants are closer than these figures suggest.) The difference may be attributed to the more sophisticated safety equipment required at nuclear plants, major corrosion problems at some nuclear plants and the fact that most older coal plants have not installed scrubbing equipment--a step assumed to increase operation and maintenance costs at coal plants by 2.5 to 3.5 mills per kilowatt hour.(24)

The Federal Power Commission figures indicate that government operation and maintenance (O&M) cost estimates made earlier are too low. In 1974 the AEC estimated that O&M costs in 1982 would be 0.8 and 2.0 mills per kilowatt hour for nuclear and coal plants, respectively. O&M costs at nuclear plants are already more than three times these estimated amounts, and costs at coal plants could also run three times as high as AEC estimates, once more stack-gas scrubbers are installed. Moreover, coal plant O&M costs will be further adversely affected by the Resource Conservation and Recovery Act and the Toxic Substances Control Act as they relate to fly ash and sludge disposal. A 1978 NERA study estimates annual O&M costs at 15.0 and 9.4 mills per kilowatt hour (in 1990 dollars) for 900 Mw coal and nuclear plants, respectively, going into operation in 1990.(25)

While escalation in coal plant O&M costs appears to be associated with scrubbers and new regulations, two factors that appear to be adversely affecting maintenance costs at nuclear plants are a corrosion problem called "denting" and strict limitations on radiation exposure of nuclear industry workers. The "denting" problem, a form of corrosion that causes leaks in pipes that carry radioactive water in pressurized water reactors, is expected to cost utilities at least $600 million in 1980 and probably much more in the future. Several nuclear plants have already experienced extended shutdowns because of the problem, and it is estimated that 11 other plants are affected to a "moderate" or "minor" degree by the leaks.(26) The radiation limits drive up nuclear costs by allowing workers only a certain level of radiation exposure, after which they are considered "burned out" and must be replaced by other workers. The result is that companies may have to train many workers to perform the same kinds of repairs, and repairs in areas where there is radiation exposure may require more time and workers than would be the case for similar repairs at nonnuclear plants. It is likely that both these factors will continue to drive up O&M costs at existing nuclear plants in the future, although new reactor plant designs oriented toward ease of maintenance and reducing radiation exposure will partially mitigate these problems at new nuclear plants.

Finally, costs at nuclear plants will soon begin to be affected by an issue to which some nuclear utilities have yet to address themselves--the decommissioning of old reactors. Because such plants would remain radioactive for hundreds of years and require constant security, most experts agree that reactors will eventually need to be dismantled and the sites decontaminated. This procedure would not necessarily occur immediately after the end of a reactor's useful life, however, as "mothballing"--placing the facility in protective storage after all radioactive waste and fuel has been removed--and "entombment"--sealing the reactor building in concrete after the fuel and waste have been removed--have also been identified by the NRC as acceptable decommissioning options. According to GE, a practical solution to the decommissioning issue would be to "mothball or encapsulate the plant for at least 30 years after which time the radioactivity would have decreased to levels low enough that workers could dismantle the facility in a much more economic fashion."(27)

The nation has not yet dismantled a commercial-size reactor, and estimates of the cost of the procedure vary widely. At the lower end of the estimates, some industry-sponsored studies say that dismantling a large reactor will cost only $40 million in today's dollars.(28) At the upper end, Peter N. Skinner, an engineer in the New York State attorney general's office, says it will cost $249 million (in 1977 dollars).(29) Overall, those utilities that are acting on the decommissioning problem by setting aside funds each year seem to be guessing that the cost will be $50 to $100 million. Utilities say that the cost of decommissioning old reactors will be insignificant when compared with total electricity generating costs. But most utilities also admit that the true cost of dismantling a large reactor won't be known until a utility trys it. "Only experience will determine whether current treatment has been adequate," TVA wrote to IRRC.(30) The eventual costs may prove so great "that people will say 'Put a fence around it and forget it,' " adds Arthur Flynn, chief of mechanical and nuclear engineering for Consolidated Edison Co.(31).

FUEL COSTS

In the area of fuel costs, both opponents and proponents of nuclear power agree that nuclear plants currently have a decisive advantage over coal-fired units. Recent Energy Information Administration figures show that fuel costs at nuclear plants in 1977 averaged 3.1 mills per kilowatt-hour while fuel costs at coal plants averaged 9.7 mills per kilowatt-hour.(32) And according to a survey of 43 utilities by the Atomic Industrial Forum, fuel costs at nuclear plants in 1978 averaged 3.4 mills per kilowatt-hour, compared with 12.4 mills per kilowatt-hour at base-load coal plants.(33)

In addition, although uranium prices rose more rapidly than coal prices during the 1970s, it appears for the moment that coal prices could outpace uranium prices over the next few years. Energy experts say that abundant new supplies of uranium, coupled with delays in bringing new nuclear plants on line, portend stable uranium prices for at least several years. Indeed, the spot market price of uranium oxide, after rising from an estimated $6 per pound in 1972 to about $45 per pound in 1979, has recently fallen to around $30 per pound as utilities have attempted to sell of unneeded uranium inventories. These trends in the price of natural uranium are shown in Figure 4.

FIGURE 4

NATURAL URANIUM AND ENRICHMENT COSTS

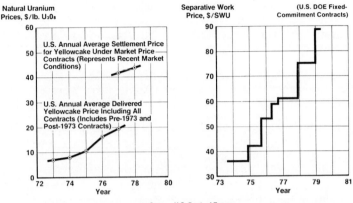

Source: U.S. Dept. of Energy

While the price of uranium oxide appears to have stabilized for the time being, the cost of government enrichment services has not. Government uranium enrichment fees, as shown in Figure 4, have tripled in the last seven years. In addition, nuclear analysts expect further increases in government enrichment fees due to the increased costs of electricity to operate the plants, sharply reduced projections of future demand for enrichment service, and a 1977 decision by Congress to require the nuclear industry to pay for enrichment as an ordinary business expense. Then-Energy Secretary James Schlesinger estimated in 1977 that the congressional action alone would cost utilities about $770 million between 1978 and 1982, adding 0.8 mills per kilowatt-hour to the cost of nuclear power.(34)

A number of other factors are likely to affect the future cost of the nuclear fuel cycle. The Carter administration's decision in 1977 to forbid spent fuel reprocessing because of its implications for weapons proliferation has created new uncertainties about the costs associated with the "back end" of the nuclear fuel cycle and about the long-term availability of uranium. Until the Carter decision, industry and government officials had assumed that there would be essentially no costs involved at the back end of the fuel cycle because the value of reusable plutonium and uranium extracted from spent fuel was expected to exceed the costs of transportation and reprocessing of spent fuel and permanent waste disposal. Preliminary estimates by the Department of Energy now place spent fuel disposal costs at around 1.0 mills per kilowatt-hour.(35) It is widely acknowledged, however, that these figures remain highly uncertain because no permanent waste disposal has ever been attempted. Meanwhile, some utilities still do not account for these costs in their estimates of nuclear power costs.

In addition, the Carter decision on reprocessing has increased utilities' concerns about the price and availability of nuclear fuel in the future. "Losing reprocessing is not insubstantial," notes Lewis J. Perl of NERA. "It drives up the price of uranium, and the economics then start to turn bad in the '90s. Sometime by the end of the century, if the light water reactor is to survive, we've got to have either reprocessing or the breeder."(36) (It has been estimated that reprocessing would extend U.S. nuclear fuel supplies by 30 to 40 percent.)

Most analysts, however, do not foresee uranium shortages, at least in the near future. In fact, many are worried about the consequences of a growing surplus. In 1979, for example, U.S. mines produced a record 37 million pounds of uranium oxide while utilities consumed only 24.8 million pounds.(37) A Resources for the Future study has estimated total recoverable U.S. uranium reserves, without reprocessing, at 1,100 quads--enough to fuel 200 1,000-megawatt nuclear reactors for about 90 years. Moreover, the study noted that "resource estimates for uranium are likely to be conservative because the uranium mining industry is still in its infancy compared with the search for coal, oil and natural gas."(38) Other studies, including two assessments by The Ford Foundation, have been even more optimistic about the adequacy of U.S. uranium supplies. A recent study sponsored by The Ford Foundation entitled *Energy: The Next Twenty Years* found that "reductions in U.S. uranium consumption of 15 to 30 percent can probably be realized relatively quickly, and with economic benefit, through such measures as improving burnup of fuel in LWRs (light water reactors) and development of the laser isotope separation technology ...."(39) Such steps would have clear economic benefits, although the use of advanced enrichment technologies would pose political problems and could increase the possibility of nuclear weapons proliferation, according to some nuclear experts.

Although debate continues over the size of the country's uranium reserve and resource base, experts in the field appear to agree on several basic points. First, recent setbacks in the development of nuclear power in the United States and around the world are lessening the possibility of near-term uranium shortages and pushing projections of the year when this fuel will be depleted further into the future. Second, experts agree that the United States is in a considerably better position regarding uranium supplies than are most other countries and thus it has flexibility and options in the use of nuclear fuel that will not be available to most countries. Finally, they note that current estimates of world uranium resources suggest that there will not be sufficient amounts of this fuel to support continued worldwide nuclear power growth far beyond the year 2000 without increasing reliance on more efficient reactors, reprocessing or breeder reactors.

Similarly, a number of factors could affect the future cost and availability of coal. Despite exhortations for increased coal production, total coal production grew only 10 percent between 1972 and 1978. Deep-mined coal production remains highly susceptible to labor strikes; strip-mined coal production may be affected by 1977 legislation requiring strict observance of standards for reclaiming strip-mined land, although there have been moves in Congress to weaken the law. The cost of coal to utilities continues to be strongly affected by plant location--its proximity to suitable coal supplies--and by the strictness of regional air quality standards. Utility officials say that a key reason burning coal has become more expensive in recent years is that railroad tariffs for transporting it have risen sharply. Railroad tariffs are forcing many utilities to take a cautious approach to coal, says Robert Price, executive vice president of the National Coal Association.(40) Finally, development of a massive synthetic fuel industry as proposed by the Carter administration in 1979 could raise serious new questions about the price and availability of coal to utilities. On the other side of the picture, however, fluidized-bed coal combustion appears to offer considerable promise as a clean, economic alternative to conventional coal-burning systems. If successfully demonstrated in large-scale power plants, utility officials say fluidized bed combustion systems are expected to cost less than conventional coal plants and allow greater use of lower cost high-sulfur eastern coal.

SUBSIDIES

In estimating the cost of electricity from nuclear and coal-fired power plants, neither industry representatives nor government officials mention the government funds used to support the development of these two power sources. This is understandable, in that most estimates are designed to show costs to utilities, but the omission does highlight an argument made by critics of nuclear power--that the competitive viability of nuclear power exists only because of the massive government funding that has been provided to the program.

Observers estimate that more than $60 billion has been spent on the development of civilian nuclear power. Of this total, about one-third--no one knows for sure--has been provided by the federal government. A report prepared in 1978 for the Department of Energy by Batelle Pacific Northwest Laboratories indicates that the federal government has spent about $217 billion since 1918 to stimulate domestic energy production. The study found that $18 billion of the total had been spent on nuclear power development and $9.7 billion had been spent on coal.(41)

Public funds are being used today in a number of areas to support the use of coal and nuclear power. It is generally acknowledged, however, that research and development funding for nuclear projects in the 1970s greatly exceeded that for coal or any other energy source. Current nuclear projects include research on safety, safeguards, waste disposal, breeder reactors, fusion, decontamination and reactor decommissioning; new reactor and spent fuel storage demonstration projects; and experiments involving recycling and the fabrication of mixed oxide fuels. Table 3 shows the Department of Energy's breakdown of its research and development activities in recent years.

TABLE 3

DOE Energy Supply Research, Technology Development Production, Demonstration and Distribution

(Budget Authority, Million Dollars)

	1977	1978	1979
Fossil	537	846	924
Solar	282	390	373
Geothermal	53	106	130
Hydro	2	10	8
Biomass	13	21	27
Fusion	316	325	334
Fission	1,099	1,125	1,000
Basic energy sciences	155	177	211
Other	7	12	25
	3,381	3,478	3,231

Source: Consumer Briefing Summary, Jan. 26, 1978, Office of Consumer Affairs, Department of Energy, Washington, D.C.

Critics of nuclear power assert that, in addition to direct government support for research, development and demonstration projects, government activities in a number of other areas act as indirect subsidies to the nuclear power industry.

Richard Morgan of the Environmental Action Foundation contends that government control and operation of the uranium enrichment process remains an important government subsidy to nuclear power--in spite of laws mandating that the government recover the cost of its enrichment operations from utilities. According to Morgan, "Each new enrichment plant, including associated power generating facilities, is expected to cost more than $4 billion. *Business Week* has noted that a $30 billion investment in uranium enrichment might be needed in the next 15 years. The same amount of money could insulate every home in the United States".(42)

Another generally recognized subsidy to the nuclear industry--and one that has received a great deal of attention since the Three Mile Island accident--is the limitation on nuclear industry liability for nuclear reactor disasters found in the Price-Anderson Act. (See Chapter IV for a full description of the act and recent attempts to change it.) Although no precise dollar figure can be attached to this subsidy, it is clear that the nuclear industry itself attaches extremely great importance to this limitation. "Removing the limitation on liability," lawyers for the Atomic Industrial Forum maintained in a June 1978 brief to the U.S. Supreme Court, "could cause utilities to refrain from completing pending projects or undertaking new projects and, conceivably, lead to the shutdown of existing reactors."(43)

A final indirect subsidy to nuclear power is government investment tax credits and depreciation allowances that aid utility power plant construction. A research team at Lawrence Berkeley Laboratory, in a study funded by the Energy Research and Development Administration, found that "effectively the federal government pays about 20 percent of the cost of each new power plant that comes on line (10 percent is tax credit and about 10 percent is accelerated depreciation allowance)."(44) While these utility tax breaks apply to both fossil-fuel and nuclear power plants, they favor nuclear plants by allowing them to be depreciated over a 16-year lifespan as compared with 22½ years for fossil-fuel plants.(45)

The Department of Energy says its policy is to use public funds only as long as necessary in areas where private funds are not available. Its aim, it says, has been to demonstrate that certain aspects of various energy industries are commercially viable. Once that is demonstrated, it expects industry to take over.

In general, industry also supports the use of government funds for these programs. Industry representatives argue that government assistance is appropriate in support of such national objectives as lowering air pollution from the burning of coal, stimulating domestic energy production, and decreasing imports of oil. The government, company representatives say, should assist industry in areas where private companies are forced to assume abnormal risks or expenditures as a result of public policy decisions. Industry officials further argue that any cost accounting that considers subsidies to nuclear power must also consider subsidies to other energy industries, especially the black lung disability program for coal miners and various tax breaks given to fossil fuel producers and solar energy companies. Southern California Edison contends that "about one-third of civilian nuclear expenditure is recoverable" by the government through sales of enriched uranium, licensing fees, and taxes on nuclear power plants and supporting facilities.(46)

Proponents of nuclear power say that the figures quoted by nuclear critics about subsidies to the industry tend to be erroneous and overstated. According to Milton Copulos of the Heritage Foundation, the charge that government uranium enrichment represents a subsidy to the nuclear industry "is so far from true that it verges on the ludicrous."(47) Copulos contends that the government actually shows a tidy profit on these operations. Moreover, he argues, because the enrichment facilities were constructed for the nuclear weapons program and would have been built with or without the advent of nuclear power, commercial enrichment operations allow the government to recoup its investment in these facilities in a way that would be impossible without the nuclear power program. Exxon Nuclear adds that "government regulations regarding investment tax credits and depreciation allowances apply to all business concerns, not just nuclear."(48)

Concerning the Price-Anderson Act, proponents say that it is not really a subsidy because the government has never made a payout under the program. In addition, they say, Price-Anderson is not unique in providing government financial protection. According to GE, "we are not aware of any industrial insurance program that has unlimited liability. Indeed, most other systems have limitations of one sort or another .... The government also provides public financial protection for coal miners and their families, federal deposit insurance for bank accounts, federal flood insurance, and federal disaster aid."(49)

OPERATING CAPACITY

Regardless of fuel, O&M, or capital costs, one of the chief determinants of nuclear power's competitiveness with coal and other energy sources will be the capacity at which nuclear plants are able to operate over their lifetime. By operating efficiently, a nuclear plant will be able to take advantage of its lower fuel costs and may overcome its initial high capital cost.

Electric utilities, in general, have three kinds of power plants, which operate to meet three levels of demand: base load, intermediate load and peak load. Base load is the minimum level of electricity demand that exists in a system around the clock, all year long. Consequently, base-load power plants are designed to run almost continuously at full capacity to meet this level of demand. Intermediate-load plants are designed to operate frequently, supplementing the output of base-load plants to meet increases in demand, above base-load levels, that occur with some regularity. Peak-load plants operate only occasionally, when demand in a system reaches unusually high levels. For example, peak demand often occurs on very hot summer days, when many air conditioning units are operating.

Nuclear power plants--and large coal-fired plants--are used almost exclusively to meet base-load requirements. The high capital and low fuel costs of nuclear plants render use of them for other than base-loading purposes very expensive, because the savings in fuel costs are modest, and the amount of capital costs to be attributed to each kilowatt hour of output becomes very high. Thus, it is important that nuclear power plants operate at close to full capacity if they are to produce electricity at a competitive cost.

In evaluating the past performance of nuclear power plants, it is important to distinguish between two measures of performance frequently used: availability and capacity. "Availability" describes the time that a plant is available for operation at some level. To say a plant was available does not mean that it actually operated during the

TABLE 4

Average Nuclear Capacity Factors by Unit, Through June 1980 For Reactors Greater than 400 Megawatts

Unit	Mega- Watts	Vendor	Years	Cumulative Capacity Factor (percent)	Rank
Arkansas-1	850	BW	6	58.4	33
Beaver Valley-1 (Pa.)	852	W	4	27.2	61
Browns Ferry-1 (Ala.)	1,098	GE	6	43.1	56
Browns Ferry-2	1,098	GE	5	55.9	41
Browns Ferry-3	1,098	GE	3	62.3	22
Brunswick-1 (N.C.)	821	GE	3	57.3	38
Brunswick-2	821	GE	5	43.9	55
Calvert Cliffs-1 (Md.)	845	CE	5	68.0	13
Calvert Cliffs-2	845	CE	3	76.4	2
Connecticut Yankee	575	W	13	76.3	3
Cook-1 (Mich.)	1,090	W	5	62.3	21
Cook-2	1,100	W	2	68.0	12
Cooper (Neb.)	778	GE	6	61.9	25
Crystal River-3 (Fla.)	825	BW	3	40.8	57
Davis-Besse-1 (Oh.)	906	BW	3	36.5	59
Dresden-2 (Ill.)	809	GE	10	57.4	37
Dresden-3	809	GE	9	52.8	50
Duane Arnold (Iowa)	538	GE	6	49.3	52
Farley-1 (Ala.)	829	W	3	57.0	39
Fitzpatrick (N.Y.)	821	GE	5	53.0	48
Fort Calhoun (Neb.)	457	CE	6	63.8	17
Ginna (N.Y.)	490	W	10	64.5	16
Hatch-1 (Ga.)	786	GE	5	57.8	36
Hatch-2	786	GE	1	52.8	51
Indian Point-2 (N.Y.)	873	W	7	54.9	46
Indian Point-3	965	W	4	58.5	32
Kewaunee (Wis.)	560	W	6	70.7	7
Maine Yankee	790	CE	8	65.6	15
Millstone-1 (Conn.)	690	GE	10	61.9	24
Millstone-2	828	CE	5	62.2	23
Monticello (Minn.)	545	GE	9	73.1	6
Nine Mile Point-1 (N.Y.)	610	GE	11	61.6	26
North Anna-1 (Va.)	907	W	2	55.3	45
Oconee-1 (S.C.)	886	BW	7	58.0	35
Oconee-2	886	BW	6	58.9	31
Oconee-3	886	BW	6	62.6	19
Oyster Creek (N.J.)	650	GE	11	62.5	20
Palisades (Mich.)	821	CE	9	34.6	60
Peach Bottom-2 (Pa.)	1,065	GE	6	60.9	27
Peach Bottom-3	1,065	GE	6	63.3	18
Pilgrim-1 (Mass.)	670	GE	8	53.4	47
Point Beach-1 (Wis.)	497	W	10	73.1	5
Point Beach-2	497	W	8	80.6	1
Prairie Island-1 (Minn.)	530	W	7	69.0	10
Prairie Island-2	530	W	6	75.3	4
Quad Cities-1 (Ill.)	809	GE	8	60.1	29
Quad Cities-2	809	GE	8	56.8	40
Rancho Seco (Ca.)	913	BW	5	55.3	44
Robinson-2 (S.C.)	707	W	9	69.9	8
Salem-1 (N.J.)	1,090	W	3	44.6	54
San Onofre-1 (Ca.)	450	W	13	67.7	14
St. Lucie-1 (Fla.)	810	CE	4	68.7	11
Surry-1 (Va.)	823	W	8	52.9	49
Surry-2	823	W	7	45.8	53
Three Mile Island-1 (Pa.)	819	BW	6	55.4	43
Three Mile Island-2	906	BW	2	11.1	62
Trojan (Ore.)	1,130	W	5	39.5	58
Turkey Point-3 (Fla.)	745	W	8	60.5	28
Turkey Point-4	745	W	7	59.5	30
Vermont Yankee	514	GE	8	69.3	9
Zion-1 (Ill.)	1,050	W	7	55.6	42
Zion-2	1,050	W	6	58.4	34

Note: Capacity factors based on original design electrical ratings.

Source: Charles Komanoff, "U.S. Nuclear Plant Performance," *The Bulletin of the Atomic Scientists,* November 1980.

time, or that it was available for operation at full capacity, only that it was available to meet some level of demand. Hence, a 1,000-megawatt plant that produces electricity during nine months of the year and is out of operation for three months would have an availability factor of 75 percent, regardless of how much electricity it actually produced. "Capacity factor" describes the level at which a plant actually has operated. A 1,000-megawatt plant producing 800 megawatts of power 100 percent of the time or 1,000 megawatts 80 percent of the time is operating with an 80 percent capacity factor. Because nuclear power plants must shut down an average of one month a year for refueling, the maximum annual realizable capacity factor of a nuclear plant is 92 percent.

Past Performance

Government officials, reactor vendors and many utilities have referred, in the past, to an 80 percent capacity factor as their performance goal. Until recently, utilities often assumed a 75 or 80 percent capacity factor in estimating the costs of generating electricity from new nuclear plants. To date, nuclear power plants have operated at an average capacity factor of about 60 percent--slightly higher than that of large-scale coal plants. (The operating history of nuclear power plants is shown in Table 4 on p. 41.) Atomic Industrial Forum figures show that nuclear plants averaged a 65.3 percent capacity factor from 1976 through 1978; base-loaded coal plants averaged 57.0 percent. The forum's figures show that coal plants had a higher availability factor during this period, however, with coal plants averaging 76.8 percent, compared with 74.9 percent for nuclear plants.(50)

Interpreting the Data

The significance of plant performance statistics is subject to some dispute, primarily because the data base is rather small. Experience with nuclear plants of the size being constructed today--1,000 megawatts or greater--is limited. Similarly, supercritical coal plants--which operate at a higher temperature and steam pressure than normal coal plants--have been in operation only since 1968.

Advocates of nuclear power have long argued that as time goes by, the industry's capacity factor record will improve. ERDA estimated that new nuclear plants would experience a three- to four-year shakedown period, after which time a higher factor could be expected. The New Jersey Public Service Electric and Gas Co. estimates that plants going into operation in 1983 will have a capacity factor for the first two years of 65 percent, rising to 74 percent in the third year and to 78 percent in the sixth year.(51) Industry representatives say that nuclear power's poorer-than-predicted performance to date is the result of "growing pains," and they argue that trends toward reactor standardization will lead to further improvements in nuclear plant reliability. The Tennessee Valley Authority, for instance, wrote to IRRC in 1980 that "the data substantiates the fact that there is a significant maturity curve." "The 60-percent average," TVA said, "is heavily weighted by newer plants that have not matured and thus tend to lower the average .... Many problems depressing nuclear capacity (primarily fuel-related) have been solved, and the outlook for new plants is much improved."(52) Many energy experts agree with this scenario. Resources for the Future's major study, *Energy in America's Future*, comments:

> Nuclear technology is relatively new, and it seems intui-tively reasonable that with further operating experience, equipment will improve in reliability. Furthermore, to the extent that new safety system requirements for plants are no longer added--in contrast to what has often happened within the past decade--problems with untried components or systems in the newer nuclear plants should become fewer. While the Three Mile Island experience could eventually lead to some new safety systems and new reliability problems, such effects, if any, are impossible to trace at this time.(53)

Nuclear critics argue that the evidence thus far does not justify the claims and optimism of the industry's supporters. They say that the capacity factor figures released by the industry are too high because they are based on a unit's maximum dependable capability or downgraded design ratings rather than the unit's design rating when it entered service.

Moreover, following up on an analysis done first in 1975 by David Comey of Business and Professional People for the Public Interest,(54) Komanoff and others have challenged industry's statements about capacity factors improving over time. Nuclear plant capacity factors suffered a significant decline in 1979 and 1980, critics say, casting serious doubts on the industry's claims about improved performance. According to Komanoff, the average capacity factor of the nation's 62 commercial-size reactors (over 400 megawatts) for the period January 1979 through June 1980 was slightly under 57 percent. "This is the industry's poorest operating record over any sustained period in five years," Komanoff wrote, "and it is over four percentage points below the 61 percent cumulative average through 1978."(55) Thus, Komanoff argues, "increased operating experience, which the nuclear industry has always claimed would provide the necessary information to improve performance, is also demonstrating that, as designed, reactors are too accident-prone and need closer surveillance and a myriad of backfits. The results may be that nuclear capacity factors are destined to fall rather than rise as the nuclear sector expands."(56)

Regardless of any improvements in capacity factors exhibited by PWRs resulting from a learning curve, many critics further contend that increasing plant size will more than offset these trends. The CEP estimates that average capacity factors decrease by 2.5 percent for every 100-megawatt increase in reactor size.(57) According to Komanoff:

> With continuing problems at large plants and the possibility that a TMI-chastened NRC will be less shy about requiring shutdowns and backfits, the prospects are not bright for high performance by the 1,150-megawatt reactors on the way. In my heart of hearts I expect them to be limited to 55 percent lifetime capacity factors, but would use 60 percent in high-level economic calculations to avert the wrath of the AIF. For the industry as a whole, I look for a return to the old tried-and-true 60 percent mark for the next few years, after the recent two-year flirtation with 65 percent.(58)

The debate over capacity factors is likely to continue as more evidence accumulates from operation of large nuclear and coal plants. Whether a substantial learning curve for nuclear plants exists, as industry argues, after which capacity factors will increase, or whether plants will encounter unforeseen problems as they age, as David Comey argued, are among the critical uncertainties that will continue to plague persons attempting to judge the economics of nuclear and coal-fired power.

While no definitive conclusions can be reached at this time concerning the economics of nuclear power versus its alternatives--largely because of uncertainties in cost trends--the following generalizations can be made:

1. The total private cost of electric power from nuclear and coal-fired power plants is currently about equal, with nuclear power slightly cheaper in some sections of the country and coal a bit cheaper in others.

2. Cost trends for all energy technologies remain subject to change and highly dependent upon political decisions concerning subsidies, degrees of safety, and environmental concerns.

3. Cost trends over the last decade have been highly unfavorable to the nuclear option and continuation of these trends would make nuclear power plants started today uneconomic before they could be completed.

NOTES

(1) Atomic Industrial Forum, INFO news release, "1978 Economic Survey Results," May 14, 1979, p. 2.

(2) R.N. Bergstrom and W.W. Brandfon, "Trends In Electric Generating Costs," presented before the WATTec Conference, Feb. 21, 1979, Knoxville, Tenn.

(3) Anthony J. Parisi, "Nuclear Power: The Bottom Line Gets Fuzzier," The New York *Times,* April 8, 1979, p. 1F.

(4) "Nuclear Power Costs," Twenty-Third Report by the Committee on Government Operations, HR No. 95-1090 (Washington, D.C., U.S. Government Printing Office, 1978), p. 44.

(5) Charles Komanoff, "Cost Escalation at Nuclear and Coal Power Plants," Aug. 15, 1980, p. 2.

(6) Atomic Industrial Forum, "Nuclear Holds Its Own... Even In An Off Year," INFO press release, July 1980, p. 2

(7) U.S. Department of Energy, *1978 Annual Report to Congress*, Volume 3: Forecasts (Washington, D.C., Energy Information Administration, 1978), p. 268.

(8) These figures do not include Three Mile Island unit #2 and the Humboldt Bay unit, both of which are shut down indefinitely.

(9) U.S. Department of Energy, *1979 Annual Report to Congress* (Washington, D.C., Energy Information Administration, 1980), Volume 3, p. 188.

(10) Komanoff, op. cit., p. 8

(11) Energy Information Administration, "Steam-Electric Plant Construction Cost and Annual Production Expenses 1977" (Washington, D.C., U.S. Government Printing Office, December 1978), p. xiii.

(12) Pacific Gas and Electric Co., "DIACOM," January 1980, p. III-A-3.

(13) Interview with Thomas E. Spink and Len R. Shasteen, Tennessee Valley Authority, August 1980.

(14) Lewis J. Perl, National Economic Research Associates, "Estimated Costs of Coal and Nuclear Generation," a seminar presented to the New York Society of Security Analysts, New York, N.Y., Dec. 12, 1978. (Estimates are for 600-Mw coal plant and 1,200-Mw nuclear plant, the presumed low cost case for each option.)

(15) U.S. Department of Energy, "Power Plant Capital Investment Cost Estimates: Current Trends and Sensitivity to Economic Parameters," Office of Nuclear Reactor Programs, June 1980, p. 15.

(16) Ibid., p. 22.

(17) Komanoff, op. cit., p. 17.

(18) William E. Mooz, "Cost Analysis of Light Water Reactor Power Plants," prepared for the Department of Energy by the Rand Corp., June 1978, p. viii.

(19) Sam Schurr et al., *Energy in America's Future: The Choices Before Us*, Resources for the Future (Baltimore, Md., The Johns Hopkins University Press, 1979), p. 31.

(20) Exxon Nuclear Co., Planning and Uranium Operations Division, comments to Investor Responsibility Research Center, October 1980.

(21) Remarks by Commissioner Richard T. Kennedy, U.S. Nuclear Regulatory Commission, before the Edison Electric Institute--Spring Conference, June 12, 1979.

(22) U.S. Department of Energy, "Power Plant Capital Investment Cost Estimates: Current Trends and Sensitivity to Economic Parameters," op. cit., p. 20.

(23) Energy Information Administration, "Steam-Electric Plant Construction Cost and Annual Production Expenses 1977," op. cit. For

46 THE NUCLEAR POWER DEBATE

fossil fuel plants see p. xxxiii; value for nuclear plants is a weighted average calculated from individual plant data, pp. 184-198.

(24) For increases in coal and nuclear O&M costs under various assumptions see Lewis J. Perl, "Review and Critique of the Council on Economic Priorities' Study *Power Plant Performance,* National Economic Research Associates, March 17, 1977, Table 7.

(25) Lewis J. Perl, "Estimated Costs of Coal and Nuclear Generation," op. cit., Table 3.

(26) Joanne Omang, "A-Plant Problem Seen Costing Millions," The Washington *Post,* May 3, 1979.

(27) General Electric Co., Nuclear Energy Group, comments to Investor Responsibility Research Center, August 1980.

(28) See for example R.N. Bergstrom and W.W. Brandfon, op. cit., p. 12.

(29) Edmund Faltermayer, "Nuclear Power After Three Mile Island," *Fortune,* May 7, 1979, p. 120.

(30) Tennessee Valley Authority, comments to Investor Responsibility Research Center, August 1980.

(31) James Feron, "Dismantling of Idle Atom Plant Called 25 Years Off," The New York *Times,* Sept. 21, 1980, p. 55.

(32) Energy Information Administration, "Steam-Electric Plant Construction Cost and Annual Production Expenses 1977," op. cit. For coal plants see p. xvi; value for nuclear plants is weighted average calculated from individual plant data, pp. 184-198.

(33) Atomic Industrial Forum, op. cit.

(34) "Nuclear Power Costs," op. cit., p. 38.

(35) U.S. Department of Energy, "Report to the President by the Interagency Review Group on Nuclear Waste Management," TID-29442 (Washington, D.C., U.S. Government Printing Office, March 1979), p. 121.

(36) Parisi, op. cit., p. 4F.

(37) Frederick Rose, "It's a Buyers' Market for Uranium; Price Plunge Is Expected to Persist," *The Wall Street Journal,* Oct. 1, 1980.

(38) Sam Schurr et al., op. cit., p. 27.

(39) Hans H. Landsberg et al., *Energy: The Next Twenty Years,* The Ford Foundation and Resources for the Future (Cambridge, Mass., Ballinger Publishing Co., 1979), p. 449.

(40) Paul van Slambrouck, "Cost discouraging utility coal switch," *The Christian Science Monitor,* Sept. 25, 1979, p. 9.

(41) Batelle Pacific Northwest Laboratories, "An Analysis of Federal Incentives Used to Stimulate Energy Production," PNL-2410-REV. (This report is an update of an earlier study by the same name.)

(42) "Nuclear Power Costs," op. cit., p. 37.

(43) Investor Responsibility Research Center, "Nuclear Power Update: Opponents, Supporters Claim Recent Victories," *News for Investors,* September 1978, p. 166.

(44) "Nuclear Power Costs," op. cit., p. 37. See also, Edward Kahn et al., "Investment Planning in the Energy Sector," Lawrence Berkeley Laboratory, March 1, 1976, p. 89.

(45) Ibid.

(46) Southern California Edison, comments to Investor Responsibility Research Center, 1975.

(47) Milton R. Copulos, "The Price of Power," *National Review*, Feb. 2, 1979, p. 156.

(48) Exxon Nuclear Co., Planning and Uranium Operations Division, comments to Investor Responsibility Research Center, October 1980.

(49) General Electric Co., Nuclear Energy Group, comments to Investor Responsibility Research Center, August 1980.

(50) Atomic Industrial Forum, op. cit., p. 3.

(51) Charles Komanoff, "Economic Analysis of the Nuclear Expansion Program of Public Service Electric and Gas Co.," testimony before the New Jersey Public Utilities Commission, June 7, 1976, pp. 43, 44. (Published by the Council on Economic Priorities, New York).

(52) Tennessee Valley Authority, comments to Investor Responsibility Research Center, August 1980.

(53) Sam Schurr et al., op. cit., p. 286.

(54) David Comey, "Nuclear Power Plant Reliability: The 1973-74 Record," *Not Man Apart*, April 1975, pp. 12-13.

(55) Charles Komanoff, "Nuclear Plant Performance: TMI and Beyond," Aug. 29, 1980, p. 1.

(56) Ibid., p. 6.

(57) Council on Economic Priorities, "Nuclear Plant Performance/Update 2," CEP newsletter, June 21, 1978, p. 2.

(58) Charles Komanoff, "Capacity Factors Take a Dive," op. cit., p. 11.

Chapter IV

THE GOVERNMENT'S ROLE IN
NUCLEAR POWER DEVELOPMENT

Both Congress--chiefly through the now-defunct Joint Committee on Atomic Energy--and the executive branch of government--through the Atomic Energy Commission and its successor agencies, have committed the United States to development of nuclear power as a major source of energy. Critics of nuclear power raise a central question in this regard: Have the political and regulatory processes allowed adequate opportunities for review of alternatives and public participation in decision making?

The dispute about the political and regulatory processes in the nuclear area is of interest for several reasons:

● Because many of the issues relating to nuclear power involve public policy, members of the public have traditionally been inclined to leave resolution of them to the government. In recent years, however, a growing number of people appear to have concluded that governmental processes are not functioning adequately, and are increasing their visibility and involvement in decision-making.

● The regulatory process is likely to have a critical impact on business performance and the economics of nuclear power. An understanding of the process is useful to an assessment of how particular actions may affect the industry.

● Major changes in the regulatory agencies and the congressional committees charged with overseeing nuclear power development have occurred in recent years. More are taking place as a result of events in 1979. Many of these changes will have direct financial and operational impact on the industry. An understanding of the past performance of those agencies and committees, and of concerns about their performance, is useful in understanding and interpreting anticipated changes.

HOW THE COMMITMENT WAS MADE

Tradition of Secrecy

The nature of nuclear fission and the unique history of its early development have greatly influenced the process by which decisions relating to the civilian nuclear industry have been made. In the early years all decisions were made in an environment dominated by national security concerns. The tradition of secrecy and the complexity of nuclear technology kept policy decisions in the hands of a few scientists, lawyers, and legislators who had expertise in the area. The Joint Committee on Atomic Energy in Congress and the Atomic Energy Commission on the executive side became the major sources of this expertise and dominated nuclear policy decision-making.

Creation of the AEC

After Hiroshima, U.S. government officials were greatly impressed by the awesome power and potential of nuclear energy. They sought to develop a program that would both preserve U.S. supremacy in nuclear military technology and allow nuclear power to be developed for peaceful purposes. In 1946 Congress adopted legislation, recommended by President Truman, to transfer responsibility for nuclear development from the military to a five-member civilian Atomic Energy Commission whose purpose was "government control of the production, ownership and use of fissionable material to assure the common defense and security and to ensure the broadest possible exploitation" of nuclear technology. The commission was put in charge of the vast existing nuclear industrial complex, together with the research and development program that had begun during World War II in support of the Manhattan Project.

Creation of the Joint Committee

Concurrently, Congress created the Joint Committee on Atomic Energy to oversee the activities of the AEC and gave it unique powers: It became the only standing joint committee of Congress with powers to recommend legislative action and to serve as the conference committee to reconcile any differences in legislation within its jurisdiction that was passed by both houses of Congress. (In general, on other kinds of legislation, the conference committees include both members of the standing committees that report the legislation and other members of Congress.) The creation of the joint committee was Congress's answer to the problem of maintaining legislative control over a highly technical program, a major portion of which was to be conducted under conditions of secrecy.(1)

As its interest and experience grew, the joint committee

expanded its oversight role to assume more direct responsibility for the civilian nuclear program. The AEC was somewhat preoccupied with cold war demands for development of military programs, according to Craig Hosmer, a former member of the joint committee, and the committee was developing a good deal of expertise concerning civilian nuclear technology. The committee came to play the primary role in what Hosmer describes as a "partnership" relationship between the AEC and the committee. While newly appointed AEC commissioners often knew little about nuclear power, six long-time members of the joint committee became very knowledgeable about nuclear power and, consequently, very influential. Hosmer recalls, "It was one instance in which power flowed to a congressional committee from the executive, rather than the other way around."(2) By 1957 the joint committee had assumed responsibility for policy development and programming, and the AEC was involved primarily with the details of program administration. The joint committee established for itself certain executive rights: in 1961 the committee's chairman wrote that the committee "reserves the right to recommend projects and levels of support which it believes necessary or important to national interests."(3) The dominant role of the joint committee went unchallenged until 1976--only a year before Congress voted to abolish the committee. In fact, with one minor exception, before 1974 no bill proposed by the joint committee was questioned on the floor of Congress. *Congressional Quarterly*, commenting on the joint committee's abolition in 1977, stated, "For most of its life, the joint committee functioned almost as a unicameral legislature within the bicameral Congress."(4)

Encouragement of Private Industry

Early on, the joint committee and certain members of the executive branch began to consider how to shift some of the responsibility for civilian nuclear power development to private industry. By 1954 the committee considered nuclear power to be at the threshold of commercial viability and began to explore methods of transferring at least a portion of the government's full control to private companies. The committee drafted the Atomic Energy Act to authorize the AEC to license private parties to work on all kinds of nuclear materials except weapons materials. The legislation was enacted in 1954.

Attracting private participation was not easy. Consequently, the government adopted a number of programs to encourage utilities to invest in nuclear power plants. Among these were government funding of research, development, and demonstration projects and a system of federally subsidized insurance and of limited liability in case of a nuclear power plant accident.

The Power Demonstration Reactor Program

Utilities were reluctant to commit large amounts of capital to nuclear technology, which they viewed as untested and not fully developed. To spur investment and demonstrate the commercial viability of nuclear power, the Power Demonstration Reactor Program was launched in 1955.

Under the program, the AEC made a major commitment to research at government laboratories on problems vital to development of a civilian nuclear industry, financed research on reactors that were more sophisticated than the first generation of light-water reactors, paid the costs of manufacturing reactor cores, and supplied nuclear fuel free of charge. The program met with considerable technical success, highlighted by the successful operation of a commercial nuclear plant at Shippingport, Pa., under the direction of Adm. Hyman G. Rickover. This led to considerably increased interest in nuclear power by manufacturers and utilities.

Price-Anderson Act

Manufacturers and utilities remained concerned about their potential liability if a major accident should occur at a nuclear power plant. A study of potential risks and damages commissioned by the AEC in 1957 made private companies even more apprehensive. General Electric made plain that it would withdraw from major participation in nuclear development unless the government came up with a program limiting the company's potential liability. "It had become clear," according to George Washington Law School professor Harold P. Green, "that private enterprise interest in nuclear power would dissipate almost entirely unless some formula were found to enable private industry to participate without risking public liability."(5) Because of the extremely limited experience with reactors, insurance companies were not willing to provide more than $60 million in liability insurance.

Responding to these concerns, in 1957 the joint committee developed and secured passage of what is known as the Price-Anderson Act. The act limits the liability of an individual company and provides government subsidies to cover liabilities well beyond those that private commercial insurers were--or are now--willing to cover. That act served the dual purpose of facilitating public compensation in the case of a nuclear power plant accident and eliminating a major barrier to the commercial development of nuclear power--easing businesses' fears about the potentially bankrupting liability that could result from a nuclear power plant disaster. It was named for its sponsors, Rep. Melvin Price (D-Ill.) and Sen. Clinton P. Anderson (D-N.M.).

The Price-Anderson Act limits overall liability for losses incurred as a result of a nuclear power accident to $560 million. The first portion of the liability is assumed by private insurance purchased by utilities from American Nuclear Insurers and the Mutual Atomic Energy Liability Underwriters, two insurance pools involving more than 140 insurance companies. Utilities are obligated to purchase as much insurance as private insurers are willing to provide--$160 million today. If liabilities from an accident exceeded this amount, each of the U.S. nuclear utilities would be assessed up to $5 million per reactor to pay the next $340 million in claims. The federal government would pay the remainder--currently $60 million--up to the $560 million ceiling. As new reactors come on line, the federal contribution will diminish. Once the combined insurance company/ utility contribution reaches $560 million, the liability ceiling will be allowed to float upward as new reactors are built. Finally, if claims far in excess of $560 million were made, Congress could pass emergency legislation to pay them. Under the act, all claims paid in this manner would be paid by the government irrespective of fault by the utility, manufacturer or architect. This provision was added in the 1960s to make recovery easier than it would be if claimants had to prove all facts under the law of a particular state.

The Price-Anderson Act survived an important constitutional challenge in 1978, but it is under renewed criticism as a result of the Three Mile Island accident. In 1978, a North Carolina district court held the act unconstitutional, ruling that it violated the due process clause of the Fifth Amendment "because it allows the destruction of the property or the lives of those affected by nuclear catastrophe without reasonable certainty that the victims will be justly compensated."(6) The U.S. Supreme Court reversed the lower court ruling, however, holding that the act's $560 million liability limitation bore a rational relationship to the legislative purpose--promoting the private development of nuclear energy. Now pending in Congress is a bill introduced by Rep. Theodore Weiss (D-N.Y.) that would remove the $560 million liability ceiling and abolish the 20-year statute of limitations provision on Price-Anderson Act claims.

Both opponents and supporters of nuclear power agree that the Price-Anderson Act represents a subsidy to the nuclear industry, but they differ as to the importance of this subsidy and whether or not it is justifiable. Supporters note that since the act's inception, the federal government has been slowly phased out of the nuclear insurance business and that it has never had to pay a claim. They acknowledge that in the event of a truly catastrophic accident at a nuclear plant, the government would probably be forced to provide emergency relief, but they argue that the probability of such an accident is exceedingly small. Moreover, nuclear supporters say, the benefits to the nation from nuclear power far outweigh the risks involved.

Critics of the Price-Anderson Act contend that its provisions would be hopelessly inadequate for dealing with a major nuclear accident and that it represents a clear subsidy of the nuclear power industry. "This issue illustrates the determination of the insurance and nuclear industries to avoid actuarial estimates that might highlight the catastrophic damages to individuals, businesses and natural resources from a nuclear power plant accident," states Ralph Nader.(7) Deputy Federal Insurance Administrator Robert Hunter agrees, saying that people near nuclear plants are paying a "tremendous subsidy" to their power companies because they will bear most of the losses in the event of a major accident. "Our position is that if there is not that much risk, then insurance should not cost much and individuals should have the right to buy it," says Hunter. "But if it is expensive, because the risk is high, policy holders and the public in general should know. That information is needed to help the public determine whether or not nuclear power is viable," Hunter adds.(8) According to Rep. Weiss, "The time has come for nuclear power to stand or fall on its own merits. No other method of energy generation enjoys a similar liability limitation," he says, "and Congress now has a clear duty to end this unfair underwriting of atomic power."(9)

Other Incentives

In general, where the industry has been hesitant to commit private funds, the AEC (and now the Department of Energy) has spent money to demonstrate various aspects of nuclear technology. In several areas--safety research, safeguarding of nuclear plants, fuel enrichment, disposal of radioactive wastes, and new reactor proto- types--the government continues to dominate.

THE REGULATORY PROCESS

Until late 1974--when the functions of the AEC were split between the newly formed Nuclear Regulatory Commission (NRC) and the Energy Research and Development Administration--the AEC was both the prime supporter and the chief regulator of the nuclear industry. Harold Green described the AEC as "by far the largest entrepreneur in the industry, the largest consumer of the industry's materials and services; it plays an active role in promoting the industry and in encouraging and subsidizing private interests to enter the industry at the same time that it is a potential competitor of these interests; and, finally, it licenses and regulates the private firms which it has encouraged and subsidized."(10)

The regulatory role of the AEC was negligible in its early years. As John O'Leary, a former AEC director of licensing, told IRRC in 1974, "The industry was only a penny industry until the early 1970s."(11) There was little system to the regulatory process; AEC engineers made ad hoc judgments about the adequacy of individual plants, O'Leary said. Until 1971, no serious efforts were made to develop standards, guidelines and routine procedures for plant construction as part of the regulatory process. According to the AEC's director of regulation, L. Manning Muntzing, in the 1960s, "at the AEC, the standards zealots could meet in a phone booth."(12) Eugene Cramer, an official at Southern California Edison Co., suggested that "until there were substantial sales of multiple units of essentially similar design at about the same time, by the same vendor, the conditions for development of standards did not exist."(13)

This situation changed markedly in the early 1970s, as the num- ber of applications for nuclear power plant licenses increased dramatically. According to O'Leary, after 1971 "the regulatory staff expanded from the dozens into the hundreds." The AEC moved to establish standards and uniform criteria to be used in the licensing process. In 1972, a full-time staff charged with developing standards was organized. Development of the AEC's regulatory processes was further stimulated in 1971 by the decision of the U.S. Court of Appeals for the District of Columbia in *Calvert Cliffs Coordinating Committee v. AEC*. The court ruled that the AEC was obliged under the National Environmental Policy Act to make a detailed assessment of the costs, benefits and environmental impact of nuclear power plants before it issued licenses for them. As NRC Commissioner Victor Gilinsky told the Joint Committee on Atomic Energy in March 1975, "the nuclear regulatory system requirements in a sense grew by accretion. Responsible persons decided that more and more requirements were useful."(14)

Following the establishment of the NRC in 1974, there was a seven-month lull in the issuance of nuclear permits and licenses, while the new commission undertook a major organizational effort. This effort brought a further expansion of the regulatory staff, the introduction of a number of new standards and guidelines, and the launching of several studies to develop means of streamlining the licensing process. At the time, these moves were considered quite comprehensive. If anything, industry officials said, the new government regulations were too strict. Government officials were optimistic. O'Leary said in 1974, "The past year has been encouraging. It looks like the technology may be maturing enough for a long period of stability in regulatory requirements. We have a good deal of confidence that there is not much wrong with the basic technology. We couldn't say that a year ago."(15)

Events in the last five years have largely discredited this optimistic view of the state of the nuclear industry and the NRC's attempts to regulate it. As NRC commissioner Victor Gilinsky noted in September 1979:

> In retrospect it appears things began to unravel in the early 1970s. The size of plants had increased rapidly; designers and builders had gotten ahead of their experience base. The government safety reviewers were thrown off balance by large numbers of applications for the new complex plants. Some utilities simply lacked the competence to supervise construction projects of this size and complexity. Construction problems multiplied and construction time stretched out.(16)

Development of Standards

The various standards affecting nuclear plants--ranging from the technical specifications governing component parts to generic standards for radioactive emissions levels or seismic guidelines in plant siting--were derived from a number of sources. Some were taken from existing engineering codes. Others evolved through ad hoc decisions made by NRC engineers reviewing individual plant designs. In many areas, industry or academic groups made suggestions that were issued as criteria in regulatory guidelines after the NRC had accepted them. Rulemaking hearings were held on generic issues such as criteria for emergency core-cooling systems, low-level radiation emissions, the environmental impact of the nuclear fuel cycle, and the impact of radioactive materials transport.

Since 1971, AEC and NRC staffs have issued more than 500 regulations and "regulatory guides" establishing procedures or acceptable levels of risk or endorsing more than 200 national standards developed through the volunteer standards program. Under the program, more than 8,000 technical specialists, primarily from industry, have served on standards-writing committees. In 1975 the NRC completed a set of "standard review plans," covering more than 1,400 pages, to be used by the NRC technical staff in reviewing nulcear power plants. At the time, the NRC said that the plans would improve the "overall quality, uniformity and predictability of staff reviews" and serve as a "well-defined basis for evaluating proposed changes."(17) Some industry and government officials expected the plans virtually to stop the proliferation of new regulations, but this has not happened to any significant degree. During 1979, for instance, the NRC issued, amended, or proposed more than 50 regulations and regulatory guides. In addition, many observers expect a plethora of new regulations and standards to result from various studies of the causes of the Three Mile Island accident.

Licensing Procedures

In order to build a nuclear power plant, a utility must follow a number of procedures, including participation in two public hearings and numerous reviews by federal and state agencies. To obtain a license from the NRC, it must be able to show, in the language of the Atomic Energy Act, that "there is reasonable assurance that the proposed facility can be constructed and operated at the proposed location without undue risk to the health and safety of the public."

The nuclear power plant licensing process has five basic steps (see Figure 5, p. 56).

Application

The utility submits to the NRC a formal application for a construction permit. The application must include general information to assure that the utility has the financial capacity to build and operate a reactor; a preliminary safety analysis of the reactor design and site, detailing aspects of operations, personnel, accident pro-cedures, radioactive releases, waste storage, and quality assurance programs; an environmental report that becomes the basis of the

FIGURE 5

Parallel Tracks in Construction Permit Review Process

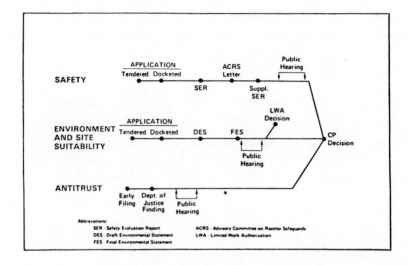

Source: U.S. Nuclear Regulatory Commission, 1975 Annual Report

NRC's environmental impact statement and sets forth probable impact, adverse environmental effects, and alternatives; and infor- mation relevant to antitrust considerations. A nonrefundable fee of $125,000 must be paid with the application.

Review by NRC Staff

If the application is accepted, it is passed along a three-track review system covering environmental, safety and antitrust con- siderations. For the environmental review, first the staff examines the utility's environmental report; then the staff drafts an environ- mental impact statement and sends it to a number of federal, state and local agencies in compliance with the National Environmental Policy Act; then it sends a final statement incorporating any agency comments to the Atomic Safety and Licensing Board--an independent review board drawn from a panel of lawyers, economists and scientists--for approval.

For the safety review, the staff reviews the preliminary safety assessment report and discusses it with utility and outside representatives. After review the staff issues a safety evaluation report which is passed to the Advisory Committee on Reactor Safeguards--an independent board whose members, mostly scientists and engineers, are appointed to four-year terms by the commission. After it reviews the staff's report, the advisory committee writes a letter to the Nuclear Regulatory Commission, and the staff submits a supplemental safety evaluation report reflecting the advisory committee's findings.

The antitrust review is conducted by the Justice Department. According to former Assistant Attorney General Thomas Kauper, the aim of the department is to ensure that utilities are making efforts "to promote efficiency, and, as part of that, to save scarce fuel. Coordination and reserve sharing of the type we have been seeking in the (NRC) proceedings enables all utilities to use large efficient units, units which produce low-cost power with less fuel."(18) The Justice Department issues an advisory opinion to the Atomic Safety and Licensing Board.

Atomic Safety and Licensing Board Hearings

When it receives completed reports from the NRC and the Justice Department, the Atomic Safety and Licensing Board holds public hearings to review any remaining issues. The hearings in the three areas--environment, safety and antitrust--may be held independently or simultaneously. Usually the environmental report is completed before the preliminary safety report and, because the utility is anxious to obtain a limited authorization to begin construction, the environmental hearings are held first. The hearings are quasi-adjudicatory. Formal notice is provided and a prehearing conference is held to consider petitions from parties wishing to intervene in the proceedings. Intervenors--those who can show they will be affected by a proposed nuclear plant--are granted the right to offer evidence and to subpoena documents and witnesses and to cross-examine witnesses at the hearings. Hearings are limited to technical and environmental issues relating to the specific application; standards, regulatory procedures and general policy questions are not reviewed. After completion of the hearings, the board decides whether to accept, conditionally accept, or reject the application.

Review of the Licensing Decision

Any person participating in the hearings as a party or an intervenor may appeal a board ruling to an Atomic Licensing Safety and Appeal Board. A further appeal may be made to the federal courts, although most observers consider it unlikely that the courts would reverse an appeals board's administrative decision.

Operating License

Once the utility has received its construction permit and completed construction, it must go through a second set of reviews and hearings, in order to obtain its operating license. The utility must file a final safety analysis report and an updated environmental impact statement. Both are reviewed by the NRC staff, and reports are filed with the Atomic Safety and Licensing Board. Further hearings at this stage are not required and are held only if an interested party achieves the status of intervenor. The board's decision on an operating license is subject to the same rights of appeal as is the construction permit. Once its operating license is approved, the utility must pay a $250,000 licensing fee and a second fee based on reactor size.

Proposals to Change Licensing

The existing procedures for licensing require about 14 years from the decision to build to the beginning of operation of a nuclear plant. Both industry and--at least before Three Mile Island--the NRC have argued that steps should be taken to speed the licensing process. The Carter administration proposed the Nuclear Siting and Licensing Act (HR 11704) in 1978, touting it as an important part of its program to increase domestic energy production. The administration-backed bill proposed:

● Standardization of reactor and plant designs, allowing the NRC to issue permits to vendors for pre-approved reactors or parts;

● Early site review, allowing NRC approval of reactor sites before a construction permit is issued;

● Reduction of the adversary public hearing process for licenses;

● Elimination of the mandatory construction permit review by the NRC's Advisory Committee on Reactor Safeguards;

● Permission for the NRC to delegate environmental reviews, as required by the National Environmental Policy Act, to state authorities; and

● Permission for the NRC to issue operating licenses together with construction permits, and to issue interim operating licenses before operating license hearings are completed.

There are differences of opinion as to how much time such a bill might save. In the past, the NRC has estimated that such measures might reduce licensing time by as much as five years. The Congressional Budget Office, however, issued a report in March 1979 that concluded that even if these proposed steps were taken, licensing times would be reduced by only about 15 months.(19) The CBO report found that most of the delays associated with nuclear plants were attributable to areas outside the direct control of government agencies--including problems with labor, materials, financing and management.

Whatever the benefits associated with streamlining the nuclear licensing process, it appears that support for such measures was dramatically reduced by events in 1979--especially the Three Mile Island incident. The chances for a licensing speedup in the near future seem virtually nonexistent, killed by a spate of public protests about nuclear safety and calls by numerous government officials for more stringent safeguards. Indeed, many high-level government officials in the NRC, Congress and agencies with jurisdiction over nuclear matters are predicting a licensing slowdown. Among the most probable changes, according to some observers, are stricter requirements for operator training, utility technical and management capabilities, plant control room design, emergency planning and evacuation procedures. In addition, it is likely that there will be new restrictions concerning the siting of nuclear plants near large population centers. As of the end of 1979, a special NRC "lessons learned" task force had recommended, and the NRC had adopted, at least 20 specific recommendations for changes in nuclear hardware and procedures.(20)

Enforcement

The NRC has about 400 staff members assigned to inspect the nuclear plants now operating or under construction. Only 20 of these, however, are federal inspectors who are permanently assigned to particular nuclear power plants.(21) Many additional staff members are currently concentrating on ensuring that operating plants comply with new regulations issued as the result of the Three Mile Island incident. NRC officials told IRRC in 1976 that a plant is inspected an average of 50 times during the period before operation and must be inspected a minimum of four times a year after it goes into operation. Any violations found during the inspections are reported orally to the plant manager, and the NRC staff writes a letter to the management of the utility asking that the problem be corrected. If necessary, the NRC will order the plant to operate at less than capacity or shut it down until the problem can be rectified. Traditionally, however, the NRC has issued shutdown orders or imposed civil fines only after repeated violations have indicated what the NRC considers "a pattern of noncompliance."

Assessments of the effectiveness of the NRC's enforcement program--both from within the agency itself and from outside observers--were dramatically altered by the accident at Three Mile Island. In 1976, for instance, the official NRC position was that civil penalties were largely unnecessary because the agency always had the power to require a plant to shut down, forcing it to buy replacement power at a cost of $100,000 to $200,000 a day. NRC officials reported that the limited use of fines and efforts to get the industry to regulate itself were working well. "By and large," one NRC official told IRRC, "I think our enforcement program is effective."(22)

Such optimistic assessments contrast sharply with the harsh indictment of the NRC's enforcement program leveled by the Kemeny Commission, a blue ribbon panel appointed by President Carter to investigate the causes of the Three Mile Island incident. The commission reported in October 1979 that:

Two of the most important activities of NRC are its licensing function and its inspection and enforcement (I&E) activities. We found serious inadequacies in both.

...Evidence for this exists in the weak and understaffed branch of NRC that monitors operator training, in the fact that inspectors who investigate accidents concentrate on what went wrong with the equipment and not on what operators may have done incorrectly, in the lack of attention to the quality of procedures provided for operators, and in an almost total lack of attention to the interaction between human beings and machines.(23)

The Kemeny Commission contended that the NRC was doing such a bad job of regulating the industry that it should be abolished. The General Accounting Office issued a report in February 1979 that presaged the Kemeny Commission's findings. The GAO report concluded that the NRC had failed to make "full and effective use" of the limited power Congress had given it to penalize companies that violated its rules. The GAO found that in one recent year the NRC had discovered violations in 2,500 of its 6,400 inspections but that it had imposed civil penalties on only 13 occasions. Even in these cases, the report noted, the fines were usually well below those permitted under the law.(24)

There were signs that the NRC was stepping up its enforcement activities even before Three Mile Island, but the accident appears to have accelerated this trend. Between April 1979 and October 1980, the NRC staff proposed more than $1 million in fines for utilities that had violated safety regulations. This included a proposed $450,000 fine, the biggest in the agency's history, against Consumers Power Co. of Jackson, Mich., for violations at its Palisades plant. In addition, the NRC has formally asked Congress to raise the limit on the civil penalties it can levy from $5,000 per violation per day to $100,000. In the words of NRC Commissioner Gilinsky, "We have made more progress in reorienting nuclear regulation this year than in the previous four years of NRC's existence.... The change which is now taking place took so long because until very recently, any effort to tighten restrictions has pitted the safety reviewers against an entrenched system designed to foster expanded participation and growth in nuclear power."(25)

THE CONTROVERSY OVER GOVERNMENT'S ROLE

The industry and major portions of the government view the political and regulatory processes as a sincere effort to protect the public interest while allowing for the necessary growth of nuclear power. Both company and government officials, however, are critical of what they see as inefficiencies in the regulatory process. Critics see the processes as detrimental to the public interest, providing few opportunities for genuine consideration of alternatives to nuclear power and other concerns of nuclear power opponents, and emphasizing the promotion of nuclear development over its regulation.

Finally, important government officials in Congress, the NRC and the executive branch have joined critics in condemning the existing regulatory system as inadequate and calling for tougher regulation of the nuclear industry.

Views of Nuclear Power Proponents

Industry and government officials dispute contentions by critics that the decision to develop nuclear energy was made without sufficient public involvement. They say that the current process of approval allows for public review of nuclear power and argue that both industry and government have made an effort to provide the public with information on issues relating to nuclear development. They also argue that the relationship between industry and government has been healthy and that government assistance to companies involved in aspects of nuclear power has not interfered with its regulatory responsibilities. If anything, industry officials say, the government has been too strict in its regulation.

Public Involvement in Decisions Relating to Nuclear Power

Government and company representatives say that the decision to proceed with the development of nuclear power was made only after conscious deliberation by public representatives. "The fact is," Westinghouse wrote to IRRC, "that the entire Congress enacted the legislation--the Atomic Energy Act. It is specious to argue that the decision to go nuclear was not adequately considered."(26)

Industry spokesmen agree with critics that the licensing process does not provide a forum for the discussion of broad public policy issues relating to nuclear power development. Those issues they consider to be political. "They were never meant to be considered in the licensing process," one utility representative told IRRC. "They belong in a political forum."

But the process does allow for public participation in the review of ongoing decisions relating to nuclear development, according to industry and government representatives. In fact, many industry officials contend that the overall regulatory process is so open that it allows a small but vocal anti-nuclear minority to jeopardize and delay nuclear plants that are endorsed by the majority of the nation's citizens. Moreover, utility representatives say, the opportunities that the public has to participate in nuclear plant hearings tend to be wasted discussing non-issues. "Sixty to seventy percent of the time spent at nuclear plant public hearings is wasted discussing trivial issues," a utility lawyer told IRRC.

Availability of Information

In general, nuclear power proponents believe that the government has not withheld important information from the public in recent years.

The AEC in 1974, and later the NRC, recognized that past restrictions on disclosure of information to the public had been overly harsh--even suppressive--but officials say the policy has changed. Muntzing of the AEC said in 1974 that "three years ago we created a revolutionary openness--we may not be perfect, but we're a lot better." He told The New York *Times* that "there is no agency as dedicated to opening up as the AEC."(27) Then-NRC Chairman William H. Anders testified in 1976 that "an examination of our record will show further that this commission has gone well beyond the requirements of the Freedom of Information Act in making information available to the public .... The NRC is committed to giving the public the facts about nuclear safety, whether the facts are agreeable or not .... Every document representing an official staff position on a reactor safety issue is routinely placed in our central public document room as well as in other locations we have established around the country." He commented that "the public may add new insights to this information and can provide us with valuable feedback, by letter or in public hearings, which we consider in reaching our determinations."(28) Marcus Rowden, who succeeded Anders as NRC chairman, commented: "It is just not in our own self-interest to cover up or appear to cover up."(29)

If anything, some nuclear proponents suggest that the NRC's readiness to make information available to the public may have gone too far. Then-NRC Chairman Joseph Hendrie, for instance, expressed alarm in 1979 at the public availability of government studies such as "Barrier Penetration Database," a document that describes security barriers at nuclear plants. According to Hendrie, because some types of information that the NRC is currently making public would aid nuclear saboteurs, he has asked Congress to give the agency new powers to withhold certain types of information from the public.(30)

Internal Dissent

Nuclear proponents argue that the regulatory process allows ample opportunity for internal dissent within the NRC. In response to allegations by critics that the agency did not allow sufficient internal dissent, then-NRC Chairman Rowden stated in 1976: "The commission is intent that there be no misunderstanding our commitment to these basic principles--that staff be able and expected to make known their best professional judgment, whether or not it corresponds with the views of other staff or management; and that this can be done with the assurance of no recrimination or retribution."(31)

Relationship with the Nuclear Industry

Company officials acknowledge that the government has played an active role in the development of nuclear power, but they argue that such assistance is fully justified. Richard McCormack of General Atomic Corp. has described the industry as "born in government and consciously weaned by statutory and administrative policies." Such government involvement was, and continues to be, necessary, he says, because the nuclear industry

> is the most technologically intensive major business in the world today. It requires enormous amounts of front-end capital to bring a system into full commercial-ization .... Traditional short-time manufacturer-customer commercial practices are breaking down because they involve time-spans and risks that simply do not allow business to proceed on an equitable basis .... The private sector first isn't investing in reprocessing and recycle because, frankly, the vendors find themselves against the wall with neither the capital nor, sadly, the desire to make new investments in an industry absolutely essential to the growth of our nation, but beset with uncertainties no prudent businessman would accept.(32)

Most industry representatives agree and say that more, rather than less, government involvement will required in the future to assist in the development of methods for waste disposal, reprocessing spent fuels, and new technologies for enrichment of uranium. Greater ex-penditure on nuclear power than on alternative technologies or conservation is justified, industry sources say, because "the costs of research increase sharply as you move up the learning curve." General Electric representatives commented to IRRC that "to compare research funds for an advanced technology with those allocated to a new technology is meaningless."(33)

But nuclear supporters categorically deny that government participation in the development of the industry has affected the NRC's ability to regulate it, and they reject charges that it has colluded with industry to spur development. "There really has developed an adversary situation," asserts Robert Szalay, the Atomic Industrial Forum's top regulation expert. "It makes me mad when some of the anti-industry people contend that there's collusion," he says.(34) And then-NRC Chairman Rowden wrote to Ralph Nader in 1976: "The strong criticism we have received from the regulated industry, responding to what it views as undue regulatory con-servatism, reflects the reality that NRC has taken measures it deemed necessary notwithstanding substantial impact on the industry."(35)

In fact, many industry officials see industry as the chief victim of the regulatory process. George J. Stathakis of General Electric has described the process as "extremely rigorous ... difficult and ex-pensive." He argues that GE's "relations with the regulatory staff had been an adversary character. We have certainly not found the NRC to be overly impressed by economic considerations. From our per-spective we have often felt that the NRC has paid excessive deference to the concerns expressed by opponents of nuclear power and has acted in an overly conservative manner."(36) The AIF's Robert Szalay adds, "There aren't many other agencies as tough or competent as the

NRC." If the commission has a problem, Szalay says, it is that "they review plant licenses in greater depth and detail than is necessary," raising costs and delaying needed projects.(37)

A major industry complaint has related to the standards set by the NRC for plant construction and operation. The absence of standards has slowed approval of plant design in certain areas, and overly strict standards have raised construction costs in others. Inefficiency in setting standards has been a major cause of expensive construction and licensing delays, these officials assert. Although many industry officials have played a role in developing standards, some industry representatives suggest that unless a more realistic approach is taken toward standards, there will be a dropoff in industry efforts to contribute to standards development. The major problems, according to McCormack of General Atomic, are ratcheting--the "practice of continuously escalating regulatory requirements on an ad hoc basis from one project to the next"--and backfitting--"requiring redesign of facilities to conform to subsequently adopted regulatory requirements."(38)

Views of Nuclear Power Opponents

Critics of nuclear power have a number of complaints about the role that government has played in its development. Until recently, they say, the growing commitment to nuclear power has never been openly reviewed in a political forum, and they argue that the current regulatory process offers little opportunity for debate on the major issues involved in its development. They also maintain that the agencies and committees involved in overseeing or administering the nuclear power program--the Joint Committee on Atomic Energy, the Atomic Energy Commission, the Energy Research and Development Administration, and the Nuclear Regulatory Commission--have been biased in its favor. As a result, they say, they have ignored energy alternatives and have failed to provide the public with a realistic assessment of nuclear power.

Joint Committee

Opponents of nuclear power are very critical of the former Joint Committee on Atomic Energy. They say the committee decided quite early that its major role was to promote nuclear power. Thereafter, they say, it made no efforts to reexamine its initial decision but concentrated instead on solving technical problems that would impede development of a civilian industry. Ralph Nader, in testimony before the committee, commented: "It is revealing to examine how poorly the committee has performed its oversight function with regard to protecting the public against the wide range of dangers associated with nuclear power development," and he accused the committee of actively assisting the AEC "in suppressing critical data on atomic plant safety hazards."(39)

Critics assert that other members of Congress chose to defer to members of the joint committee on the theory that they possessed the experience and technical knowledge required to review nuclear power. Thus, according to Green of George Washington Law School, "the development of atomic energy policy has taken place largely within a closed circle of government atomic energy specialists, on the apparent assumption that atomic energy represents a totally unique and isolated problem separate from other technical concerns of the government."(40) Until recently, this isolation, critics say, made it impossible for questions about nuclear power to get a full hearing in Congress.

AEC

During its lifetime, the AEC was criticized heavily by opponents of nuclear power. They considered the commission to be schizophrenic, with its dual purpose of regulation and promotion, and they argued that its performance was unbalanced in favor of promotion. Anthony Roisman, then a lawyer for a number of groups intervening in hearings to oppose nuclear plant licenses, said in 1974 that "promotion has often clouded the AEC's regulatory judgment."(41) Daniel Ford of the Union of Concerned Scientists emphasized this point in December 1974 in a letter to IRRC:

> For the most part, we sense that people in the country generally have thrown up their hands in despair when it comes to any serious discussion of the nuclear power controversy . . . . Instead, they have trusted the AEC to make expert impartial decisions on nuclear safety matters in the public interest. In fact, however, the AEC has acted much more to promote nuclear power than they have to protect the public health and safety . . . . The fact that the agency entrusted with making the safety decisions cannot itself be trusted is a factor that must weigh heavily in the country's acceptance or nonacceptance of nuclear power. No one doubts the need for strict controls over nuclear power, and if the agency insuring such strict controls is seriously compromised, then it's a major institutional barrier to the society's use of nuclear power.(42)

Not only did the AEC overlook safety, the critics say, but the commission also tried to keep information concerning safety problems from the public. David Burnham of The New York *Times*, after examining a number of AEC documents written before 1973, concluded that "AEC documents show that for at least 10 years, the commission has repeatedly sought to suppress studies by its own scientists that found nuclear power was more dangerous than officially acknowledged or that raised questions about reactor safety devices."(43)

ERDA

A number of observers--including most critics of nuclear power--argue that the Energy Research and Development Adminis- tration was dominated by former AEC employees and also that its programs were too heavily focused on the development of nuclear power. Jimmy Carter commented during the 1976 presidential campaign that because ERDA "is an off-shoot of the now defunct Atomic Energy Commission, its entire slant is toward the nuclear industry. Sixty-five percent of its research resources for fiscal year 1977 are oriented toward nuclear fission and fusion, while only 5 percent will go to energy conservation and 6 percent for solar power."(44) Carter described this distribution as "folly," and most nuclear critics agree with that description.

DOE

Since ERDA's functions were incorporated into the new Department of Energy in 1977, critics acknowledge that there has been some reorienting of the nation's energy research and development effort away from nuclear power and toward alternatives such as conservation and solar power. Nevertheless, they say that DOE continues--like its predecessor organizations--to be obsessed with nuclear power to the detriment of more promising energy sources. Critics say that the department's R&D budget allocations--where spending for nuclear programs remains higher than that for fossil fuel or solar technologies--indicate that DOE continues to exhibit a pro-nuclear bias. In addition, they note that the department's first head, James Schlesinger, was a former chairman of the AEC and outspokenly pronuclear, and that its next head, Charles W. Duncan, called for continued large use of nuclear power.

NRC

Many of the same complaints raised about the AEC continue to be voiced by critics of the Nuclear Regulatory Commission. Critics of nuclear power say that the commission's regulatory objectivity suffers from conflicts of interest among its staff members, many of whom are drawn from--or will eventually go to--the industry they regulate. Common Cause charged, in a study released late in 1976, that relationships between NRC staff and consultants and the industry it regulates offer serious potential for conflict of interest. The study reported that 72 percent of the NRC's top 429 employees have been employed by private energy companies and that 90 percent of these employees came from companies with which the NRC had current contracts or licenses. Sixty-five percent of the NRC's consultants are working as well for companies that have received NRC licenses or contracts. "Our findings," Common Cause wrote in the study, "point to potential conflicts of interest, and the possibility of serious agency bias, throughout the executive bureaucracy."(45)

Some of the criticism for the NRC's practices has originated within the agency. In 1976, for instance, several engineers left the NRC in protest over what they considered to be an inadequate concern for safety. Robert Pollard, a reactor engineer and project manager with the NRC until February 1976, testified that, "as a result of my work at the commission, I believe that the separation of the Atomic Energy Commission into two agencies has not resolved the conflict between the promotion and regulation of commercial nuclear plants. Because I found that the pressures to maintain schedules and to defer resolution of known safety problems frequently prevailed over reactor safety, I decided I had to resign."(46) Today, as a member of the Union of Concerned Scientists, Pollard remains highly critical of the NRC. "The NRC program is superficial, inadequate and does not attack the fundamental problems," Pollard asserts. "The only things being fixed are the particular matters that went wrong at Three Mile Island, not the broad range of safety problems the commission knows exist," he says.(47)

In October 1976, Ronald Fluegge, an NRC engineer, resigned and asserted that he had been repeatedly "frustrated in (his) efforts to make the agency deal honestly with pressing nuclear safety problems."(48) Fluegge stated, "We are issuing safety evaluation reports that are carefully censored to conceal major safety problems. We are withholding from the public NRC staff technical analyses of a wide range of unpleasant nuclear safety difficulties. We are giving the public glib assurances about the nuclear plant safety that we know lack an adequate technical basis."(49)

In addition, at least two of the NRC's present commissioners--Victor Gilinsky and Peter Bradford--believe that the agency has long sacrificed safety in order to promote the development of nuclear power. Bradford described the problem in November 1979 as primarily one of attitude. "The primary blockages to safety in the Nuclear Regulatory Commission have not been analogous to some set of frayed wires in a complex electrical circuit," Bradford states. "Rather they have been the willful shunting aside of not only the specific bad news, but of procedures and people who have inclined to raise and pursue bad news to a reasonable conclusion on anything other than the most urgently obvious safety questions."(50) Gilinsky, who feels that the NRC has made some impressive changes since the accident at Three Mile Island, describes the pre-TMI NRC as inheriting a flawed system of priorities from the AEC:

> NRC was established to make sure that expansion was not bought at the price of safety. Unfortunately, there was a flaw in the system of priorities inherited from the AEC. For while NRC's mandate was safety, its top priority was licensing nuclear power plants. Performance in the new regulatory agency tended to be measured in terms of how many licenses were granted and how fast the proceedings were closed; the assumption was that the level of safety attained was already well beyond what was needed. This

turned out not to be, so the flaw turned out to be
fundamental. It took Three Mile Island to grind it out.(51)

Finally, nuclear critics' complaints about a bias in the NRC have
been given additional legitimacy by the Report of the President's
Commission on Three Mile Island (Kemeny Commission). That commission reported in October 1979:

> ... We have seen evidence that some of the old promotional
> philosophy still influences the regulatory practices of the
> NRC. While some compromises between the needs of safety
> and the needs of an industry are inevitable, the evidence
> suggests that the NRC has sometimes erred on the side of
> the industry's convenience rather than carrying out its
> primary mission of assuring safety.(52)

Public Involvement in Decision-Making

Critics of the Nuclear Regulatory Commission argue that the way
it structures licensing hearings--with the intent of reviewing the
applicant's capacity to meet safety standards--does not allow the
debate of what intervenors see as the major issues of substance--plant
safety, safeguards, waste storage, and energy alternatives. Intervenors see the licensing process as limited to discussion of technical
issues, many of which are irrelevant. The problem, according to
Harold Green of George Washington, is that intervenors "are driven to
contest issue of the license on grounds with respect to which they have
the least technical resources and the least competence. The
experience is characteristically one of frustration, and the opponents
of nuclear power emerge from their inevitable defeat with a feeling of
alienation and resentment about the stacked deck of cards."(53) The
recently released report of a special inquiry group established by the
NRC to investigate the causes of the Three Mile Island accident went
even farther in condemning the NRC's licensing process. The inquiry
group, headed by Washington lawyer Mitchell Rogovin, stated in a
draft report that "insofar as the licensing process is supposed to
provide a publicly accessible, adversary forum for the resolution of
safety issues relevant to the construction and operation of a nuclear
power plant," the process "is a sham."(54)
Critics also assert that the NRC's policy of discussing generic
issues in rulemaking hearings further limits the opportunity to challenge nuclear development. They say that by removing major issues
from adjudicatory licensing to administrative rule-making hearings,
the NRC potentially inhibits the intervenors' ability to raise questions
and to get important information before the public.

THE FUTURE ROLE OF GOVERNMENT

The last five years have seen a growing decentralization of the decision-making process related to nuclear power. The AEC's responsibilities were split, and the congressional oversight functions once handled exclusively by the Joint Committee on Atomic Energy have been spread among several congressional committees. Responsibility for setting standards in such areas as radiation limits and transportation procedures no longer rests exclusively with the NRC but is shared with agencies such as the Environmental Protection Agency, the Department of Energy, the Department of Health and Human Services, and the Department of Transportation. In some areas, state and local governments have passed laws or ordinances that are beginning to have a profound effect on nuclear development. Finally, discussion of nuclear power has entered the political arena, where debate over various aspects of its development is exerting increasing pressure to slow the speed at which it develops.

The Future of the NRC and Federal Involvement

The future role of the NRC is uncertain, but signs suggest that it will continue much as it has in the past--albeit with a larger budget, more safety inspectors, a new and more powerful chairman, and a greater emphasis on power plant safety. The President's Commission on the Accident at Three Mile Island concluded that the NRC, as now organized, was incapable of carrying out its mandate of ensuring nuclear plant safety and recommended that the agency be totally restructured as an independent agency within the executive branch, headed by a single administrator. The NRC's own special inquiry group reached much the same conclusion after stating in a draft report that the NRC was "an organization that is not so much badly managed as it is not managed at all."(55) President Carter, however, announced in December 1979 that he intended to keep the five-member commission but that he would appoint a new chairman from outside the agency and ask Congress to strengthen the role of the chairman to "clarify assignment of authority and responsibility and provide this person with the power to act on a daily basis as a chief executive officer . . . . "(56) In July 1980, Carter nominated Albert Carnesale, a nuclear engineer and professor of public policy at Harvard, for the NRC chairmanship.

Outside of some reform of the NRC and the regulatory process, the federal government's role in nuclear power development appears likely to remain somewhat schizophrenic and highly dependent upon the perspectives of the President. Overall federal involvement in the nuclear fuel cycle appears certain to increase as the government is forced to confront such issues as permanent waste disposal, plant decommissioning, evacuation procedures for areas near nuclear plants, growing international disputes over the issues of reprocessing and the use of breeder technology, and efforts by states to impose restrictions or moratoriums on nuclear plant construction and waste disposal. In addition, many observers believe that responsibility for the protection of the public, and perhaps even ownership of nuclear plants themselves, will inevitably shift from the utility companies to the federal government. In many ways, the shift in responsibility for safety has already occurred. As a high-level NRC official recently noted with respect to the Three Mile Island accident:

> After several days of confusion, when concern about a core meltdown was still very great, the NRC made clear that from then on it would have the last word in the potentially life-and-death decisions. In relieving the owner of the damaged reactor from responsibility for final decision making, the federal government, in fact if not in law, took over the responsibility for protecting the public. The absurdity of the previously held notion that a utility company could develop the resources necessary to protect large populations against the hazards of massive releases of radioactivity, which could easily extend over many states and several decades in time, has now become apparent.(57)

The Future Role of State and Local Governments

One factor that is beginning to have a significant impact on nuclear development--and appears likely to have an ever larger impact in the future--is decisions by state and local authorities forbidding or restricting nuclear power development. It is unclear exactly how far such efforts will go, as many unanswered questions remain concerning final jurisdiction over nuclear matters, but for the moment states' decisions about future nuclear plant construction have not been strongly challenged by the federal government.

The state energy boards or public service commissions in at least six states--California, Connecticut, Iowa, Maine, New York and Wisconsin--have enacted what amount to statewide moratoriums on future nuclear plant construction.(58) In California, Connecticut and Maine, laws have been passed requiring that nuclear waste disposal methods be demonstrated before new nuclear plants can be approved. In Iowa and Wisconsin, state regulatory commissions have announced that they will not consider approving new nuclear plants, citing unresolved issues concerning waste disposal, economics, and plant decommissioning. In New York, Gov. Hugh Carey, the New York Public Service Commission and the New York State Energy Board have all announced their opposition to new nuclear plant construction and have effectively blocked all recent utility attempts to site nuclear plants in that state.

In addition, in four states--Hawaii, Montana, Oregon and Vermont--statewide initiatives have been passed by voters attaching such stringent conditions to nuclear plant construction that it is extremely unlikely that any utility would attempt to build new plants there.(59) (Statewide antinuclear initiatives in a number of other states, including a September 1980 initiative in Maine that would have prohibited the continued operation of that state's only nuclear plant, have been rejected by voters.)

Finally, state utility commissions in some states, notably California, Illinois, North Carolina and Wisconsin, have begun penalizing utilities whose construction programs have emphasized nuclear power over alternative energy sources. In California, the public utility commission recently penalized Pacific Gas & Electric $7.2 million per year for failing to stimulate more industrial cogeneration projects, but said it would refund the money if PG&E signed up 600 megawatts of cogenerated power within two years.(60) In North Carolina, the state commission ordered Duke Power Co., Carolina Power & Light Co., Virginia Electric & Power Co., and Nantahala Power & Light Co. to establish, operate and finance a North Carolina Alternative Energy Corporation. The commission ordered Duke Power to set aside $1 million per year from a recent rate increase as its share of the operating costs of the corporation and said that it would assess the other companies in future rate cases.(61) In Illinois, the Illinois Commerce Commission initially granted Chicago's Commonwealth Edison only a 1.65 percent rate increase (the company had asked for an 18.3 percent increase), citing unanswered questions about nuclear plant performance and consumers' wage concerns. In response, Commonwealth Edison temporarily halted all construction on its half-finished Braidwood nuclear plant.(62) Finally, in Wisconsin, the Wisconsin Public Service Commission issued an order in February 1980 designed to encourage Wisconsin Electric Power and two minority partners to abandon their plans to build the proposed Haven nuclear plant. The commission offered the utilities two options: one, pursue the Haven application, write off $36 million in pre-certification costs and receive no rate of return on the amortization of those costs; or two, abandon the application and receive a return on the amortization of the $36 million. A staff source on the commission described the order as "dangling a carrot in front of (the utilities) to abandon the application." In March, the utilities announced they were canceling the Haven project.(63)

As this list illustrates, some state authorities are becoming increasingly critical of nuclear power development. The trend is likely to accelerate. Anti-nuclear legislation is under consideration now in the legislatures of Arkansas, Arizona, Colorado, Illinois, Iowa, Louisiana, Michigan, New Hampshire, New York, Ohio, Oklahoma and Pennsylvania. Many state public utility commissions are reexamining the financial implications of utilities' nuclear construction programs and some of them are ordering independent financial audits in the face of skyrocketing utility cost estimates. Statewide antinuclear initiatives were on the Nov. 4, 1980, ballot in five states--Oregon, Washington, Montana, South Dakota and Missouri. The initiatives were passed in Oregon and Washington but rejected in Missouri, Montana and South Dakota.(64)

In addition to this increased opposition at the state level, nuclear power proposals are encountering rising opposition at the local level. The most prevalent local actions have been restrictions by cities or counties on the transportation of nuclear materials. But the construction of a nuclear plant typically requires various local zoning permits, and there are signs that these will become increasingly tough for utilities to get, especially in heavily populated areas or in areas of great scenic beauty. Of the two local referendums concerning nuclear plant construction that have taken place since the Three Mile Island accident, one approved and one rejected continued nuclear power projects. In Austin, Tex., on April 7, 1979, voters narrowly approved continuation of the city's participation in the South Texas nuclear project.(65) But on Nov. 6, 1979, voters in northwestern Washington's Skagit County voted by a margin of 71.6 percent against a proposal to renew a zoning contract that would allow Puget Sound Power & Light Co. to build two plants in the Skagit River Valley. The company has since announced that it is considering building only one plant instead of two, deferring the project for up to three years, and examining other possible sites.(66)

Another area where local opposition appears to be having a significant impact is in New England, where a number of local municipalities have forbidden small local power companies from buying a stake in the Seabrook nuclear plant. Public Service Co. of New Hampshire is attempting to sell a major portion of the much-delayed plant and had lined up power companies to buy shares in the plant, but public opposition has forced a number of companies to back down from their offers. According to *The Wall Street Journal*, the biggest controversy developed in Massachusetts, where public opposition forced Massachusetts Municipal Wholesale Electric Co., a consortium of 31 municipal power companies, to reduce its planned new stake in the Seabrook plant from 14 percent to 6 percent.(67)

State and local sentiments also will soon become an important factor in the siting of temporary and permanent waste disposal sites. Major controversies have already developed in several areas of the country that are likely candidates for a permanent geologic waste depository. Tensions will undoubtedly increase as the federal government begins choosing preliminary sites and building waste disposal demonstration facilities.

NOTES

(1) For a history of the early relationship between the nuclear industry and government, see Harold P. Green, "Nuclear Technology and the Fabric of Government," 33 *George Washington Law Review* 121, 1964, pp. 121 ff.; Arthur D. Little Inc., "Competition in the Nuclear Power Supply Industry," a report to the AEC and the U.S. Department of Justice (Washington, D.C., U.S. Government Printing Office, December 1968); Irwin C. Bupp Jr., "Priorities in the Nuclear Technology Program," Ph.D. thesis, Harvard University, Cambridge, Mass., 1971.

(2) Craig Hosmer, telephone interview with Investor Responsibility Research Center, 1974.

(3) Green, op. cit., p. 129.

(4) *Congressional Quarterly 1977 Almanac*, 95th Congress, Vol. XXXIII (Washington, D.C., Congressional Quarterly, 1978), p. 660.

(5) Green, op. cit., p. 141.

(6) "Nuclear Power Update: Opponents, Supporters Claim Recent Victories," IRRC *News for Investors*, September 1978, p. 196.

(7) Larry Kramer, "Insurance Regulator Decries Nuclear Accident Coverage," The Washington *Post*, April 18, 1979, p. A10.

(8) Ibid.

(9) "Nuclear Insurance: How Much Is Enough (and from Whom)?" *Technology Review*, June-July 1979, p. 73.

(10) Green, op. cit., p. 148.

(11) John O'Leary, interview with Investor Responsibility Research Center, 1974.

(12) L. Manning Muntzing, speech before the American Nuclear Society, 1972.

(13) Eugene Cramer, interview with Investor Responsibility Research Center, 1974.

(14) Victor Gilinsky, testimony before the Joint Committee on Atomic Energy, March 2, 1976, Vol. I, p. 306, "Investigation of Charges Relating to Nuclear Reactor Safety."

(15) O'Leary, op. cit.

(16) Victor Gilinsky, speech before the American Newspaper Publishers Association, Washington, D.C., Sept. 19, 1979 (reprinted in NRC news release, Vol. 5, No. 35, Oct. 2, 1979).

(17) Westinghouse comments to Investor Responsibility Research Center, March 16, 1976; U.S. Nuclear Regulatory Commission, *1975 Annual Report*. Also, Bernard Rusche, testimony before the Joint Committee on Atomic Energy, March 2, 1976, p. 316.

(18) Interview with Investor Responsibility Research Center, 1974.

(19) Congressional Budget Office, *Delays in Nuclear Reactor Licensing and Construction* (Washington, D.C., U.S. Government Printing Office, 1979).

(20) U.S. Nuclear Regulatory Commission, news release, Vol. 5, No. 44, Dec. 6, 1979, p. 4.

(21) Edward Walsh, "Most A-Sites Lack Federal Inspectors; First Urged in '77," The Washington *Post*, April 3, 1979, p. A6.

(22) Telephone interview with Investor Responsibility Research Center, December 1976.

(23) "Excerpts from Presidential Panel's Report on the Three Mile Nuclear Accident," The New York *Times*, April 13, 1979, p. A11.

(24) David Burnham, "Nuclear Officials Believe Accident Will Bring Many New Regulations," The New York *Times*, April 13, 1979, p. A11.

(25) Victor Gilinsky, speech at Brown University, Nov. 15, 1979 (reprinted in NRC news release, Vol. 5, No. 44, Dec. 6, 1979. p. 3).

(26) Westinghouse remarks to Investor Responsibility Research Center, Dec. 17, 1974, p. 29.

(27) David Burnham, "AEC Files Show Effort to Conceal Safety Perils," The New York Times, Nov. 10, 1974, p. 1.

(28) William H. Anders, testimony before the Joint Committee on Atomic Energy, March 2, 1976, Vol. I, op. cit., p. 263.

(29) David Burnham, "Atomic Energy Agency Completes Report Amid Charges It Stifles Criticism," The New York Times, Oct. 21, 1976.

(30) Glenn Frankel, "Power to Withhold Sensitive Reports Sought by Agency," The Washington Post, July 25, 1979.

(31) Hal Willard, "NRC Acts on Safety Warnings," The Washington Post, Nov. 6, 1976, p. A1.

(32) Richard A. McCormack, "Assessing Today's Nuclear Power Licensing Process," speech at the Atomic Industrial Forum, July 28-31, 1975.

(33) General Electric comments to Investor Responsibility Research Center, Jan. 10, 1975, p. 5.

(34) Walter S. Mossberg, "Nuclear Agency Seeks to Strengthen Its Role in Promoting Safety," The Wall Street Journal, Aug. 7, 1979, p. 1.

(35) Marcus Rowden, letter to Ralph Nader, Oct. 28, 1976.

(36) George Stathakis, testimony before the Joint Committee on Atomic Energy, March 2, 1976, op. cit., p. 175.

(37) Walter S. Mossberg, op. cit.

(38) McCormack, op. cit., p. 14.

(39) Ralph Nader, testimony before the Joint Committee on Atomic Energy, Jan. 28, 1974, pp. 1, 7, 8.

(40) Green, op. cit., p. 152.

(41) Anthony Roisman, interview with IRRC, 1974.

(42) Daniel Ford, letter to IRRC, Dec. 19, 1974.

(43) Burnham, "AEC Files Show Effort to Conceal Safety Perils," op. cit.

(44) Jimmy Carter, "On Energy Reorganization, "press release, Sept. 21, 1976.

(45) Common Cause, "Serving Two Masters" (Washington, D.C., October 1976), pp. i, ii.

(46) Robert Pollard, testimony before the Joint Committee on Atomic Energy, Feb. 18, 1976, Vol. I, pp. 97, 98.

(47) David Burnham, "Nuclear Safety Campaign Aims at the Old Reactors," The New York Times, Dec. 2, 1979.

(48) Thomas O'Toole, "Atom Power Risks Said Disregarded," The Washington Post, Oct. 21, 1976, p. A7.

(49) Burnham, "Atomic Agency Completes Report Amid Charges It Stifles Criticism," op. cit.

(50) Peter A. Bradford, speech before the Seminar on Problems of Energy Policy, New York University, Nov. 21, 1979 (reprinted in NRC news release, Vol. 5, No. 44, Dec. 6, 1979, p. 5).

(51) Victor Gilinsky, speech at Brown University, op. cit.

(52) "Excerpts from Presidential Panel's Report on the Three Mile Nuclear Accident," op. cit.

(53) See Harold Green, Hearings before the Subcommittee on Reorganization, Research and International Organizations, Senate Committee on Government Operations, March 12, 1976, pp. 172 ff.

(54) David Burnham, "Closing Nuclear Plants Suggested If People Can't Evacuate the Area," The New York Times, Dec. 27, 1979, p. 1.

(55) "Rogovin Draft Urges Major NRC Changes and Moratorium on CPs," Nucleonics Week, Vol. 21, No. 1, Jan. 3, 1980, p. 5.

(56) Text of President Carter's statement on the Kemeny Report on Three Mile Island, Congressional Quarterly Weekly Report, Vol. 37, No. 50, Dec. 15, 1979, p. 2856.

(57) R.A. Brightsen, "The Way to Save Nuclear Power," Fortune, Sept. 10, 1979, p. 132.

(58) For information on state actions, see Energy Daily, June 22, 1979; Nucleonics Week, June 14, 1979, and Not Man Apart, August 1979.

(59) Ibid.

(60) Tom Murnane, "Calif. Orders Utilities: Buy Firms' Cogenerated Elec.," Energy User News, Vol. 4, No. 52, Dec. 24, 1979, p. 5.

(61) "North Carolina Commission Urges Formation of Alternative Energy Unit," Energy Users Report, No. 323, Oct. 18, 1979, p. 15.

(62) Paula Ellis, "Utility, Irked by Rule, Stops N-Work," Energy User News, Sept. 17, 1979, p. 5; and "Tight Money Freezes Illinois Nuke Project," In These Times, Oct. 2, 1979, p. 4.

(63) Rob Laufer, "Wisconsin Utilities Offered Incentive to Cancel Nuclear Unit," Nucleonics Week, Vol. 21, No. 8, Feb. 21, 1980, p. 1.

(64) "Five States Will Hold Antinuclear Initiatives," Nucleonics Week, Vol. 21, No. 38, Sept. 18, 1980, p. 3.

(65) "President Names Panelists to Investigate Nuclear Accident," Energy Users Report, No. 296, April 12, 1979, p. 4.

(66) "Local Anti-Nuclear Sentiment Noted as Washington Utility Revises Project," Energy Users Report, No. 328, Nov. 22, 1979, p. 18.

(67) William M. Bulkeley, "Battle-Scarred Seabrook Still Is Facing a Planned 'Occupation,' Financing Woes," The Wall Street Journal, Sept. 14, 1979, p. 15; and Scott Armstrong, "Costs Peril Seabrook Plant More Than Protestors," The Christian Science Monitor, Oct. 5, 1979, p. 5.

Chapter V

CHANGES IN THE NUCLEAR POWER INDUSTRY

The commitment to nuclear power by private industry--including manufacturers of nuclear plants, utilities, banks that finance nuclear projects, and businesses that ultimately must rely on the electricity supplied by these plants--appears to be waning after a decade of steady growth. Events in recent years suggest that the industry may have reached a zenith in the mid-1970s and that it may now be entering a no- or slow-growth phase. Portions of private industry that have been highly supportive of nuclear power are now reexamining their positions. Although some parts of the nuclear power industry have replaced the government as the most vociferous supporter of continued nuclear development, it is unlikely that the industry will regain its former dynamism unless major sections of the public, private industry and government become significantly more supportive than they are at present.

UTILITIES' COMMITMENT TO NUCLEAR POWER

Early Interest

Initially, two factors, in addition to government incentives, encouraged utilities to invest in nuclear power plants. One, according to former Joint Atomic Energy Committee member Craig Hosmer, was that utilities were looking for a competing source of fuel that would help keep down the price of coal and oil.(1) The other, according to MIT's Irwin Bupp, was that "the private utilities were extremely nervous about the evolving AEC power reactor development program. They were inclined to see it as potential camouflage for federal support of publicly owned utilities which in secret with the government would eventually 'squeeze' private utilities out of the power business with massive atomic TVAs."(2)

The 1960s

A report issued in 1968 by Arthur D. Little Inc. noted that growing government experience with nuclear plants and rising fossil fuel prices were complemented by the willingness of General Electric and Westinghouse to supply and construct nuclear power plants on a fixed-price--or "turnkey"--basis. "The utilities needed the reassuring presence of known suppliers (GE and Westinghouse) who had demonstrated through past fossil projects technical resourcefulness in coping with unforeseeable difficulties, and reasonableness in sharing with the utilities the consequent burden of these difficulties,"(3) the study said. GE and Westinghouse, the report suggested, had built up large nuclear engineering divisions in support of government projects, and had a major stake in development of a civilian nuclear power industry.(4)

The result was an early, large commitment to nuclear technology. The report stated: "The fact is that utilities and manufacturers committed themselves to the installation of nearly 60,000 megawatts of generating capacity (representing an investment of over $10 billion) at a time when the only operating experience with nuclear plants was limited to installations which were, in some cases, only one-sixth the size of plants being ordered and having technical performance considerably less strenuous than the plants being ordered."(5)

The Decision-Making Process

The Arthur D. Little report described the process by which utilities decided to purchase nuclear power plants as follows: "In the typical utility process whereby a utility arrives at a choice of power plant supplier, the normal sequence of events is to proceed from a determination of the need for additional capacity, to the selection of a supplier, without an extensive intermediate phase of analyzing potential energy sources. The operating experience and the geography of the utility usually serve to pre-screen various energy sources, excluding some without the need for elaborate analysis."(6)

Utilities argue that this is no longer the case. They say that they carefully consider the costs and benefits of all potential energy sources before investing in new plants. Detroit Edison Co., for example, in response to a shareholder resolution in 1979 asking the company not to meet its energy needs with nuclear power, stated that "In its planning, the company has always considered such things as capital costs, fuel availability and costs, other operating costs, and environmental requirements, before building these plants of the future."(7) The utility added that recent studies by it and other utilities "continue to indicate that generation by nuclear fuel is more economical than generation by coal, oil and gas."(8) Pacific Gas and Electric Co., in response to a similar shareholder resolution in 1979, said it "is already seriously considering and will continue to consider all alternative sources of energy production and energy conservation measures, along with nuclear power proposals."(9) However, the company added that "the oil, gas, coal, hydroelectric, geothermal and purchased power sources available to the company are not sufficient to meet the increasing demand for power" and "there is, at present, no method whereby the company could generate sufficient power from solar or wind-powered sources to meet this demand and it is unlikely that such sources will be available in sufficient quantity in the foreseeable future."(10)

Nuclear opponents are highly critical of the decision-making process that led many utilities to build nuclear plants and largely dismiss utilities' claims that such decisions were made only after a thorough study of alternative sources. David DeVarti, a Detroit Edison shareholder who is opposed to the company's decision to build nuclear plants, says the utility has done less in the area of conservation than a number of other utilities and most of its conservation programs have come about only because the Michigan Public Service Commission ordered the utility to undertake them. According to DeVarti, the utility's shareholders and ratepayers would both be better served if the company concentrated on conservation, cogeneration, hydroelectric and wind power instead of building more nuclear plants.(11) Similarly, W.R.Z. Willey, an economist with the Environmental Defense Fund, did an econometric study of Pacific Gas and Electric's future construction plans and concluded that of the 10 large nuclear and coal-fired power plants that PG&E plans to build between now and 1996, only one 800-megawatt coal unit should be built. The rest of the company's projected demand could be met better through alternative energy sources, the EDF study found. "As investments are shifted out of the nuclear- and coal-based PG&E plan and into the alternative energy developments," the study states, "there are clear economic benefits--for PG&E, for PG&E shareholders, and for PG&E ratepayers--to be gained; and the benefits increase with the size of the shift."(12) Moreover, according to EDF counsel David Roe, the PG&E example is widely applicable to other utilities. "Public utility companies...could meet their own projected electricity demands for the foreseeable future, essentially without building any more large baseload power plants," by using alternative sources of energy that are already available "at lower cost and higher profit," says Roe.(13)

These two examples illustrate the growing debate between utilities and their critics as to the need for additional nuclear plants and the adequacy of utilities' efforts to develop and utilize alternatives to large nuclear and coal-fired power plants. Most of the nation's major electric utilities face similar criticism. And while the merits of critics' arguments in favor of alternative energy generation methods remain, to some extent, untested, it is clear that these arguments are having an impact on the utility decision-making process. Utilities' decisions about new generating facilities are no longer being accepted passively. Increasingly, utility ratepayers, public service commissions, state and federal agencies, the press, and even utility shareholders are challenging utilities' construction plans--especially those that concern nuclear plants. Moreover, a few major electric utilities have begun to reorient their construction programs away from new nuclear and coal-fired generating capacity and toward renewable technologies. Southern California Edison, for instance, announced in September 1980 a "major change in corporate policy regarding the sources of future electricity for its customers." The utility said that by 1990, it would meet 30 percent of its anticipated six million kilowatts of additional generation needs with "renewable and alternative sources," including wind, geothermal and solar power, fuel cells, hydroelectric facilities and cogeneration.(14)

It is still unclear exactly to what extent utility companies will be forced to relinquish control over the decision-making process concerning new generating facilities, but the trend is in that direction. (See Chapter IV for a summary of state and local governmental anti-nuclear activities.)

Status Today

The first civilian nuclear power plant began operation in 1957. By the end of 1970, 15 plants were operating, and by September 1980, 74 nuclear plants had operating licenses, representing about 9 percent of U.S. generating capacity.(15) Another 108 reactors were under construction or had been ordered, although a number of these units will probably be canceled (see Figure 6 on p. 80).

Future Development

The extent to which utilities will order nuclear power plants appears to be tied closely to two factors: growth in electricity demand and government actions on such issues as fuel reprocessing, nuclear plant safety and waste disposal. The desire of electric utilities to build more nuclear plants is likely to diminish in importance as a factor in determining the number of plants that actually get built--because of the increasing involvement of the public and government authorities in the decision-making process--but it will nevertheless remain an important determinant of the future of nuclear power.

Many utilities continue to support full-scale development of nuclear power. Most say that nuclear power is cheaper than the alternatives, that nuclear plants can be operated safely, and that the problems of waste disposal, plant decommissioning and nuclear proliferation are all amenable to solution with known technology. Nuclear power would prosper, these utilities say, if only the government had the resolve to implement solutions to these problems and cut the endless red tape involved in siting and constructing nuclear plants. In spite of this general support for continued nuclear power development, however, not a single electric utility in the country

FIGURE 6

Nuclear Power Plants in the United States

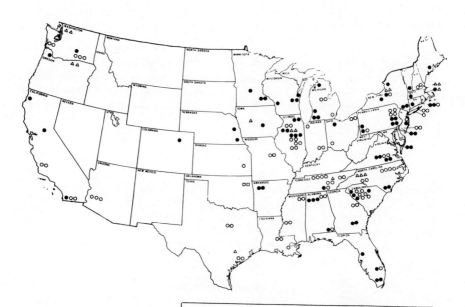

Key
- ● Operable
- ○ Under Construction
- □ With Limited Work Authorizations
- △ On Order

Atomic Industrial Forum, Inc.

The following figures are current as of September 22, 1980:

74 Reactors With Operating Licenses[1]	54,988 MWe[2]
87 Reactors With Construction Permits	95,839 MWe
2 Reactors With Limited Work Authorizations	2,300 MWe
19 Reactors On Order	22,282 MWe
182 Total	175,409 MWe

[1]Includes 69 reactors (50,904 MWe) in commercial operation; 2 reactors (North Anna 2 = 850 MWe; Sequoyah 1 = 1,148 MWe) with full-power licenses and in power ascension phase; 1 reactor (Salem 2 = 1,115 MWe) with low-power license; and 2 reactors (Humboldt Bay = 65 MWe, TMI 2 = 906 MWe) shut down indefinitely.

[2]Represents rated capability of all operable reactors and, as of 6/30/80, accounted for 9.2% of the total U.S. installed electric generating capacity. For the first 6 months of 1980, nuclear power plants generated 114.6-billion kwh, or 10.3% of the total U.S. output of 1,110.0-billion kwh.

NOTE: As of 6/30/80, U.S. commercial nuclear reactors accumulated approximately 565 years of operating experience. Over 1,800 reactor years have accumulated worldwide.

today appears eager to begin the process of siting and constructing a new nuclear power plant given the current regulatory environment. It is clear that, in the minds of many utility executives, the risks associated with building nuclear plants are now perceived as being much greater than they were a few years ago. As an editorial in *Electrical World*, an industry trade journal, noted: "An executive who chooses the nuclear option is, in effect, because of the huge capital cost, betting his company that the facility will be built, and operated for at least a major part of its economic life. (General Public Utilities) may have lost that bet .... This brutal lesson will not be lost on the industry."(16)

Case Studies

The attitude of utilities toward nuclear power today is perhaps best illustrated by several examples.

Carolina Power and Light

Carolina Power and Light (CP&L) is a rapidly growing electric utility that supplies electric service to about half of North Carolina and one-fourth of South Carolina. The company has three nuclear reactors in operation now and is building four more. CP&L says its nuclear plants in 1978 provided 47.1 percent of the company's power requirements and saved its customers $129 million in fuel costs when compared with its coal-fired units. The company's 1978 annual report states that it is in favor of "full exercise of the nuclear option" including the reprocessing of spent fuel.(17) Its 1979 proxy statement adds, "Nuclear power plants have been proved to be clean and safe, and their use has allowed this company to save substantial amounts of money on fuel, thereby reducing the total cost of generation."(18) Despite this favorable attitude toward nuclear power, however, CP&L has canceled plans to construct two additional nuclear units that had been scheduled for completion in 1989 and 1991 because of downward revisions in its latest demand forecast. In addition, the company announced in its 1978 annual report that because of federal inaction on the waste disposal and reprocessing issues and because of the regulatory climate, it did "not believe it is possible to license and construct a new nuclear facility within a reasonable time period."(19) Thus, even before the accident at Three Mile Island, CP&L had decided that various political factors and uncertainties precluded it from planning additional nuclear plants. Meanwhile, the four nuclear units that CP&L has under construction--originally scheduled for completion in 1977, 1978, 1979 and 1980--are now scheduled for completion in 1985, 1988, 1992 and 1994 at a cost of $4.4 billion.(20)

Detroit Edison

Detroit Edison is a large, primarily electric utility serving Detroit and southeastern Michigan. The company has no nuclear generating capacity and relies on coal-fired units to generate about 82 percent of its power needs. However, Detroit Edison has one nuclear unit in an advanced stage of construction and had plans to construct three additional nuclear units.

Detroit Edison placed the order for its first nuclear plant--Enrico Fermi #2--in August 1968. The plant was originally scheduled for completion in 1974 at an estimated cost of $300 million. The company now says that it hopes to have the plant completed by November 1983 at a cost of about $1.8 billion.(21) The most recent setback for this much-delayed plant came in March 1980, when Detroit Edison announced that work on the plant was being delayed by the need for additional safety-related systems.

The company placed orders for three more nuclear units in 1972--Enrico Fermi unit #3 and Greenwood units #2 and 3. In 1975, the utility canceled the second Fermi unit because of lower-than-expected demand growth. Meanwhile, work on the two Greenwood units was halted in 1974 as part of a cash-conservation plan. In 1978, work on these units was resumed and the company announced that they were slated for completion in 1987 and 1989--at a total cost of more than $3.8 billion. In May 1979, the company moved the target completion dates for the two units back to late 1990 and 1992 because of uncertainties over licensing and the need for additional safety equipment. At the time, the utility maintained that it was not considering canceling or scaling back its nuclear projects and that its studies continued to indicate that nuclear power was economical. In March 1980, however, Detroit Edison announced that it was canceling the two Greenwood units because of regulatory uncertainties resulting from the Three Mile Island accident, financial constraints and a lowered demand forecast. "It was our judgment that (the nuclear project) couldn't be completed as scheduled or within current estimates of cost," William Meese, the company's chairman and chief executive officer, said. "To continue with the design and engineering of these units simply wouldn't be a prudent allocation of the resources of the company."(22) Detroit Edison officials now concede that, at least for the time being, nuclear power has been ruled out as a source of additional generating capacity.

Pacific Gas and Electric

Pacific Gas and Electric (PG&E) is the nation's second largest electric utility, serving northern and central California. The company has traditionally relied on oil and gas to provide the bulk of its electricity needs, but it is attempting to reduce its dependence on these fuels by building geothermal, coal and nuclear plants. PG&E has no major coal-fired or nuclear generating capacity, although it did operate a small 63-megawatt nuclear reactor at Humboldt Bay for a number of years before the unit was ordered to shut down in 1976 for seismic modifications.

PG&E has two large nuclear units at Diablo Canyon which the company ordered in 1966 and 1968. Construction has been completed on the first unit and the second is nearly finished, but neither plant has been granted an operating license. The company originally estimated that the plants would cost about $320 million, but it now expects to complete them for a total cost of about $1.8 billion.(23) Much of this cost overrun has resulted from extensive modifications to the plants that the company was forced to make after it was discovered in 1973 that the plants are located only two-and-a-half miles from a major, active earthquake fault.(24) PG&E maintains that the plants are economic, safe and capable of withstanding a major earthquake. But a number of groups have petitioned the NRC to deny an operating license, citing safety considerations. Many local residents are vehemently opposed to the plants, and California Gov. Edmund G. Brown Jr. has called upon the NRC to deny an operating license permanently, adding, "I hereby serve notice that I personally intend to pursue every avenue of appeal if the NRC ignores the will of this community."(25)

In addition to the two Diablo Canyon units, PG&E filed a Notice of Intention in 1978 stating that it planned to begin development on two additional nuclear units. The California Energy Commission rejected the company's application for the plants, however, and the company has put its plans for the units in abeyance pending the outcome of court suits to overturn various state laws that block the development of nuclear power. A federal district court invalidated all of California's antinuclear laws in April 1980, contending that the Atomic Energy Act gives the federal government exclusive power to regulate nuclear energy, but to date PG&E has shown no signs of reactivating its plans for the two additional nuclear units.

These examples illustrate the current attitude of many utilities toward nuclear power. All three companies say that ideally they would like to build and operate more nuclear plants, but their actions--in view of the political and regulatory environment--suggest that they have begun to turn away from the nuclear option. The problems faced by these three are typical of those faced by other utilities attempting to build nuclear plants. The three utilities themselves, however, are perhaps atypical in that they are larger, and stronger financially, than most of the utility companies in the country.

Delays and Cancellations

Even utilities that remain bullish about nuclear power have been forced to reexamine their projected needs and commitments to build new power plants in light of financial constraints and reduced demand projections. Between January 1974 and February 1980, utilities: ordered 39 nuclear plants, canceled orders for 52 nuclear plants, deferred indefinitely orders for at least seven other reactors, and suffered more than 200 delays of more than a year at nuclear plants planned or under construction.(26) (Some of these delays have occurred at the same plants.) Most utilities, in announcing delays or cutbacks, explain that their decisions are based in part on reassessments of growth in electricity demand, reflecting conservation by residential customers and industry. Cancellations of nuclear plants have far outpaced orders in the last two years, and many nuclear analysts expect this trend to continue, at least for the next several years. In fact, an informal survey of Wall Street analysts by the trade journal *Nucleonics Week* in 1979 found a consensus that from 30 to 53 nuclear plants planned or under construction will probably be canceled as an indirect result of the accident at Three Mile Island.(27)

Financing Problems

In addition to uncertainties about demand and regulatory requirements, many utilities continue to be plagued with uncertainties about their ability to raise capital. Rate increases, while hefty in recent years, have not kept pace with rising construction and fuel costs. Utilities that were able to meet 60 percent of their capital needs internally in the 1960s have been forced to borrow an increasing amount of capital from external sources in the 1970s. This trend hit a peak in 1974 when utilities reached the limit of the industry's ability to raise capital, borrowing 71 percent from external sources.(28)

Although the capital market eased in subsequent years and many utilities were granted rate increases, many analysts are predicting a renewed credit crunch for utilities in the 1980s. Bankers Trust Co. reports that it "expects that the external financing ratio for the electric utility industry will begin to rise again." The bank notes that "fuel, environmental and construction costs will probably rise considerably in the next few years, but recent indications are that state regulators will be reluctant to raise rates in accordance with cost increases." As a result, the bank predicts, "the share of financing from cash flow will be diminished and the industry will be forced to turn increasingly to the financial markets."(29) James G. King, a utility analyst with David L. Babson & Co., agrees, saying that "many of the industry's long-standing problems are beginning to resurface."(30) Gordon Corey, vice chairman of Commonwealth Edison Co., goes even further, saying that "the financial condition of the electric power industry is the worst it has ever been." Corey told a conference of energy analysts in 1980 that unless something was done to make the utility industry more profitable "we can't proceed with the nuclear program or any of the things we are talking about."(31)

Many utilities faced with capital shortages are inclined to cut back on plans to construct new nuclear plants because they are more expensive to build and require longer lead times than fossil fuel plants. Utilities are canceling or delaying nuclear projects with the expectation that even if demand growth should rise, they will be able to meet their power needs by constructing a coal-fired plant or by utilizing alternative technologies—both of which have shorter lead times than nuclear plants. "The uncertainties make you pause and say, 'gee, let me wait another year,' " noted Clyde A. Lilly, former president of The Southern Co. Services Inc. "And if you do that a couple of times, then you don't have time to put in a nuclear unit."(32)

In sum, uncertainties about growth in demand, availability of capital, and regulatory requirements have led to a self-imposed partial moratorium on nuclear power development by the utility industry. Industry representatives believe this may lead to serious problems in the late-1980s—including possible power shortages—but critics of nuclear power and some government regulatory bodies are viewing it as an opportunity to reexamine the country's nuclear power program.

MANUFACTURERS' COMMITMENT TO NUCLEAR POWER

As noted earlier, the existence of General Electric and Westinghouse as suppliers of nuclear reactors was an important factor in utilities' decisions to buy nuclear plants. There are only four reactor manufacturers in the United States today—GE, Westinghouse, Combustion Engineering, and Babcock & Wilcox—and the commitment of these firms to remain in the nuclear business could have an important influence on nuclear power development in the United States. At present, each of the four reactor manufacturers says that it intends to stay in the nuclear business for the foreseeable future. Nevertheless, some important changes appear to be taking place in the supplier segment of the nuclear industry. As domestic orders have dried up, manufacturers are being forced to scale back their nuclear work forces, convert their reactor manufacturing facilities to non-nuclear projects, and concentrate on profitable fuel and servicing contracts rather than the manufacture of reactor vessels. In addition, many component suppliers and subcontractors which supply parts and services to the major manufacturers are leaving the industry altogether.

Westinghouse

Westinghouse Electric Corp. appears to be the reactor manufacturer most dedicated and able to stay in the nuclear power business. This assessment is based on a number of factors: Its size ($7.3 billion in sales in 1979) and dominant position in the reactor market (29 of the country's 74 licensed commercial reactors were built by Westinghouse) give it some advantages over the other manufacturers; it has the largest backlog of reactor orders of the four manufacturers (approximately 65 reactors); its nuclear operations, unlike those of the other three manufacturers, have been marginally profitable; and most importantly, the company's top management appears totally dedicated to sticking with the nuclear power business. Gordon C. Hurlbert, president of Westinghouse Power Systems, contends that the United States' worsening energy mess leaves the country with no alternative to more nuclear power, and he says he expects U.S. reactor suppliers to be getting about 20 orders per year from domestic and foreign markets by 1982. "Just watch," Hurlbert told one interviewer in January 1979, "if they don't get the Iran situation straightened out . . . there are going to be gas lines to where you can't stand it. And there will be massive new orders for nuclear power plants. I'm just confident of that. A year, two years, three, it doesn't really matter when it comes. I'm looking at nuclear power to pay my pension when I retire."(33)

Even the accident at Three Mile Island appears not to have shaken Westinghouse's confidence in the soundness of its approach. Asked if his company was having any thoughts about leaving the business in the wake of that accident, Leo W. Yochum, the company's senior executive vice president of finance, replied, "No. Why should we?" "Our nuclear work has been very profitable for us," Yochum said. "I just don't understand this talk about nuclear being dead. The market is going to return. After all, there's a nuclear imperative for this country. We know it, Wall Street knows it, and we're prepared to meet it."(34) In spite of such optimism, however, Westinghouse admits that the current lull in reactor orders is having an impact. The company recently announced that it was closing by the end of 1981 its big nuclear steam-generator plant in Tampa, Fla., and consolidating the plant's operations with those of a nuclear parts plant in Pensacola.(35) Westinghouse said that the 1,000 employees in its Tampa plant would be laid off.

General Electric

General Electric is the second largest force in the domestic reactor manufacturer market. The company shares Westinghouse's advantage of size (1979 sales of $22.5 billion), but it also suffers from a unique disadvantage: some utilities remain convinced that GE's boiling-water reactors are inherently inferior to the pressurized-water reactors manufactured by the other three reactor manufacturers. (For many years, capacity factors for BWRs were consistently lower than those at PWRs, although in 1978 and 1979 BWRs outperformed PWRs.) GE's commitment to nuclear power also suffers from the fact that the company has never been able to make a profit on its nuclear business. "It's no great secret that GE has lost more money in this business than anyone," a GE spokesman told IRRC in October 1979. "We're making a good profit off fuel sales and servicing contracts for operating plants," he added, "but it doesn't offset the losses we're taking building nuclear steam supply systems."(36)

For years, rumors have persisted in the nation's financial community that GE is on the verge of exiting the nuclear business. In 1977, GE announced a reorganization of its nuclear division which

The Wall Street Journal suggested might be a preliminary step toward dropping out of the reactor business if profits failed to materialize. And a February 1979 article in *The Wall Street Journal* stated that of the four reactor makers, "it is GE that in the view of many observers is the company that will ease out of the nuclear business."(37) Although the company is much larger than its rivals, it "wants each of its divisions to stand on its own and be profitable," the *Journal* quoted a Wall Street analyst as saying.

GE insists that it intends to stay in the reactor business. The company appears to have been encouraged in recent years by the improved performance of BWRs, accidents and shutdowns at PWR plants, and the belief that continued instability in world oil markets will dictate increased reliance on nuclear power. "We are willing to take losses until things straighten up," says A. Philip Bray, a GE manager.(38) "People tend to look at the rise or fall of the nuclear boiler business and say that that is the nuclear business," adds Hugh Hexamer, GE's manager for communication and nuclear power information. "But we have a three-part nuclear business--boilers, fuel and services," Hexamer told IRRC in 1980, "and two of those are prospering."(39) Hexamer said that GE's commitment to the nuclear business was reflected in the fact that it had just completed a new BWR maintenance training center and several other test and development facilities at its nuclear operations in San Jose, Calif. Nevertheless, GE hasn't received a new domestic reactor order since 1974, and many industry observers say it is only a matter of time before the company will be forced to drop out of the reactor-building business. Robert T. Cornell, first vice president of Paine Webber Mitchell Hutchins Inc., says he "would not be surprised" to see GE attempt to reduce its nuclear commitment by taking on a foreign partner.(40) GE's 1979 annual report says the company had a $5.3 billion backlog of nuclear work at the end of 1979, but the company has acknowledged that it has already begun using its nuclear production facilities to do work on hydroelectric generators, wind tunnels, offshore drilling platforms, and other non-nuclear projects.(41) And one GE source confided to IRRC that the company was very excited about the prospect of a national commitment to develop a synthetic fuels industry because that would allow it to employ part of its nuclear work force building synthetic fuels plants.

Combustion, Babcock

The two smaller reactor manufacturers, Combustion Engineering and the Babcock & Wilcox subsidiary of J. Ray McDermott & Co., appear to be in precarious positions in the reactor business. Neither company has ever won a foreign order and Babcock & Wilcox is nearing the end of its work on domestic orders. They "don't have the backlog to stay with it," *Business Week* quoted one industry source as saying at the end of 1978.(42)

It appears that Babcock & Wilcox, supplier of the ill-fated Three

Mile Island plant in Pennsylvania, may be forced out of the reactor-building business by the accident at that plant. Since the accident, utilities have canceled orders for seven B&W reactors and the company decided in June 1979 to close its major reactor manufacturing plant at Mt. Vernon, Ind., by the end of 1979. "For economic reasons we couldn't justify keeping it open," observed Paul Bergson, a Babcock & Wilcox Washington representative.(43) The company is "still interested in serving the utility market," according to Louis M. Favret, executive vice president of B&W's Power Generation Group, but so many of the company's previous orders are now subject to delay or cancellation that some industry analysts foresee the company's role reduced to that of a component supplier.(44)

Combustion Engineering appears to have a large enough backlog of orders to take it through the 1980s, but its design and engineering teams are likely to run out of work in the mid-1980s unless the company can win more new orders.(45) The company is trying to keep its nuclear facilities and employees busy by supplying "part of the plant we currently go out and buy," according to Howard M. Winterson, president of the company's Power Systems Group.(46) Company officials say Combustion Engineering will simply produce whatever kind of power plants its utility customers want but it has no intention of abandoning the nuclear business. In fact, the company predicts that its refueling and servicing business for on-line reactors will be generating $200 million in annual revenues by 1992.(47)

Component Suppliers

A less visible but vital aspect of manufacturers' ability to continue to supply nuclear plants is the willingness and ability of large numbers of small firms that supply parts and services to the major manufacturers to remain in the nuclear business. Industry sources have reported that large numbers of such firms are likely to depart the industry during the next two years because of the stagnant domestic reactor market and the difficulties these firms face in storing deferred equipment, maintaining their nuclear ratings, and dealing with the paperwork demanded by government regulatory agencies. According to Nucleonics Week, a report written in June 1980 by Westinghouse top management says: "Many suppliers have abandoned the nuclear field. Certification of a new supplier takes about one year--if he has appropriate facilities and personnel, and the desire to repeat a previously frustrating experience. Manufacturing facilities for many nuclear components will be virtually empty in another year or two."(48) A GE source quoted by Nucleonics Week agrees:

We're going to lose the little guys. I bet we buy supplies from 30 states. We stimulate the entire economy by buying from hundreds of companies. DOE thinks that big companies like GE and Westinghouse are so strong that, one day, the government can say, 'Give me six plants,' and we can go right out and do it. Well, we can't. We're not 'make shops.' I'm afraid that the next time there's a push for nuclear--and mark my words, there'll be one--there's not going to be anyone to bid on the vending list.(49)

THE BUSINESS COMMUNITY'S ATTITUDE
TOWARD NUCLEAR POWER

Over the years, in general, the nuclear power industry has been highly regarded by the American business community. Industrial corporations have looked to nuclear utilities as an assured source of electric power, banks and insurance companies have provided financial services to the nuclear industry on generally favorable terms, and investors have regarded utilities with heavy nuclear commitments as among the most stable and least risky investments available. In recent years--but particularly following the accident at Three Mile Island and its ramifications for the owner of that plant, General Public Utilities Corp.--segments of the country's business community have moderated, and in some cases ended, their previous support for nuclear power.

Industry

While support for further nuclear power development continues to be strong among much of the U.S. industrial sector, it is clear that some corporations now perceive investments in nuclear power-- whether in the form of uranium mining capacity, nuclear research, or the building of industrial plants in areas served by nuclear utilities--to be more risky than they had previously assumed. A number of the nation's leading uranium producers, including Kerr-McGee and Atlantic Richfield, have recently closed uranium mines and abandoned plans for opening new ones. Exxon Corp. told participants at its 1979 Energy Research and Development Symposium that it had recently "scaled back" its R&D activities in the nuclear field and that in the future the company expected twice as much R&D growth in coal, shale and tar sands technologies as in nuclear and solar energy. E.E. David, president of Exxon Research & Engineering, said the move came in response to government actions and attitudes, but it was not meant as a "message" to the business community.(50) And Ron Smith, project engineer for General Motors' energy management section, says that GM is acting on its concerns about the risks of nuclear power. According to *Energy User News*, Smith has said that when GM decides to locate future plants that will depend on electricity, it will shy away from utilities planning substantial additions of nuclear generating capacity because it expects delays in the licensing of new nuclear power plants.(51)

Banks and Insurance Companies

In general, the nation's banks, insurance companies and other financial institutions continue to be highly supportive of the nuclear industry. General Public Utilities, for instance, was able to arrange a $409 million revolving credit agreement with 43 banks after the Three Mile Island accident. Burt Proom, president of American Nuclear Insurers, told The New York Times during the Three Mile Island accident that the nuclear industry remained an excellent insurance risk. "The ratio for risk in an industry of this kind of technology, like the chemical industry, might be twice as high," Proom stated. "So we are very happy about insuring the nuclear industry."(52) And James Wyatt, senior vice president of the Hartford Insurance Group, agreed with this assessment:

> My reaction is that I don't think this (accident at Three Mile Island) is a catastrophe. We're around to insure accidents. We don't think there have been an unusual number. From an insurance standpoint, this latest accident gives us no concern. So far, though, I think the safety record has been outstanding.(53)

In spite of this generally favorable attitude toward nuclear power among banks and financial institutions, some institutions have clearly moderated their support for further nuclear development. Bank of America, for instance, announced at its 1979 annual meeting that it was putting additional credit for the nuclear industry in a "holding pattern" until the safety questions raised by the accident at Three Mile Island were answered. Since that announcement in April 1979, the bank has begun to extend loans backing utilities' issuance of commercial paper to finance nuclear fuel, but it has not granted any direct loans for the construction of nuclear facilities. But even before the accident, Bank of America executive Roger Roberts told reporters that commercial banks did not want to participate heavily in nuclear projects because of "the vulnerability of the nuclear industry."(54)

Investors

Perhaps the greatest indication that the nuclear industry is confronting some changed attitudes in the nation's business and financial community comes from investors. The stock prices of utilities that are heavily dependent upon nuclear power dropped more sharply than those of the utility industry as a whole in 1979; some nuclear utilities had their bond ratings downgraded; many nuclear utilities were forced to offer more generous yields on their bond offerings than comparable non-nuclear utilities; and some institutional investors decided to divest their portfolios of nuclear industry stocks.

Most investment advisers now say that the risks associated with investments in the nuclear industry are higher than was previously thought. Steven Leuthold, a portfolio manager for Funds Advisory Inc. and a consultant to Piper, Jaffray & Hopwood, contends that "investments in utilities heavily committed to nuclear power clearly have a significantly higher level of risk than they did a couple of short months ago. The risk, of course, has always been there, but it was not perceived as it is now."(55) Paine Webber Mitchell Hutchins, in a recent utility industry review paper, adds that although investor concern about nuclear power appears to be subsiding from the levels it reached immediately after the Three Mile Island accident, "the probability and financial consequences of nuclear accidents are higher than previously thought."(56) And Anne Faber, vice president for corporate ratings at Standard & Poors, told an Atomic Industrial Forum conference in 1980 that her organization had lowered its bond ratings on 37 utilities in 1979 and raised only six. "In many instances," she said, "this is due to nuclear commitments."(57)

Institutional investors appear to have been in no great rush so far to sell nuclear-related stocks, but interest in divestment is clearly growing. A survey by *Pensions & Investments* in May 1979 found that of the five largest public and corporate pension funds, only one--the $10-billion New York Retirement Systems--was actively divesting its nuclear holdings as a result of the Three Mile Island accident. The fund said it had liquidated its holdings in Kerr-McGee, Westinghouse, Southern Co., and Babcock & Wilcox, according to *Pensions & Investments*.(58) But while few institutions appear to have established policies against investing in the nuclear industry, a number of institutions seem to be evaluating such a move. Charles H. Jones, vice president and senior trust officer of Mid Atlantic Banks Inc., says he is sure that bank trust divisions are reevaluating utility stocks that are dependent upon nuclear power. According to Jones, his company hasn't disposed of nuclear utility stocks yet, but it is "thinking about it. You have to consider it a possibility in order to be prudent," he said.(59) The assistant treasurer of a major university concurred. "Send me everything you've got on the nuclear industry," he told IRRC in 1979. "We've got to review our portfolio to determine its vulnerability."

Institutional investors remain generally unsympathetic to antinuclear shareholder resolutions, but institutional support for such resolutions clearly rose between 1979 and 1980. In 1979, not one of the institutions responding to IRRC's annual survey of how institutions voted on shareholder resolutions voted in favor of any of the six resolutions in 1979 requesting utilities to restrict their use of nuclear power. In 1980, however, several colleges and universities, a number of church groups, the California State Teachers' Retirement System, and a bank voted in favor of at least one of the 26 antinuclear proposals brought to a vote.(60) Finally, concern about investments in the nuclear power industry has increased dramatically at church-related institutions in recent years. In May 1979, the National Council of Churches voted to support a national energy policy opposing the further development of nuclear power; during the 1980 proxy season, church investors affiliated with the Interfaith Center on

Corporate Responsibility sponsored 15 shareholder resolutions opposing the further development of nuclear power; and in December 1980, church investors indicated that they would again be active in sponsoring antinuclear shareholder resolutions in 1981.

THE CONTROVERSY OVER INDUSTRY'S ROLE

Critics of the nuclear industry's role in nuclear power development raise four principal issues: (1) that the manufacturers misled the utilities in their projections, and concurrently that the utilities failed to challenge those projections; (2) that the utilities jumped into nuclear power too fast, without adequate consideration of the alternatives or the consequences; (3) that both manufacturers and utilities have failed to inform the public adequately about their programs and the problems involved; and (4) that the industry has been socially irresponsible by failing to consider the environmental, nuclear weapons proliferation, and health implications of nuclear power development.

The Manufacturers' Role

As noted earlier, the number of manufacturers is small but the influence they wield in the nuclear industry remains quite strong. Because of their expertise in the field, they often operated at an advantage as sellers, and utilities relied on them for information on plant operation and for projections of power plant costs and reliability. Critics contend that the manufacturers used this informational advantage to dupe utilities into buying nuclear plants and that utilities did not adequately question manufacturers' assessments of power plant costs and reliability.

Manufacturers' Assessments

Manufacturers in general agree with the criticism that some of their projections have been too optimistic and that there have been problems with many plants, but they do not agree with assertions that they deliberately misled the utilities. The manufacturers assert that most of the problems were unforeseen and that many arose as a consequence of either regulatory decisions or inadequate performance by others in constructing or operating the plants. Some observers point to the heavy losses the manufacturers have sustained --particularly on early turnkey projects--as added evidence that the problems with nuclear plants were as much a surprise to the manufacturers as to the utilities. One former industry marketing executive has estimated that GE and Westinghouse together suffered losses of between $800 million and $1 billion on 18 nuclear plants built on a turnkey basis.

Utilities' Views

Many utility officials admit that they were--and to some extent still are--dependent on manufacturers for information about nuclear plant operations. They generally agree that manufacturers' projections of nuclear plant capacity factors and fuel, operation and maintenance costs have been optimistic. "It's painfully true," the vice chairman of one large utility told IRRC, "that manufacturers' projections have been overstated. But where else do you go?" Most utilities--with several notable exceptions like Commonwealth Edison--have limited experience with nuclear power. "Of 9,000 presidents, chief executives and chief engineers in utilities," Milton Levenson of the Electric Power Research Institute noted in 1974, "less that 1 percent have a nuclear background."(61)

Another major problem for utilities that arose out of this "seller's market" is the problem of obtaining warranties from the manu-facturers that come close to covering the potential losses to utilities. W.H. Arnold of Westinghouse explained his company's position on warranties to IRRC. He said the basic warranty runs for one year from the date of "plant acceptance," provided the equipment is installed in accordance with Westinghouse specifications. Under the warranty, he said, Westinghouse will fix or replace any defective equipment it supplied. It will not pay for damages to other equipment or for consequential damages such as the cost of buying power from other utilities to replace power that cannot be generated as a result of equipment failure.

According to Arnold, Westinghouse is "not very flexible" about negotiating the basic terms of the warranty. The nuclear reactor, he said, represents only about 10 percent of the value of the plant. For Westinghouse to assume enormous contingent liabilities when its involvement is so limited would not be prudent, he asserted. However, he noted, on the question of who bears the risk of loss due to changes in regulatory requirements, the company is willing to assume some responsibility.(62)

The Nuclear Commitment

The utilities' desire to go nuclear, according to many critics, is attributable at least in part to financial motives. Utility rates are computed by public service commissions to allow for a certain rate of return on capital investment. Critics say that because nuclear plants are extremely capital-intensive, this method of computing rates makes it financially attractive for utilities to buy nuclear plants rather than coal-fired plants that will cost less and have somewhat higher operating costs. Worse yet, critics argue, the regulatory incentives for utilities to promote conservation or decentralized solar tech-nologies are virtually nonexistent. A study by Thermo Electron Corp. summed up the situation in 1976:

> Conservation does not yet receive the favorable treatment in rate design that it deserves....A utility that does conserve fuels, and saves operating costs, is placed at a disadvantage when the next round of rate increases comes about. A utility that encourages its customers to conserve electricity is confronted with a reduced revenue. There are no accounts for conservation type activities that would allow full treatment of expenses coming from conservation efforts.(63)

Critics contend that while the situation described in the Thermo Electron study has changed in some states, such as California, it still applies in many states.

Many observers agree that the utility industry tried to go too far too fast with nuclear power. Harold Green criticizes what he describes as a "leapfrogging technical experience,"(64) and James Conner, then director of planning and analysis for the AEC, wrote in 1973 that "in retrospect it is clear that the initial cost and time schedules for nuclear power plants were wildly optimistic, given the industry's lack of experience with the technology ....Utility schedules have had to be lengthened by over 40 percent to accommodate the delays attributable to increasing size and evolving technology." But "most unsettling of all," Conners related, "utility executives have discovered that they are responsible for these troublesome new plants. By law, the AEC licenses the utility itself--not the manufacturer--to build and assure safe operation of a nuclear plant."(65)

Some observers are more critical. Irwin Bupp of MIT describes the prevalence of a "stainless steel mentality." Utility officials, he says, need to feel that they are in the forefront of the industry; they believe that coal technology represents the 19th century and that fission technology represents the science of the future.(66)

Others are more charitable. They point to uncertainties about the price and availability of fossil fuels as having a major role in utilities' thinking. "We know we have problems with supply from the Arabs or the United Mine Workers," one official told IRRC. B.B. Parker, former chairman of the Atomic Industrial Forum, maintains that uncertainty continues to be the main problem confronting utilities wishing to build new power plants; "uncertainty as to load growth, uncertainty as to constraints of government regulation, uncertainty as to the allowed rate of return and to the ability to finance new generating capacity, and uncertainty as to the reaction of shareholders, ratepayers, the public and the media to any one of a host of decisions that must be made by utility management--many of them in anticipation of events over which management has no control."(67)

Informing the Public

Critics assert that the nuclear industry has shared with government a failure to keep the public adequately informed on the problems of nuclear power. "There has been a tacit conspiracy on the part of the atomic energy establishment--industry and government--for the last 20 years to hide from the public view the risks inherent in nuclear power," Harold Green of George Washington Law School has testified. "I do not use the phrase 'conspiracy' in an invidious sense. The fact of the matter is that the establishment fears that the public discussion of the risks will unduly alarm the public and slow the introduction of nuclear power which the establishment honestly believes is acceptably safe and in the public interest."(68)

What critics see as a failure by industry to disclose information on nuclear power may be seen by industry--at least in part--as a proper withholding of proprietary information. Critics, however, argue that industry has hidden behind claims of confidentiality in order to avoid discussing its problems openly.

Perhaps the overriding complaint of critics is that in its discussion of nuclear power, the industry has focused on selling its benefits to the public, rather than on assisting the public to reach an understanding of its implications. The desire to sell, some say, has encouraged industry to mislead. Concerning safety issues, critics point to the Three Mile Island incident--where statements by utility officials about the potential seriousness of the accident conflicted sharply with statements by NRC officials during the first several days of the incident--as evidence that the industry is more concerned with its own public image than with public safety. Critics also say the industry has attempted to deceive the public on economic issues. In 1975, for instance, the Council on Economic Priorities challenged Consolidated Edison's claims that the company's nuclear plants had saved consumers $90 million. The claims, according to the council, failed to take into account capital and operating costs.(69) Although the company maintained that it was clear that its statement referred only to savings in fuel costs, New York Public Service Commissioner Kahn sided with the council. In a letter to Con Ed's chairman, he said he could not see how the company's claims "could fail in some degree to mislead the public" about the comparative costs of nuclear and fossil fuel.(70) More recently, nuclear critic Charles Komanoff has charged that an Atomic Industrial Forum survey of coal and nuclear plant costs released in 1979 "relied upon a distorted data base, and its conclusions are misleading to the point of falsehood."(71) According to Komanoff, the survey excluded 21 nuclear plants whose costs were higher than average and a number of coal plants with lower than average costs. Komanoff contends that there is only a "75,000 to 1" chance that such a "skewed distribution" could have occurred at random, "indicating beyond any reasonable doubt that the bias in the AIF sample was no accident."(72)

Concern with industry's efforts to sell nuclear power is further

compounded by its ability to spend large sums on its own behalf.
Critics are particularly incensed about the size of corporate contributions in opposition to the anti-nuclear initiatives on state ballots
across the country in recent years. In 1976, Pacific Gas & Electric
spent $500,000 and other power companies contributed more than
$300,000 in a successful effort to defeat a California proposition that
would have slowed nuclear growth in that state.(73) In Arizona in
1976, groups favoring nuclear power--including labor and professional
as well as industry donors--are reported to have spent $1.1 million
compared with $17,000 for those opposed to nuclear power. In Oregon
the spending ratio was 4 to 1, and in Montana nuclear proponents spent
$120,000 to the $600 spent by nuclear critics.(74) Finally, in 1980,
opponents of a resolution calling for the shutdown of the Maine
Yankee nuclear plant disclosed spending more than $800,000 compared
with $179,000 spent by supporters of the resolution.(75)

Critics also point out that utilities have frequently been able to
bill customers for the entire cost of their advertising expen-
ditures--even for ads that were clearly political in nature. In 1977, for
instance, Virginia Electric & Power Co. ran full-page ads in several
Virginia and Washington area newspapers stating, "The only thing
frightening about nuclear power is the thought of facing the 1980s
without it . . . . One fact that stands out about nuclear generation is
that it's safe. The scientific problems of storing nuclear waste were
solved years ago . . . . If we are going to have the electricity we'll need
in the 1980s, we'll need nuclear power as part of a balanced generating
system."(76) The ads were part of a $140,000 "educational" ad
campaign that Vepco ran in 1977 for which customers were billed. As
Vepco's advertising manager at the time told The Washington *Post*,
these advertisements "are not promoting anything. They are simple
statements of fact on the energy situation and how it affects our
customers."(77)

Industry's Position

Supporters of nuclear power agree that they have not been able to
provide information sufficient to convince the general public of the
benefits of nuclear power, but they deny vigorously all charges that
they have withheld important facts or misled the public. They say
that critics of nuclear power have been irresponsible in their
statements, using sensationalism to attract public attention, and
making thoughtful public discussion of the issues very difficult.

Many persons in industry say that the public mood and the nature
of the news media are not conducive to a fair hearing of the industry's
position. H.D. Hexamer, manager of GE's department of communications and nuclear power information, wrote to IRRC in 1975:

> It's common knowledge . . . that during the past 25 years,
> popular respect for science and its corollary congressional
> support reached its apogee shortly after World War II, and
> has continually declined since then. Many of the

critics...have been demonstratively adept at sensing this aspect of the public mood and have chosen to place the blame for pollution, energy shortages, and other national ills on science and technology. Of course they have reinforced their efforts with attacks on the Atomic Energy Commission, the utility industry, Congress, and a sensationalist discussion of the various so-called safety problems of radiation, reactor emergency cooling, and so forth....(As a result), it's industry's position the evidence is very strong that the determined citizen who wishes to be heard, particularly if he opposes the government, a utility, or the establishment in any form, gets attention, magnified by a receptive press, far out of proportion to his single vote. The industry believes the need is not so much for just the opportunity to speak but rather for an informed and active public willing to responsibly and thoughtfully express its opinion.(78)

It is also difficult to generate positive news coverage, industry representatives say. Some utility officials contend that the media spend a disproportionate amount of time covering nuclear protests or that reporters tend to be biased against nuclear power. A Commonwealth Edison official told IRRC, "It is much more likely that a newspaper will be interested in running a headline describing cracks in a minor steam pipe at a nuclear plant than reporting that the plant is operating at full capacity and saving consumers' dollars."(79) Industry officials further contend that critics exaggerate the disparity between the amounts of money spent by the industry and its critics in the debate over nuclear power. They say that the industry is forced to spend more money to balance the effect of celebrities, film stars and rock groups who donate their efforts to stopping nuclear power development. One industry representative wondered rhetorically, "How much is it worth when Jane Fonda speaks against nuclear power or Jackson Browne does an anti-nuclear benefit concert?"

Another problem, according to industry officials, is that utilities are often ill-equipped to handle public relations questions. In the past, most utilities have relied mainly on the Edison Electric Institute and the Atomic Industrial Forum to speak for the industry on nuclear power. Eugene Cramer of Southern California Edison wrote to IRRC that "since public utilities commissions in general have proscribed in recent years any extensive mass communications, it is doubtful if utilities have been able to afford the luxury of more than an occasional weak defense against a high-bill complaint. It should also be recognized that a utility would logically tend to provide excellent information readily available (from a trade or professional source), rather than reinventing the wheel."(80)

Finally, as concerns technical information, industry spokesmen say they must have the right to withhold some information that they consider to be proprietary. Spokesmen say industry is willing to make available to the public all necessary information on plants and operation. But they agree with Westinghouse's Arnold that "unrestricted disclosure of proprietary information would harm significantly the interests of the commission and the public. Unrestricted disclosure could discourage initiation of research and development by private parties, limit the knowledge of the existence of such information, impair the commission's independent review process, and endanger the position of the U.S. as the world leader in nuclear power reactor technology...."(81) GE and Westinghouse, however, have told IRRC that they have made proprietary information available to the NRC, congressional committees, or even intervenors "under appropriate protective agreement."(82)

Recent Changes in Industry Tactics

Until the mid-1970s, efforts by the nuclear industry to inform the public of its nuclear power program concentrated almost exclusively on trying to persuade members of the public to accept those programs. Little effort was made to discuss the pros and cons of nuclear development. Few people questioned statements by reactor vendors and government officials that nuclear power would be the predominant source of electrical energy in the future. Most utilities accepted vendors' claims and left response to questions about nuclear power to government information officers, vendors or organizations financed by the industry such as the Atomic Industrial Forum. In 1974, for instance, IRRC sent a questionnaire to 82 companies involved in all phases of the nuclear industry asking for data on companies' experience with nuclear power, cost analyses, and copies of statements or studies relevant to controversy over nuclear power development. Virtually all the materials that IRRC received that had been prepared for distribution to the general public were public relations pieces emphasizing the merits of nuclear power. The only major issue of public concern that was discussed meaningfully in these materials by several companies was power plant safety. None included any extensive comparison of costs of nuclear and coal-fired power plants or alternatives to nuclear power development, and few mentioned issues such as reactor siting, safeguards or waste disposal.

The last several years, however, have seen a good deal of change in the quantity and quality of information available from the industry and in the industry's approach toward informing the public. Some utilities, the reactor vendors and industry trade associations have dramatically increased the amount of information available to the public. They have designed materials that respond to specific concerns about reactor safety and reliability, economics, reprocessing, waste disposal and other issues. Their publications have become increasingly sophisticated as the industry has been forced to respond to more sophisticated and informed critics. Increasingly, the industry has commissioned high-powered engineering, economic consulting and research firms to do studies buttressing its position. At the same time, however, much industry information--especially that available from utilities--continues to reflect a traditional public relations approach to issues. This seemed to be especially true in the wake of the Three Mile Island accident.

In addition to its growing informational effort, the nuclear industry has begun to respond to critics' challenges in other ways. In a number of states, representatives of the industry, their families, business organizations, scientific and engineering associations, and some labor groups have joined together to support organizations such as Citizens for Jobs and Energy, Nuclear Energy Women, and Citizens for Energy and Freedom--groups that advocate continued development of nuclear power as part of a comprehensive energy program. Such groups receive some financial support from the industry. Utilities also help finance a number of traveling energy education shows through Oak Ridge Associated Universities in Tennessee. The shows, with titles such as "This Atomic World" and "Energy: Today and Tomorrow," stress the need for nuclear power to high school classes around the country. Staffed by about 60 "teacher-demonstrators" from Oak Ridge, the traveling shows have a budget of about $1 million which comes from "utilities, banks and other private sources," according to Robert Potter, public information officer for Oak Ridge Associated Universities.(83) Finally, through the Atomic Industrial Forum and other representative groups, the nuclear industry has greatly increased the tempo of its lobbying efforts on behalf of nuclear development in recent years. Since it moved to Washington in 1975, the AIF has become one of the most effective lobbying organizations in town, according to political observers.

Even before Three Mile Island, the nuclear industry had clearly come to the conclusion that informing and persuading the public was critical to the future of nuclear power. Westinghouse, for instance, wrote to IRRC in 1976: "We view the major problem which must be overcome to be educating the public to the point at which they can rationally weigh the arguments of both opponents and proponents of nuclear power. The nuclear industry firmly believes that once the public understands nuclear power and the manner in which nuclear plants are designed, built and operated, the great majority of the issues now in public controversy will be laid to rest. This is the reason why the industry is now putting greater emphasis on public information systems."(84)

Whether the industry's increased effort to sell nuclear power will help the industry to regain some of its lost credibility is the subject of some debate. NRC Commissioner Victor Gilinsky is skeptical. "If the industry does not survive and the technology succumbs to pressures of costs, safety concerns, and the nagging worry about what to do with nuclear wastes, it will be at least in part because 25 years of hard sell of an all-nuclear future has stood in the way of common sense," Gilinsky says.(85) Thomas G. Leighton, a public relations consultant who has represented utilities and other nuclear interests for years, disagrees. "The men who manage America's nuclear industry must learn to speak now or forever hold their peace," Leighton says. Failure to "speak, relate and communicate effectively will mean the certain decay and eventual destruction of the industry," he insists.(86)

Industry Social Responsibility

A final criticism made of the nuclear industry by its opponents is that it has been socially irresponsible. Critics contend that the industry has been concerned mainly with profits and that it has largely ignored the externalities associated with nuclear power--radioactive waste, the potential for catastrophic accidents, and the worldwide proliferation of nuclear weapons. They point to examples of uranium mining companies and companies involved in the storage of nuclear waste. After years of profiting from their role in the nuclear industry, the critics say, these companies then abandon the business--leaving enormous clean-up problems to be dealt with by the government.

Industry officials respond that the risks associated with nuclear power are smaller than those associated with the alternatives to it. They maintain that, overall, the industry has done an excellent job of minimizing those risks that do exist and that critics are woefully uninformed about the industry's efforts to develop solutions to the waste problem, safer reactors, and proliferation-resistant fuel cycles. Finally, industry representatives note that the nuclear power industry exists largely because the U.S. government decided that it was in the country's best interests to develop a nuclear power program and to encourage the use of nuclear power abroad.

NOTES

(1) Craig Hosmer, interview with Investor Responsibility Research Center, 1974.

(2) Irwin C. Bupp Jr., "Priorities in the Nuclear Technology Program," Ph.D. dissertation, Harvard University, Cambridge, Mass., 1971.

(3) Arthur D. Little Inc., "Competition in the Nuclear Power Supply Industry," report to the U.S. Atomic Energy Commission and the U.S. Department of Justice, December 1968, p. 361.

(4) Ibid.

(5) Ibid., p. 124.

(6) Ibid., p. 358.

(7) Detroit Edison Co., 1979 Proxy Statement, p. 9.

(8) Ibid., p. 10.

(9) Pacific Gas & Electric Co., 1979 Proxy Statement, p. 11.

(10) Letter from John C. Morrissey, Pacific Gas & Electric Co. Vice President and General Counsel, to the Securities and Exchange Commission, Jan. 8, 1979, p. 4.

(11) Telephone interview with Investor Responsibility Research Center, 1979.

(12) W.R.Z. Willey, "Alternative Energy Systems for Pacific Gas & Electric Co.: An Economic Analysis," The Environmental Defense Fund, 1968.

(13) "Alternative Fuel Use Feasible in Powerplants, EDF Attorney Says," *Energy Users Report*, No. 303, May 31, 1979, p. 10.

(14) Laurel Leff, "S. California Edison Raises Commitment to Alternative Energy in Major Change," *The Wall Street Journal*, Oct. 20, 1980, p. 21.

(15) These figures from the Atomic Industrial Forum include two reactors—Indian Point 1 and Humboldt Bay—which are in indefinite shutdown status and the two Three Mile Island units which were shut down due to an accident at unit 2 in March 1979. They also include the Shippingport and Hanford-N reactors, dual-purpose reactors operated by the Department of Energy that supply electricity to commercial grids.

(16) Quoted in *The Power Line*, Environmental Action Foundation, Vol. 4, No. 11, June 1979, p. 1.

(17) Carolina Power & Light, 1978 Annual Report, p. 2.

(18) Carolina Power & Light, 1979 Proxy Statement, p. 7.

(19) Carolina Power & Light, 1978 Annual Report, p. 3.

(20) "Demand Uncertainties, Construction Delays Take Heavy Toll in Plans for Power Plants," *Energy Users Report*, No. 371, Sept. 18, 1980, p. 23.

(21) See Detroit Edison Co., 1979 Proxy Statement, and "Detroit Edison Sets New Delay, Higher Cost for Nuclear Facility," *The Wall Street Journal*, Aug. 26, 1980.

(22) "Detroit Edison Drops Twice-Shelved Plan for 2 Additional Nuclear Power Plants," *The Wall Street Journal*, March 25, 1980

(23) Robert J. McDevitt, Senior Nuclear Generation Engineer, Pacific Gas & Electric Co., interview with Investor Responsibility Research Center, August 1980.

(24) For further background on the controversy surrounding the Diablo Canyon plant, see "Nuclear Power Development: Pacific Gas & Electric Co.," Investor Responsibility Research Center, Analysis I, Supplement No. 1, March 27, 1979; and David L. Lenderts, "Decision at Diablo Canyon," the Abalone Alliance, 1977.

(25) Text of speech by Gov. Edmund G. Brown Jr. to nuclear protestors at Diablo Canyon, June 30, 1979. (Reprinted in *Not Man Apart*, Friends of the Earth, August 1979, p. 16.)

(26) Atomic Industrial Forum figures.

(27) Jim Harding, "Can Nuclear Plants Be Scrapped," *Not Man Apart*, November 1979, p. 10; see also *Nucleonics Week*, Aug. 10, 1979.

(28) Bankers Trust Co., Energy Group, "U.S. Energy and Capital: A Forecast," (New York, 1978), p. 22.

(29) Ibid., p. 23.

(30) Mark N. Dodosh, "Electric Utilities, Hit by Cost of Money, Rate-Increase Delays, See Lackluster Year," *The Wall Street Journal*, March 22, 1979, p. 48.

(31) Eliot Marshall, "Planning for an Oil Cutoff," *Science*, July 11, 1980, p. 247.

(32) Quoted in "Why Atomic Power Dims Today," *Business Week*, Nov. 17, 1975, p. 98.

(33) Mark Hertsgaard, "Is Nuclear on the Ropes?" *Not Man Apart*, November 1979, p. 9.

(34) Ibid., p. 8.

(35) "Westinghouse Plans to Close Nuclear Plant Parts Facility," *The Wall Street Journal*, Sept. 30, 1980, p. 19.

(36) Conversation with Richard S. Alben, GE Manager, Technology Evaluation Operations, Oct. 11, 1979.

(37) John R. Emshwiller, "Nuclear Industry Faces Bleak Future as Orders Get Increasingly Scarce," *The Wall Street Journal*, Feb. 2, 1979, p. 23.

(38) Ibid.

(39) Hugh D. Hexamer, interview with Investor Responsibility Research Center, August 1980.

(40) "Nuclear Plant Orders Melt Away," *Business Week*, Nov. 19, 1979, p. 44.

(41) General Electric Co., 1979 Annual Report; and Emshwiller, op. cit.

(42) "Nuclear Dilemma: The atom's fizzle in an energy-short world," *Business Week*, Dec. 25, 1978, p. 57.

(43) Richard Pollock, "The Great Nuclear Fizzle," *Critical Mass Journal*, June 1979, p. 5.

(44) "Nuclear Plant Orders Melt Away," op. cit., p. 44.

(45) For further discussion of U.S. and foreign reactor manufacturers, see Mans Lonnroth and William Walter, "The Viability of the Civil Nuclear Industry," International Consultative Group on Nuclear Energy, 1979, pp. 71-92.

(46) "Nuclear Dilemma: The atom's fizzle in an energy-short world," op. cit., p. 57.

(47) Hertsgaard, op. cit., p. 9.

(48) Brad Ferguson, "Departure of Subsuppliers from U.S. Nuclear Market Seen on Horizon," *Nucleonics Week*, Vol. 21, No. 35, Aug. 28, 1980, p. 1.

(49) Ibid., p. 2.

(50) Remarks of E.E. David, president, Exxon Research & Engineering Co., before the 1979 Exxon Energy Research and Development Symposium, New York City, Oct. 11, 1979.

(51) Paula Ellis, "Plant Siting: Supplier of Energy Vital," *Energy User News*, July 2, 1979, p. 5.

(52) N.R. Kleinfield, "Nuclear Insurers Confident," The New York *Times*, March 30, 1979.

(53) Ibid.

(54) Gloria C. Duffy and Gordon Adams, *Power Politics - The Nuclear Industry and Nuclear Exports* (Council on Economic Priorities, New York, N.Y., 1979), p. 33.

(55) Steven C. Leuthold, "Comeback for 'Nuke' stocks not likely in current climate," *Pensions & Investments*, June 4, 1979, p. 26.

(56) "Three Mile Island--II: A Sequel Featuring an Investment Strategy for Electric Utilities," Paine Webber Mitchell Hutchins Inc., Aug. 7, 1979, p. 2.

(57) "Growing Investor Risks Threaten Needed Capital for Utilities," *Nucleonics Week*, Vol. 21, No. 27, July 3, 1980, p. 7.

(58) Charles Epstein, "Portfolios suffer shocks after nuclear accident," *Pensions & Investments*, May 21, 1979, p. 33.

(59) "After TMI, Big Institutions Take Second Look at Utility Stocks," *Energy Users Report*, April 19, 1979, p. 12.

(60) "How Institutions Voted in the 1980 Proxy Season," Investor Responsibility Research Center, October 1980.

(61) Milton Levenson, interview with Investor Responsibility Research Center, 1974.

(62) W.H. Arnold, interview with Investor Responsibility Research Center, 1974.

(63) *A Study of Inplant Electric Power Generation in the Chemical, Petroleum Refining and Paper and Pulp Industries*, prepared for the Federal Energy Administration by Thermo Electron Corp., Report No. TE 5429-97-76, June 1976, pp. 6-68.

(64) Harold P. Green, Hearings before the Subcommittee on Reorganization, Research and International Organizations of the Committee on Government Operations, U.S. Senate, March 12, 1974.

(65) James E. Conner, "Prospects for Nuclear Power," reprint from "The National Energy Problem," *Proceedings of the Academy of Political Science* (December 1973), pp. 66, 67.

(66) Irwin Bupp, telephone interview with Investor Responsibility Research Center, 1974.

(67) "Uncertainty Plagues Industry, AIF Conference Speakers Report," *Energy Users Report*, No. 275, Nov. 16, 1978, p. 13.

(68) Green, op. cit., p. 229.

(69) Charles Komanoff, "Responding to Con Edison: An Analysis of the 1974 Costs of Indian Point and Alternatives," Council on Economic Priorities, 1975.

(70) Alfred Kahn, letter to Charles Luce, Feb. 27, 1976.

(71) "Antinuclear Economist Charles Komanoff Finds Major Flaws in an AIF Survey," *Nucleonics Week*, Vol. 21, No. 10, March 6, 1980, p. 3.

(72) Ibid.

(73) "Money From Dominoes," *The Power Line*, Environmental Action Foundation, Vol. 2, No. 1, June/July 1976, p. 3.

(74) Figures from the Utility Project, Environmental Action Foundation (Washington, D.C., November 1976).

(75) Joanne Omang, "Nuclear Plant Preserved by Maine Voters, 3 to 2," The Washington *Post*, Sept. 24, 1980, p. A2.

(76) Joanne Omang, "Group Assails Vepco Ads on Nuclear Power as One-Sided," The Washington *Post*, Dec. 13, 1977, p. C8.

(77) Ibid.

(78) Hugh Hexamer, letter to Investor Responsibility Research Center, Jan. 10, 1975.

(79) Telephone interview with Investor Responsibility Research Center, 1974.

(80) Eugene Cramer, letter to Investor Responsibility Research Center, Jan. 3, 1975.

(81) W.H. Arnold, interview with Investor Responsibility Research Center, 1974.

(82) Ibid.; see also GE's testimony before the Joint Committee on Atomic Energy, Feb. 24, 1976, pp. 170 ff.

(83) Quoted in Karl Grossman, "Get them while they're young," *Environmental Action*, Environmental Action Inc., November 1979, p. 7.

(84) Westinghouse Electric Corp., letter to Investor Responsibility Research Center, March 17, 1976, p. 14.

(85) Victor Gilinsky, remarks before the American Newspaper Publishers Association, Sept. 19, 1979 (reprinted in Nuclear Regulatory Commission news release No. 35, Oct. 2, 1979, p. 3).

(86) Thomas Petzinger Jr., "Nuclear Power Industry Spokesmen Face Job of Calming Fears Over Such Energy," *The Wall Street Journal*, April 9, 1979.

Chapter VI

THE STATUS OF NUCLEAR TECHNOLOGY

Virtually all the nuclear power plants that are operating, under construction, or on order in the United States use "light-water" nuclear reactors to generate electric power. Eventually, some may use other types of "converter" reactors but these have not yet been able to break into the American reactor market, and only one is currently operating. For the future, government and industry research and development efforts continue to place heavy emphasis on the "breeder" reactor, which is expected to produce more nuclear fuel than it consumes and thus provide a virtually unlimited supply of energy.

Because the safety and weapons proliferation issues raised by nuclear opponents relate in large part to the ways nuclear power is generated, this chapter outlines the status of nuclear technology. Subsequent chapters will discuss the potential effects of the use of nuclear technology and the steps that are being taken and might be taken to prevent adverse consequences.

THE LIGHT-WATER REACTORS

There are two kinds of light-water reactors: boiling-water reactors (which are made by General Electric) and pressurized-water reactors (which are manufactured by Babcock & Wilcox, Combustion Engineering and Westinghouse). Light-water reactors run on energy created by the fission, or splitting, of uranium atoms, which throw off two or three neutrons and release heat in the process. The neutrons in turn run into other atoms, dislodging more neutrons, and, if properly controlled, set up a chain reaction that provides a steady source of heat.(1)

The light-water reactors now in operation use "enriched" uranium, containing about 3 percent of the isotype U-235, as their fuel. Natural uranium contains less than 1 percent U-235; almost all the remainder is U-238. The proportion of U-235 is increased through a complex gaseous diffusion process at special Department of Energy uranium enrichment plants. (U-235 can be used to make atomic weapons; U-238 cannot. Uranium enriched to more than 20 percent U-235 is considered to be weapons usable material.)

For use as a reactor fuel, the slightly enriched uranium is oxidized and formed into fuel pellets, which are placed into 12-foot rods clad in zirconium. The rods are assembled in bundles and placed vertically in the reactor core. The reactor core is surrounded by a heavy steel pressure vessel, and the pressure vessel and supporting cooling systems are placed inside a large reinforced-concrete containment dome. The chain reaction is controlled by rods--usually made of boron--which are partially raised from the reactor core and by boric acid which circulates in water around the fuel bundles. Boron is a neutron-absorbing element; when the rods are dropped into the fuel core, the boron absorbs neutrons being thrown off by the splitting atoms and controls the chain reaction. Removing the control rods from the core starts up the reactor; thrusting them back into the core terminates, or "scrams," the reactor's operation.

The reactor operates until the fuel is "spent," when it is no longer able to sustain a chain reaction economically because it has used up a major portion of its fissile material and has accumulated too many neutron-absorbing by-products. The spent fuel is composed of a variety of materials, including plutonium produced through the fissioning of U-235, amounts of unused U-235 and smaller quantities of U-238, and radioactive wastes. The plutonium, which itself is highly radioactive, and uranium may later be extracted from the unusable wastes to be reprocessed and made into fuel for light-water or breeder reactors. Current U.S. government policy, however, holds that reprocessing is both uneconomic and unwise from a nuclear weapons proliferation standpoint.

The Boiling-Water Reactor

In a boiling-water reactor, the heat from the fission process —contained in the reactor core--boils water that is passing through the core and thus creates steam. (See Figure 7) The steam drives the turbines that generate the electricity. After the steam passes through the turbines, it is condensed, and the water formed is returned to the reactor core. There, the water is boiled again, cooling the reactor core in the process, and so the cycle continues.

The Pressurized-Water Reactor

A pressurized-water reactor operates in much the same fashion, except that the water is kept under pressure, which prevents it from

FIGURE 7

Boiling-Water Reactor Power Plant

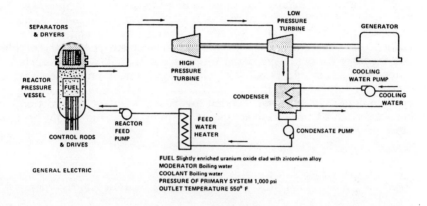

FUEL Slightly enriched uranium oxide clad with zirconium alloy
MODERATOR Boiling water
COOLANT Boiling water
PRESSURE OF PRIMARY SYSTEM 1,000 psi
OUTLET TEMPERATURE 550° F

GENERAL ELECTRIC

Source: Atomic Energy Commission, *"The Nuclear Industry 1974,"* WASH 1174-74.

FIGURE 8

Pressurized-Water Reactor Power Plant

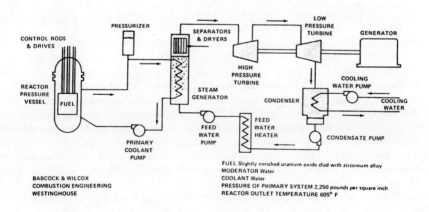

FUEL Slightly enriched uranium oxide clad with zirconium alloy
MODERATOR Water
COOLANT Water
PRESSURE OF PRIMARY SYSTEM 2,250 pounds per square inch
REACTOR OUTLET TEMPERATURE 605° F

BABCOCK & WILCOX
COMBUSTION ENGINEERING
WESTINGHOUSE

Source: Atomic Energy Commission, *"The Nuclear Industry 1974,"* WASH 1174-74.

becoming steam, and the radioactive coolant is isolated from the steam turbine by a heat exchanger. (See Figure 8) The heated water flows through the heat exchanger, where it is cooled, and water in a secondary system is boiled to create steam to drive the turbines.

Although most diagrams of light-water reactors make them appear quite simple in design, and nuclear power plants often are said to operate in essentially the same manner as fossil fuel plants, in fact the design of nuclear power plants is very complex. A maze of pipes is needed for the primary-water, cooling-water, and emergency-core-cooling systems. Over the years, government regulatory officials and industry experts have often emphasized that it is inappropriate to compare nuclear and fossil fuel plants. Nuclear plants, they say, are more complex, are harder to build, and require special cooling and containment systems not needed by fossil plants. In addition, the consequences of potential accidents at nuclear plants would be much more severe.

OTHER CONVERTER REACTORS

Other types of commercial reactors--which, like LWRs, burn U-235 to release energy--have been built in countries such as Canada, the Soviet Union and Britain. To date, the two major alternatives to LWRs consist of the Canadian CANDU reactor and the high-temperature, gas-cooled reactor (HTGR).

The CANDU Reactor

The Canadian CANDU reactor, a pressurized heavy-water reactor, is the only commercial reactor that has been able to compete in world markets with American LWR designs. Its principal advantage is its ability to operate on natural uranium ore, bypassing the need for costly enrichment facilities. Another important attribute of the CANDU is that it uses approximately 20 percent less uranium than LWRs assuming a once-through fuel cycle.(2) So far, despite these advantages, CANDU has not been able to woo much of the foreign reactor market from LWRs and has been unable to penetrate the U.S. market. A major factor in this may be the relatively higher capital costs associated with the CANDU. Although rising uranium prices and enrichment fees have generated renewed interest in the CANDU in the last few years, few observers believe it will ever crack the U.S. market. A recent study by Resources for the Future and the Ford Foundation, for instance, estimates that heavy-water reactors "will probably continue to command 8 to 10 percent of the market for the remainder of the century. Consideration has been given to their introduction in the United States, but this prospect seems unlikely because of the entrenched--even though newly furnished--position of LWRs, the licensing problems with a new reactor, and the fact that access to enrichment service is unlikely to be a problem for American utilities."(3)

The High-Temperature, Gas-Cooled Reactor

Another alternative to the light-water reactor is the high-temperature, gas-cooled reactor. Gas-cooled reactors have been developed most fully in Britain, where the civilian nuclear power industry currently relies on a carbon dioxide-cooled reactor. In the United States, ERDA had a program to develop HTGRs and test them for commercial marketability, but there has been little support for the program in recent years. HTGRs were removed from the domestic market in 1975 when General Atomic Corp., the only U.S. manufacturer, encountered financial and technical difficulties and dropped out of the reactor business. One 330-megawatt plant, at Fort St. Vrain, Colo., is currently operating on a commercial basis, but plans for eight other such plants have been dropped. Continuing technical problems at the Fort St. Vrain plant have kept it from operating at full commercial power for the last six years.(4)

The HTGR differs in several important respects from the light-water reactor:

Fuel: Highly enriched uranium 235 mixed with thorium is formed into cylindrical rods about one-half inch in diameter by two inches long and inserted into graphite blocks. Thorium is more naturally abundant than uranium.

Coolant: Pressurized helium is circulated through cylindrical passages in the graphite of the reactor core. The helium carries the heat from the reactor through a heat exchanger which in turn generates the steam to drive the turbines.

Fission products: During the fission process, uranium 233 is produced from the thorium, which captures neutrons from the uranium 235. Spent fuel assemblies are reprocessed to extract the U-233, which is then recycled for use as fuel.

The arguments that have arisen over certain technological aspects of the HTGR can be summarized as follows:

Arguments for the HTGR

Proponents of the HTGR say the following characteristics make it superior to the light-water reactor: (a) It is more efficient in converting energy to power--40 percent compared with 32.5 percent for the light-water reactor--and uses 30 to 40 percent less uranium than a light-water reactor of equivalent size. (b) Its higher thermal efficiency means less thermal pollution, which could save up to 9 million gallons of water a day. (c) Use of graphite as a moderator increases safety and eliminates the need for an emergency cooling system in the event of accidental rupture of the coolant line. (d) It produces less plutonium and thus reduces plutonium safeguards and waste disposal hazards.

Arguments Against the HTGR

Those who remain skeptical about the HTGR say: (a) While the use of graphite eliminates the need for an emergency cooling system, the HTGR still requires a second means of forced circulation of the coolant in emergency situations. (b) Although the HTGR produces no plutonium, it uses highly enriched uranium 235 and produces uranium 233, both of which are weapons-grade material. Like the light-water reactor, it produces long-lived fission products in its wastes. (c) The HTGR's efficiency should be compared not with the light-water reactor but with the breeder reactors. (Proponents of the breeder believe it is economically more attractive than the HTGR, although neither system has yet had any commercial operating experience.)

BREEDER REACTORS

The difference between breeder reactors and converter reactors is that in addition to burning up U-235, breeders also convert some U-238 into fissionable plutonium. Theoretically, breeders could produce, or "breed," more fissile material than they consumed at the expense of consuming U-238. Because more than 99 percent of natural uranium is U-238, however, breeder technology would dramatically extend uranium reserves. Breeders might allow nuclear power to become an important energy source for thousands of years.

In the United States, breeder development has focused since the 1950s on the liquid metal (sodium) fast breeder reactor (LMFBR). This attention has continued in spite of technical and regulatory problems and opposition from the Carter administration. In the LMFBR, plutonium initially produced in LWRs would be used together with U-238 in the fuel assembly. Liquid sodium would be used as a coolant, and the LMFBR would generate higher temperatures than LWRs and operate at close to 40 percent efficiency.

In recent years, the breeder program has been the federal government's largest energy research and development project, consuming more than 20 percent of the Energy Department's research and development budget. In fiscal 1979, the government spent $742 million on the breeder program, including $80 million for the controversial Clinch River, Tenn., LMFBR demonstration project that was opposed by the Carter administration.(5) Estimates of the cost of the 350-megawatt Clinch River plant have escalated from the $400- to $500-million range in 1974 to $2.6 billion today.(6) The costs of the overall program through 2020 were estimated in 1971 to be $3.9 billion; by 1980, government estimates of the total cost of the program had reached $10 billion.(7)

Opposition to the LMFBR has grown in recent years, particularly in the United States, where opponents have been aided by the Carter administration's call for the termination of the Clinch River demonstration plant. The Carter administration contended that uranium supplies were ample to last for a least 30 years and that the design of the Clinch River project was awkward, outmoded and uneconomical. The breeder program continued to command powerful support from Congress, the nuclear industry, the General Accounting Office and foreign governments, however. In 1978, President Carter attempted to kill the Clinch River project by cutting all funding for the project in his 1979 budget proposal. Congress restored the funds, however, and a Carter administration threat to use the authorized funds to phase out the project was turned back when U.S. Comptroller General Elmer B. Staats ruled that such an action would be illegal and that any government official who approved the spending of funds to terminate the project would be held personally liable for the debt. In 1979, the administration again mounted a major lobbying effort against Clinch River, but Congress appropriated $183.8 million for continued construction on the project. With the election of Reagan in 1980, however, many congressional sources now believe that the Clinch River project may be continued.

Opposition to the breeder in the United States has clearly slowed institutional momentum for its introduction into commercial use. The Clinch River demonstration project was originally scheduled to begin operation in the mid-1980s, with commercial plants following within several years. Today, the government's timetable calls for completion of the first commercial breeder in 2009 at the earliest.(8) Overseas, on the other hand--particularly in England, France and the Soviet Union--plans for the construction of commercial breeders continue to receive unswerving governmental support.

As with the HTGR, arguments over the technology of the breeder reactor (as distinct from arguments over its safety, which are discussed in the following chapters) abound. The points can be summarized as follows:(9)

Arguments for the Breeder

Supporters of the breeder say it is needed to extend dwindling uranium reserves and ensure an adequate and economic energy supply for the future. In June 1971, President Nixon committed the United States to successful development of LMFBR technology by 1980 as "our best hope today for meeting the nation's growing demand for economical clean energy."(10) Carl Walske of the Atomic Industrial Forum concurs: "Without the breeder we have decades; with it we have centuries."(11) Others say that the operation of the LMFBR is likely to present fewer safety problems than do light-water reactors. As the Department of Energy told IRRC, "A liquid-metal fast breeder reactor is cooled by liquid sodium which is at a very low pressure compared to the pressure of the water coolant in a light water reactor. In a breeder system, steam for the turbine is produced in secondary heat exchangers which greatly reduce the chances of it becoming radioactive, even in the event of a leak in the reactor sodium system."(12) Finally, some supporters of the breeder say that because it can use recycled plutonium as its fuel, it provides one answer to the problem of disposing of plutonium wastes.

Arguments Against the Breeder

Critics of the breeder reactor believe that much of the evidence presented in support of the LMFBR is flawed, that breeders will be uneconomic compared with alternative technologies by the time they could be commercialized, and that breeder technology involves hazards that far outweigh any potential economic gains. Many critics, including the Carter administration, dispute the contention that rapid development of the breeder is essential to assure low-cost fuel for the nuclear power industry. They argue that the size of U.S. uranium reserves has never been accurately determined, and that they may be far greater than current estimates. Others, pointing to the spiraling costs of the Clinch River project and other enormous construction projects, assert that solar and alternative technologies would be cheaper than the breeder if the government gave them equal R&D support. Thomas Cochran of the Natural Resources Defense Council contends that breeders "will go the way of the SST" with France and possibly some other countries actually building the plants before they discover that they are economic disasters.(13) Finally, breeder opponents say that industry cost-benefit analyses are based on flawed assumptions in such critical areas as plant capital costs, fuel cycle costs, performance characteristics of the LMFBR, and the demand for electric power.

NOTES

(1) For a description of light-water reactors, see Atomic Energy Commission, "The Nuclear Industry 1974," WASH 1174-74 (Washington, D.C., 1974), p. 23; and Fred H. Schmidt and David Bodansky, *The Fight Over Nuclear Power* (San Francisco, Albion Publishing, 1976).
(2) Hans H. Landsberg et al., *Energy: The Next Twenty Years* (Cambridge, Mass., Balinger Publishing for Resources for the Future and the Ford Foundation, 1979), p. 431.
(3) Ibid.
(4) *Nucleonics Week*, Vol. 19, No. 45, Nov. 9, 1978, p. 7.
(5) "DOE Fiscal 1980 Budget Requests More Solar, Less Fossil Fuel Spending," *Energy Users Report*, No. 285, Jan. 25, 1979, p. 3.
(6) Richard Halloran, "House Defies Carter and Backs Breeder Reactor Project," The New York *Times*, July 27, 1979.
(7) U.S. Department of Energy, "Nuclear Proliferation and Civilian Nuclear Power: Report of the Nonproliferation Alternative Systems Assessment Program," Volume IX: Reactor and Fuel Cycle Description, June 1980, p. 190.

(8)   Ibid., p. 191.

(9)   For additional information on the LMFBR, see Brian G. Chow, *The Liquid Metal Fast Breeder Reactor* (Washington, D.C., American Enterprise Institute, 1975); Thomas B. Cochran, *The Liquid Metal Fast Breeder Reactor* (Baltimore, Johns Hopkins University Press for Resources for the Future, 1974); U.S. Department of Energy, "Nuclear Proliferation and Civilian Nuclear Power," op. cit.

(10)   President Richard Nixon, Energy speech to Congress, June 1971.

(11)   J.P. Smith, "Nuclear Breeder Program on Back, Back Burner," The Washington *Post*, Dec. 9, 1978, p. A2.

(12)   U.S. Department of Energy, comments to Investor Responsibility Research Center by the Office of Plans and Analysis, Nuclear Reactor Programs, Aug. 14, 1980.

(13)   Conversation with Investor Responsibility Research Center, December 1979.

Chapter VII

NUCLEAR REACTOR SAFETY AND RADIATION

A major component of the debate over nuclear power has been and continues to be the safety with which nuclear plants can be operated. Concern about nuclear safety has inspired public opposition to plant construction and prompted increased regulatory activity. It also has led to delays in construction and shut-downs in operation and, in doing so, has imposed growing costs on the industry. For many persons, concern over the safety of nuclear plants reached new heights in 1979 due to the accident at the Three Mile Island plant.

Few people disagree that the potential for danger exists at nuclear power plants from accidents that would result in an extensive release of radioactive materials. But there continues to be widespread disagreement on the likelihood that major accidents will occur at nuclear plants, the potential danger from radioactive emissions and the efficacy of measures that are being taken or might be taken to ensure that accidents do not occur.

THE POTENTIAL FOR DANGER AT NUCLEAR PLANTS

The potential for danger at nuclear power plants consists of two distinct risks, both associated with the release of radiation. One danger stems from the risks associated with routine emissions of low-level radiation at nuclear plants and at various points in the nuclear fuel cycle. Such emissions are an inevitable consequence of operating nuclear plants, but their actual effects on the health of workers in the nuclear industry and people living near nuclear plants are the subject of an intense scientific controversy. A second distinct danger is associated with the possibility of catastrophic accidents at nuclear plants, involving the widespread release of massive amounts of radiation. Here, experts are closer to agreement on the disastrous health effects of such a release, but there are sharp differences of opinion over the probability of such accidents.

Dangers Associated with Routine
Radioactive Emissions

A light-water reactor of the average size now being built contains a great deal of radioactive material when in operation, including such known carcinogens as strontium 90, cesium 137, barium 140 and iodine 131. Small amounts of these and other isotopes are routinely emitted during normal operations of nuclear plants. In addition, varying amounts of radioactive elements are present at various points in the nuclear fuel cycle--in uranium mining and milling, fuel fabrication, fuel reprocessing and waste storage and disposal. All authorities agree that the accidental release of a large quantity of radioactivity, either from a plant or from elsewhere in the fuel cycle, could have catastrophic effects on human beings. Extremely high levels of radiation can cause almost immediate death. Lower dosages cause cancer of the thyroid, lung or bone and can lead to genetic damage. But the likely health effects of the small amounts of radiation that are typically associated with nuclear plant emissions have sparked a heated controversy in the scientific community in recent years.

The debate over the health effects associated with nuclear power arises out of a widespread split among scientists over both the postulated health effects of low-level radiation and the actual amount of nuclear power-related radiation that atomic workers and the general population are being exposed to. Alvin M. Weinberg, director of the Institute for Energy Analysis, notes, "There is the strongest kind of disagreement among scientists as to the effect of very low levels of radiation, even levels as low as our natural radiation background. Indeed, the whole question of low-level radiation is so critical to the acceptance of nuclear energy that I would judge this to be a leading, if not the leading, scientific issue underlying the nuclear controversy."(1)

The National Academy of Sciences' Committee on the Biological Effects of Ionizing Radiation estimates that the average American is exposed to between 109 and 140 millirem of radiation each year. This exposure is from the following sources:(2)

Source	Dose (millirem)
Cosmic rays (sea level/5,000 ft.)	23-50
Radioactive constituents of body	28
Gamma radiation from external sources	26
Medical and dental X-rays	20
Radiopharmaceuticals	2-4
Weapons testing fallout	4-5
Radioactive consumer products	4-5
Nuclear power	1
Air travel, research, military and industrial applications	1

As these figures indicate, the radiation dose to the *average* American resulting from the nuclear power industry is quite small when compared with medical-related exposures and is dwarfed by that received from natural background sources. Nevertheless, because some people receive much higher radiation exposure than the average, and because scientists have been unable to find a "threshold" level of exposure--a level of radiation exposure below which there are no harmful effects--the Environmental Protection Agency, the NRC and various other government agencies have set standards and established procedures intended to ensure that emissions levels are "as low as reasonably achievable." In practice, this meant adoption by the NRC and EPA of standards set in 1960 by the old Federal Radiation Council. The standards effectively set a maximum annual exposure level from all sources of 5,000 millirem for employees exposed to radiation in workplaces and 500 millirem for the general population. Recently, the EPA, which inherited the radiation council's responsibilities in 1970, set a new and significantly lower standard for overall public exposure--25 millirem a year above normal background exposure.(3) In addition, the NRC requires that nuclear plants be designed so as to limit radioactive emissions to levels that would keep radiation exposures of persons living near the plants to less than 5 millirem a year.

The Debate Over Low-Level Radiation

The federal government has long maintained that existing radiation standards for the nuclear industry are safe, although it concedes that U.S. light-water reactors and associated fuel-cycle activities can be expected to cause 1,100 cancer deaths and 2,100 genetic defects between 1975 and 2000.(4) The nuclear industry and many prominent scientists in the field agree, and they believe that attempts to lower existing radiation standards tend to be politically motivated. Exxon Nuclear Co. wrote to IRRC that "the routine emissions of low-level radiation from nuclear plants and at various points in the fuel cycle should not be considered seriously dangerous. The literature is full of comparisons of these small emissions with other risks readily accepted by our society."(5) Similarly, G. Hoyt Whipple, a radiation expert at the University of Michigan, says that "viewed as a question of health and safety for workers and the public, there is no apparent need to lower the radiation limits. The limits are not being abused by the nuclear industry. Actual exposures are, in fact, appreciably lower than the limits and, if these exposures are producing any effects, they are undetectable."(6)

Over the last decade, however, a small but growing segment of the American scientific community--including some of the most distinguished scientists in the field--has come to challenge the government's assertions that existing levels of radiation exposure pose minimal dangers to atomic workers and virtually no danger to the general population. Concern among scientists and the public about the effects of low-level radiation increased dramatically in the 1970s as a result of a number of controversial studies relating increased risks of cancer to prolonged exposure to low-level radiation.

One study looked at employees of the federal government's Hanford nuclear facilities and showed that the average radiation exposure for employees who died of cancer was higher than for those who died from other causes. Another study of naval shipyard workers in Portsmouth, N.H., alleged that nuclear shipyard workers have a sixfold higher chance of developing leukemia than the general population. Still another study found a higher-than-expected incidence of leukemia among 300,000 military men involved in observing nuclear bomb tests between 1945 and 1962. While all these studies were highly controversial and drew heavy criticism from a considerable portion of the scientific community, they did sway some prominent experts in the field to the belief that existing standards for low-level radiation might be inadequate. Scientists such as Carl Z. Morgan of the Georgia Institute of Technology, the "father of health physics," and Edward P. Radford of the University of Pittsburgh's School of Public Health have come out in favor of lower radiation limits. According to Radford, who heads the National Academy of Sciences' Committee on the Biological Effects of Ionizing Radiation, "occupational exposure limits should be dropped by a factor of 10," to 500 millirem.(7) Morgan thinks the limit should be cut in half for now, as a more drastic reduction would kill the nuclear power industry.(8)

Many other scientists seem determined not to take sides on the issue until more facts are known. Arthur C. Upton, director of the National Cancer Institute, declares that "Radiation is bad, it causes cancer, and you don't have to have large doses to do it. But you have to weigh the risks against the benefits."(9)

At the center of the debate over the effects of low-level radiation is a split among scientists over the question of what dose-response model should be used in extrapolating low-level radiation effects. Scientists believe that they have a relatively good understanding and a good data base about the health effects of exposures to high doses of radiation. They have little direct information about the carcinogenic effects of low doses of radiation, however, because the statistical sample sizes needed to obtain such information are impracticably large. So scientists have derived estimates of the health effects of low-level radiation by extrapolating from the known risks of exposure to high-level radiation. But there is little agreement among them over how such risks should be extrapolated, with many scientists believing that the linear (proportional) extrapolations used in government safety studies overestimate the risks of low-level radiation and others contending that they underestimate the risks.

The radiation issue is further complicated by the fact that knowledge about radiation effects does not easily translate into simple decisions about radiation standards. As Robert Minogue of the NRC commented to *Science*, "what's conservative (in setting radiation standards) is not self-evident," because if the linear hypothesis understates the risk (as some antinuclear scientists believe), then lowering existing radiation standards could be unwise because it would result in more workers being exposed to low-level radiation. On the other hand, if the linear hypothesis overstates the risk (as many pronuclear scientists contend), "we should lower the standard right now," Minogue says, "because that implies a quasi-threshold beneath which there would be no detectable risk."(10)

The controversy over low-level radiation and the safety of nuclear facilities shows few signs of abating. In 1978, congressional concern over the issue prompted President Carter to appoint an Interagency Task Force on Ionizing Radiation to reevaluate the federal government's research and regulatory responsibilities in the area. In 1979, radiation releases associated with the accident at Three Mile Island, combined with controversial new findings by 14 West German scientists that NRC estimates vastly understated the radiation dose that persons living near nuclear plants could expect to receive, heightened the low-level radiation controversy. The German study contends that NRC estimates of radiation exposures are meaningless because they fail to include some of the most important pathways by which radiation from the plants would enter the body--especially through radioactive elements in the food chain. The study says that in measuring radioactive fallout's journey from nuclear reactors to the body, NRC figures are "either at the lower end of the range given in the literature or far below the values that may be regarded as realistic," and asserts that NRC judgments on how much plutonium, cesium and strontium crops pick up from the soil, because they are based on a series of rigged experiments by the AEC, are "between 10 and 1,000 times too low."(11) The NRC staff has called the German report "flawed" and contends that its own calculations are "supported by a large majority of the scientific community."(12)

Whatever the merits of arguments in favor of keeping or lowering existing radiation limits, the scientific and public controversy over this issue appears certain to remain intense, and its outcome will be crucial in determining the level of public acceptability of nuclear power. A number of major health studies--most of them under the control of various federal agencies--are being planned to resolve the questions resulting from earlier studies. Overall, about the only thing a majority of experts in the field now agree on is that a great deal more research is required before any definitive conclusions about the effects of low-level radiation can be made. As U.S. Comptroller General Elmer Staats recently testified to a Senate subcommittee, "In spite of over 70 years of study, millions of dollars of research, and tens of thousands of scientific papers on the subject, many questions remain unanswered about the action of radiation on people. Scientists are still trying to understand exactly how many cancers are caused by a given amount of radiation."(13)

Postulated Health Effects of Low-Level Radiation

The postulated adverse health effects attributable to low-level radiation from the nuclear power industry remain highly contingent upon resolution of the debate over the effects of low-level radiation exposure. As mentioned earlier, official NRC documents estimate that there will be 1,100 cancer deaths between 1975 and 2000 directly attributable to the nuclear power industry--although these estimates are based on assumptions about rapid nuclear industry growth that now appear to be unrealistic. This estimate, according to the NRC, assumes "exposures of very large populations to very small doses" and "no major nuclear plant accidents."(14) A National Academy of Sciences report entitled "Risks Associated with Nuclear Power," released in 1979, estimates 2,000 additional cancer deaths between 1975 and 2000 resulting from the use of nuclear power.(15) The report says the additional cancer deaths will result from the mining of radioactive materials, their fabrication into fuel elements, the exposure of plant employees, the release of small amounts of radioactive materials into the atmosphere, and the transportation, reprocessing and storage of nuclear materials. This study also assumes no major plant accidents.

These estimates represent the prevailing thought of the mainstream of America's scientific establishment. A number of distinguished scientists believe that these estimates overstate the risks of low-level radiation; an equally distinguished group contends that they understate the risks.

One further issue that arises from an examination of the health hazards of low-level radiation is its effect over time. While scientists do not agree on the precise effect that a given amount of low-level radiation will have on humans, they do agree that some of the radioactive elements (radioisotopes) responsible for its effect will continue to cause fatalities for hundreds, and in some cases thousands, of years. Thus, the effect of low-level radiation from today's nuclear power programs will not be confined to people alive today. It will continue to add up for thousands of years.

Two of the most commonly discussed long-lived radioisotopes are carbon-14 and the decay elements (or "daughters") of radon. Carbon-14, which is routinely emitted from nuclear reactors, has a half-life of 5,470 years. Scientists believe that its effective half-life is much shorter, however--perhaps as little as 40 years--because it tends to be absorbed into the depths of the ocean. Radon, which is a radioactive gas that is emitted by uranium tailings piles and from uranium mining operations, has a half-life of only about four days, but it is continuously produced by other elements having a half-life of about 80,000 years. Scientists expect that these two elements, together with other long-lived radioisotopes, will cause a few cancer deaths each year for thousands of years to come unless costly measures are taken to reduce plant emissions and bury millions of tons of uranium mill and mine tailings. William Ramsay of Resources for the Future, as part of a major study on the health impacts of nuclear and coal-fired electrical generation, makes the following estimates:

...the number of deaths attributed to radon from a nuclearized United States in the first year after its emission ranges between 0.8 and 2, while the carbon-14 fatalities range from 2 to 4. But the number of predicted fatalities over all time from the same sources is large for carbon-14 (100 to 300), while the prediction for radon (as many as 200,000) is huge. After all, we are adding up a virtually constant rate of fatalities (assuming that populations stay about the same) over many thousands of years.(16)

In summary, although more is known about radiation than is known about most other carcinogenic materials, the extent of the dangers posed by low-level radioactive emissions from the nuclear power industry remain largely unknown. Scientists believe that they have established some of the limits of the risk posed by low-level radiation and are convinced that the risks attributable to radiation from the nuclear power industry are small in comparison with the risks from other sources of radiation. But they are less confident today than they were 10 years ago that they can accurately predict the effects of small amounts of radiation on the human body. Their best estimates suggest that low-level radiation from the nuclear power industry, assuming there are no major accidents, might result in from 40 to 80 cancer deaths a year during the existence of an active nuclear power program, falling to a few deaths a year thereafter for thousands of generations. This compares with approximately 360,000 cancer deaths per year that result from all causes.

Dangers from Catastrophic Nuclear Plant Accidents

Despite renewed interest in the question of the effects of low-level radiation, the major fear in connection with the safety of the nuclear industry is not of low-level radiation, but of high levels of exposure as the result of a serious accident. For years, anti-nuclear activists and groups such as the Union of Concerned Scientists have argued that a major accident at a nuclear plant, involving failure of the plant's safety systems and the widespread release of radioactive materials, is not only possible, but likely. For years, the industry and the government have countered with studies showing that the plant's safety systems are reliable and that the chances of an accident that would release large amounts of radiation to the atmosphere are exceedingly small. A major shift in the attitude of both the public and the government appears to have occurred as a result of the Three Mile Island incident in 1979, however, and the issue of reactor safety is again in the forefront of concern by the industry, the media, Congress and the NRC. As a writer for The Washington *Post* observed, "Ironically, the accident at Three Mile Island raised the issue of nuclear safety all over just as it had become the least urgent of the three basic parts of the debate on nuclear power. The last few years had seen the threats of the spread of nuclear weapons and the disposal of radioactive waste become more central to the debate than the issue of safety."(17)

Loss-of-Coolant Accident

The kind of accident most experts postulate could produce a large release of radiation is a loss-of-coolant accident, or LOCA, resulting from the failure of several plant cooling systems. Such an accident could be initiated by the rupture of a large pipe in the primary cooling system. The water in the system is under high pressure, so a large pipe break would lead to rapid expulsion of water out of the reactor core and into the containment vessel. In some cases this loss-of-coolant, or "blowdown," could take less than one minute.

The loss of water from the core of a reactor would lead to an automatic shutdown, or "scram," of the reactor, but residual radioactive decay from the fuel rods would continue to generate vast amounts of heat. At shutdown, heat from residual decay is equal to about 7 percent of the total generated by the reactor; for a power plant producing 1,000 megawatts of electric power, then, residual heat would amount to about 230 megawatts when the efficiency of conversion from thermal to electrical energy is taken into account. As isotopes with very short half-lives decay, the heat rate initially falls rapidly, dropping to 3 percent after 100 seconds and to less than 1 percent after two hours.(18) However, radioactive elements with longer half-lives then begin to dominate, and the reactor core continues to generate considerable quantities of heat for a period of days. During this time, unless cooling water is continuously supplied to the core, the zirconium cladding around the fuel pellets is likely to deteriorate, and the fuel pellets will melt into a molten mass that could be hot enough to burn its way through the bottom of the reactor vessel, through the containment building and into the ground below. Where it would stop is not really known; the phenomenon has been dubbed "the China syndrome."

If an extensive core melt were to occur, it is possible that radioactive gases could escape from underground into the atmosphere. It is also possible that such gases could cause a steam or chemical explosion large enough to burst the containment building, releasing radioactive materials directly into the atmosphere. Such a chemical explosion--in this case involving oxygen and hydrogen--was what experts feared during the Three Mile Island accident, although government safety officials later said that these fears were groundless.

Safety Systems

To guard against the possibility of a loss-of-coolant accident, nuclear plants are constructed with what the industry describes as three levels of safety in a "defense-in-depth" or multiple-barrier system. The first level of safety results from conservative design and quality assurance for materials, design and construction. The second level is based on redundant back-up safety systems, some of which are designed to shut down the reactor in case of emergency. As a third line of defense, the NRC requires that all light-water reactors be equipped with an emergency core-cooling system designed to flood the reactor core with water in the event of a failure in the primary system. The emergency system is supposed to begin functioning quickly enough after any loss of coolant to prevent the cladding on the fuel rods from rupturing as the heat builds up. It also is designed to cool the radioactive materials sufficiently to safeguard the containment building from destruction or rupture.

Before Three Mile Island, no major loss-of-coolant accident had ever occurred. In the few cases where portions of the emergency systems were required, they functioned properly. At Three Mile Island, operator errors and mechanical failures led to extensive damage to the reactor's fuel rods. Although the accident failed to breach the plant's containment building, non-negligible amounts of radioactive gases did escape into the atmosphere.(19)

Industry and government officials express confidence that the emergency safety systems at nuclear plants will work. Their views are based on extensive research, including computer modeling and semi-scale testing to predict the ability of safety systems to respond in case of a loss-of-coolant accident. Over the years, however, there has been a continuing debate about the extent to which the tests that have been conducted are meaningful. Industry representatives contend that the tests provide reliable information about how a full-sized reactor would respond in an emergency. Critics question this assumption and contend that the safety research to date--especially that concerning the emergency core-cooling system--has been incomplete and inadequate. They also say that both the government and the industry have misrepresented the results of safety research to the public.

Tests of Core-Cooling Systems

Recent developments have provided mixed evidence as to the adequacy of emergency core-cooling systems. In July 1977, tests conducted under the auspices of the NRC at the U.S. government's Sandia Laboratories revealed that certain kinds of electrical connectors essential to emergency systems failed under loss-of-coolant conditions. There was no immediate response from the NRC to the test results. However, in the fall of 1977, the Union of Concerned Scientists called public attention to the tests and petitioned the NRC to close down affected reactors. In November 1977, as a result of that petition, the NRC closed a nuclear power plant in Michigan and ordered studies that resulted in temporary shutdowns of 12 other plants.(20)

In December 1978, however, a planned "accident" at the LOFT--Loss of Fluid Test--reactor in Idaho was hailed by the nuclear industry and the NRC as a success. During the reactor test, which simulated the break of a primary coolant pipe, everything went as expected except that the nuclear core cladding did not reach the predicted temperature and cooled off more rapidly than expected.

Although the LOFT reactor was not designed to determine whether full-scale emergency core-cooling systems would work, but rather to provide data and confirm existing computer projections, industry officials claimed that the tests showed that back-up safety systems worked even better than expected. "I pronounce this a successful test. Very good," declared Thomas E. Murley, the NRC's director of reactor safety research.(21)

A second test at the LOFT reactor on May 12, 1979--with the reactor operating at a higher power level--achieved results similar to the first LOFT test. Again, core temperatures did not reach the predicted levels, and the core cooled off more quickly than expected.(22) The NRC has continued semiscale testing at the LOFT facility, allowing successively higher temperatures in the reactor core before activating the emergency core-cooling system.

Undoubtedly the most significant test of nuclear plant emergency safety systems took place not at the LOFT facility, however, but at the Three Mile Island nuclear plant--again with mixed results. Reactor safety experts are still trying to determine the exact sequence of events that led to damage to the reactor's core, but it is clear that both mechanical failures and operator errors were involved.

Predictably, nuclear critics have emphasized that the equipment failures and operator blunders at Three Mile Island prove that reactors cannot be run safely, and nuclear enthusiasts have emphasized that, in spite of all the mistakes, the reactor was eventually brought under control and no one was killed. While nuclear experts will probably debate the significance of various factors involved in the accident for years, the available evidence suggests that some of the plant's safety systems performed quite well and others were virtually useless. The plant's emergency core-cooling system appears to have performed reasonably well under the circumstances. However, this system does not appear to have played a major role in cooling the reactor's overheated core because plant operators turned the system off at an early stage in the accident, apparently after they received confusing signals from instruments measuring pressure in the reactor's core.(23) Overall, the fact that the plant's safety systems were able to contain the accident even after many of them were rendered useless by mechanical failures or operator errors attests to the effectiveness of highly redundant safety systems. Nevertheless, the fact that so many things could go wrong almost instantaneously at a nuclear plant--and that plant operators tended to take actions that made the situation worse, at least during the first crucial hours of the accident--suggests fundamental flaws in the nation's nuclear power safety programs.

Safety Concerns of Nuclear Critics

A specific focus of critics' safety concerns has been the emergency core-cooling system, the principal back-up safety system that must operate in case of a serious accident. The Union of Concerned Scientists says that the AEC and NRC testing programs have been narrow in scope and that experimental results for a loss-of-coolant accident and response by the emergency core-cooling system cannot be predicted accurately. The group made the ineffectiveness of emergency cooling systems its primary complaint during hearings before the AEC in 1972 and 1973. The AEC subsequently imposed tougher standards, but the Union of Concerned Scientists and other highly regarded nuclear critics continue to be skeptical about the effectiveness of the emergency core-cooling system. In 1975, the computer codes designed to simulate the functioning of the emergency core-cooling system were described as "inaccurate and unverified" by Carl Hocevar, a safety research engineer who did contract work for the AEC but resigned in 1974 to join the Union of Concerned Scientists.(24) A recent U.C.S. publication sums up the situation as follows:

> The public is being asked to accept the word of the nuclear industry that the currently installed emergency core-cooling system can function properly to prevent this most dreaded of disasters. The fact remains, however, that there has been only limited testing of the emergency core-cooling system--and some of the tests reveal design defects and indicate that ECCS might fail if actually called upon. Sworn testimony of experts in the field reveals that the effectiveness of this critical reactor safety system has not been properly demonstrated.(25)

Nuclear critics contend that the size of the LOFT facility--it generates about one-sixtieth the heat of a commercial-size plant-- makes tests on it largely irrelevant. "It's like testing a tire one-third of an inch high and saying it's safe to ride on in your car," says James Cubie of the Union of Concerned Scientists.(26) Nuclear critics also argue that the computer codes--which recent tests at the LOFT facility were attempting to confirm--have been proved inaccurate and thus the safety systems that relied on them cannot be deemed safe at all. The fact that temperatures in the LOFT facility did not rise as high as predicted makes the tests a failure rather than a success, the U.C.S. maintains, because it shows an inability to predict accurately what will happen in the reactor. They note that a group of academic and industry experts from the American Physical Society has stated that "a code which has made conservative predictions for the LOFT facility cannot be considered 'verified' because it is not necessarily true that it will give conservative results for a large reactor."(27) Critics also fault the testing program as too little, too late. They say that the NRC's LOFT tests are something of an afterthought now that 74 plants are in operation.

On a related issue, in August 1974 David Comey of Business and Professional People in the Public Interest wrote to the AEC to challenge the operating efficiency of the diesel engines that are to power the emergency core-cooling system in case of a loss of off-site power coincident with a loss-of-coolant accident. Comey pointed out that a number of the diesels had a reliability factor of less than 92 percent--the AEC's reliability standard is 99 percent--and cited one with a reliability factor of 51 percent. He concluded: "Fortunately, although there have been well over a hundred diesel generator failures at operating nuclear plants in the last few years, none of them has occurred coincident with a major accident .... If, however, the diesel generators were to fail to start in the event of a major loss-of-coolant accident with a loss of off-site power, then the plant emergency core-cooling system would be without power, and a delay of even 120 seconds in getting the diesels started by manual means would probably lead to onset of a fuel core meltdown."(28)

At the time, the AEC said it shared Comey's concern and would take steps to deal with the problem. Some nuclear critics contend that little has been done, however, and that the loss of off-site power continues to represent a major safety threat at nuclear plants. The NRC, although it maintains that steps have been taken to alleviate the problem, continues to list the loss of offsite and AC power as a generic unresolved safety issue at light-water reactors for which it is considering additional regulations.(29)

Finally, a safety issue that is receiving increased attention from nuclear critics and government authorities in the wake of the Three Mile Island accident is reactor emergency planning. According to Jan Beyea, a nuclear physicist and senior energy scientist of the National Audubon Society, the traditional regulatory approach of the AEC and the NRC--where regulation of reactor designs is presumed to reduce the probability of a large release of radioactivity to such a low level that this possibility can essentially be ignored--"has led to an imbalance between the enormous resources which have been devoted to *accident prevention* and the almost negligible resources which have been devoted to the development of *consequence mitigation strategies.*"(30) In a study conducted with Frank von Hippel, a physicist in the Program on Nuclear Policy Alternatives at Princeton University's Center for Energy and Environmental Studies, Beyea argues that current reactor emergency planning is insufficient because it focuses on the evacuation of areas close to nuclear plants whereas a significant percentage of the long-term health impacts from a major radiation release would result from the exposure of persons at distances beyond 50 miles downwind from the reactor site. Because evacuation "may not be feasible beyond a distance of tens of miles from the reactor," Beyea and von Hippel conclude, the government should give greater priority to measures which would reduce the consequences of a major radiation release.(31) Among the measures the study advocates are: the backfitting of the containment buildings of existing reactors with a system capable of filtering large volumes of radioactive gases; the virtual nationwide distribution of potassium iodide, a compound that could be ingested during a reactor accident to block the uptake of radioactive iodine by the thyroid gland; the sheltering of people in closed buildings and the use of makeshift cloth filters for breathing during the period when the radioactive cloud was passing overhead; and increased government research efforts on radioactive decontamination.

The NRC is already considering requiring filtered venting containment on reactors located near major population centers and is conducting preliminary studies on the sheltering concept, but the NRC staff apparently opposes the advance distribution of thyroid blocking agents on economic grounds. According to an NRC cost-benefit analysis, stockpiling potassium iodide "appears only marginally cost-effective at best."(32) Frank von Hippel contends, however, that the commission's refusal to implement a thyroid protection strategy has less to do with economics--von Hippel and Beyea estimate that the program would cost less than $10 million per year nationwide(33)--than with political ramifications. According to von Hippel, "The question of stockpiling potassium iodide is a sensitive issue because if the commission visibly prepares for the possibility of a large release of radioactivity, the public may become convinced that such an accident is not only possible but probable."(34) But "it is no longer part of the NRC's job description . . . to make the political environment safe for nuclear energy," von Hippel says.

Nuclear Proponents' View of Safety

Supporters of nuclear power say that extensive research on plant safety systems and the series of tests on the LOFT reactor in Idaho provide adequate evidence that emergency core-cooling systems would operate as predicted during an accident. They also disagree with critics' analysis, saying much of it is based on outdated information. According to Exxon Nuclear Co., "The ECCS codes are inaccurate in the sense they are purposely made inaccurate in the conservative direction to compensate for uncertainties. The LOFT tests have verified the conservatism of the codes."(35)

Industry representatives also reject critics' contention that full-scale tests are required to assure that nuclear plants are sufficiently safe. "A full-scale test is much less demanding on the system being tested," W.H. Arnold of Westinghouse has stated, "than a well-devised series of component tests coupled with a good program of analytical predictions of the effect of system failures on components. In a full-scale test, one takes what one gets. One has little or no control of influences a particular component will experience. In individual tests, one can subject individual components to conditions two, three, or even 10 times worse than they might receive in the full-scale test."(36)

Not only is a full-scale test unnecessary, nuclear proponents say, but to ask that one be performed is unreasonable. "Even if such a test (pushing a plant to a true-core melt and destruction) were done, the test would be met with the claim we tested it the wrong way," GE's Philip Bray comments. "We could say that more plants should be tested to destruction, thus leading to the wasteful expenditure of billions of dollars and, more importantly I think, the wasteful diversion of our technical talent toward areas of reactor design that don't add to overall safety."(37)

Nuclear proponents admit that the Three Mile Island accident uncovered some safety deficiencies at nuclear plants, but they say that steps taken by the industry since the accident have largely resolved these problems. They add that two new industry-sponsored safety organizations, the Institute of Nuclear Power Operations (INPO) and the Nuclear Safety Analysis Center (NSAC), are already at work ensuring that nuclear plants are operated safely. According to Edwin Zebroski, director of NSAC, "Improvements already undertaken together with those being developed and committed should...make it highly improbable for the rest of this century that another accident with severe core damage will occur within the population of reactors and utilities that rigorously apply the improvements."(38)

OPERATING HISTORY

The Nuclear Regulatory Commission requires nuclear plants and facilities "to report incidents or events that involve a variance from the regulations such as personnel overexposures, radioactive material releases above prescribed limits, and malfunctions of safety-related equipment."(39) The NRC investigates all reported events, and its findings are circulated "to the industry, the public, and other interested groups." They are also available through the NRC's 122 public document rooms across the country. In addition, the NRC reports quarterly to Congress on any of these incidents that could be considered an abnormal occurrence," defined as "an unscheduled incident or event which the commission determines is significant from the standpoint of public health and safety."(40)

In 1978, the NRC received reports on 2,835 "reportable occurrences."(41) Every nuclear plant in operation that year had at least one unscheduled shutdown. In 1979, utilities filed reports of 2,300 occurrences.(42)

Events may occur singly or at more than one plant--in which case they may be labeled a generic problem. Some of the areas in which nuclear plants have suffered recurring difficulties, although not usually of a serious enough nature to be ruled an abnormal occurrence under current NRC criteria, are as follows:

Valves

Valve failures continue to be blamed for more abnormal occurrences at nuclear plants than any other component; valve mechanism malfunctions recur in every nuclear plant, in every size, type and brand of valve. Valve failures in areas of the plants unrelated to the reactor have resulted in several deaths; other valve failures have led to the exposing of a reactor core, cooling system failures, and the exposure of workers to high doses of radiation. Valve failures played a major role in exacerbating the accident at Three Mile Island.

Instrument Sensors and Switches

Instrument switches and electronic sensors malfunction with great frequency. AEC officials told IRRC in 1974 that instrument switch set points were "constantly beyond required safety limits" and were so frequently out of calibration that the AEC suggested weekly inspections. Misaligned, loose and undersized switches have been responsible for rendering high-pressure coolant systems inoperative. Sensors give conflicting signals or stop functioning during emergency situations.

Pipes

A number of reported events concern pipes, pipe fittings, hangers and supports. Corrosion problems leading to cracked or leaking pipes have already caused extended shutdowns at a number of nuclear plants in the United States and abroad. Several have affected the primary cooling system. Recently, cracks began appearing in some large diameter stainless steel pipes that experts had thought were immune to the cracking problem, leading the NRC to reestablish a pipe crack study group it had previously disbanded.

Fuel

Potential problems have developed as a result of shrinkage of fuel pellets within the fuel rods and possible swelling of the fuel cladding at high temperatures. The shrinkage problem occurred at a number of pressurized-water reactor plants, leading to a collapsing of the fuel rods, an increase in fuel temperature, and the danger of leakage of fissionable materials from the fuel assemblies.

The AEC temporarily reduced ("derated") the permissible level of power generation at a number of plants until the problems could be corrected. In late 1979, research at Oak Ridge National Laboratories found that fuel cladding would swell more than was previously thought before it would burst, possibly blocking the flow of cooling water in the event of a loss-of-coolant accident. The NRC, after urgent meetings with fuel suppliers, determined that no major changes were necessary.

Human Error

A large number of reported events have been attributed to human error. Specific incidents of human infallibility include upside-down insertion of tubes in the control rods, incorrect installation of valves, shoddy welding, connection of waste disposal lines to an employee water fountain, and most recently, shutting valves and turning off emergency cooling systems during a loss-of-coolant accident at the Three Mile Island plant.

Interpreting the Record

Opponents of nuclear power say the performance record of nuclear reactors now in operation is replete with design, fabrication, installation, operation, maintenance, and human errors affecting plant safety. Proliferation of nuclear plants, they say, will unduly increase the risk that similar errors will result in a serious accident. Proponents argue that the record of operating reactors provides evidence of the safety of nuclear power, not cause for concern. They say a combination of stringent regulations, safeguards and contingency systems has enabled utilities to identify and deal safely with a number of minor problems; after hundreds of reactor-years of operation, there has not been a single nuclear-related accident affecting public health.

Critics' Interpretations

Critics claim that the number of events or incidents being reported demonstrates that the industry, despite its extensive efforts at quality assurance, is not able to plan for contingencies and thus is not able to provide the systems and equipment required to guarantee public safety. In support of their claim, critics often cite AEC or NRC sources, or the reports of several recent investigations into the accident at Three Mile Island.

Critics give a number of reasons for these problems. They contend that the NRC is overly theoretical in its approach to safety or too vague in its guidelines. They say that the commission, often for commercial reasons, will allow old plants to operate without meeting new standards or will fail to halt operation of new plants that do not meet safety criteria. Or they say that utilities are simply not prepared to handle the complications of operating a sophisticated nuclear technology.

The resignation of three engineers from GE and two from the NRC gave new impetus to these complaints in 1976. Gregory Minor, formerly of GE, testified before the Joint Atomic Energy Committee that "the industry, with the concurrence of the NRC, has overemphasized the theoretical approach to design verification with insufficient prototype, laboratory or field test verification." The result, he said, "is an inadequate and unsafe design."(43) And in later testimony, the GE engineers and Robert Pollard of the NRC focused their criticism on specific design defects. The engineers from GE criticized aspects of the reactor core, the control rods, the reactor vessel, the primary containment, and the supporting system.(44) In a report to the NRC after his resignation, Pollard expressed concerns about the location of certain valves, problems with turbines, and the placement of electrical equipment. "There is at least one but probably several serious safety problems in every plant now operating," Pollard asserted in 1979.(45)

In part, nuclear critics say, the problem lies in utilities' inexperience with nuclear plants. Opponents of nuclear power have argued for a number of years that many utilities were not qualified to run nuclear reactors--a conclusion that has recently been endorsed by a number of the groups investigating the Three Mile Island accident. But opponents contend that although the government is aware of the problem, it is unwilling to take dramatic actions against those utilities that fail to meet government safety standards. They cite a 1973 report by the AEC which commented that "utility management, for the most part, has been slow to recognize the distinction between the organization and controls required to operate a nuclear power plant and the traditional controls employed in operating fossil fuel plants."(46) They also cite the testimony of various safety officials who contend that there are still virtually no minimum qualifications for utility companies that wish to own nuclear plants. As NRC Commissioner Victor Gilinsky stated in 1979,

> ... The AEC encouraged all utilities to buy nuclear plants. It wasn't then going to rule the smaller ones ineligible for licenses .... While the NRC is charged with determining the qualifications of electric utilities to operate nuclear plants, this rule was never vigorously applied. Of course, the obvious shortcomings of the Three Mile Island management will lead to sharper scrutiny of license applicants, but if NRC should try separating the sheep from goats among the utility companies, I suspect a mighty battle will ensue.(47)

At the base of this resistance may be a utility's financial concerns. The commercial prospects of nuclear power, critics say, may conflict with an effective safety program. "The tremendous cost, schedule and political pressures experienced make unbiased decisions, with true evaluations of the consequences, impossible to achieve," the three GE engineers said in testimony to the Joint Committee on Atomic Energy after they had left the company. "The primary focus of the (assessment) program has been to 'prove' the plants are safe enough for continued operation--not to openly assess their true safety....It is unfortunate that the commercial and technical proprietary pressures of the business world also work to the detriment of the maximum achievement of safety."(48)

Even if industry and the NRC were able to correct all design defects and resolve conflicts between safety concerns and commercial interests, however, many critics question whether it will be possible to achieve what they would consider to be an adequate level of safety. They say that nuclear plants are subject to Murphy's law--whatever can go wrong, will go wrong--and that many of the problems in nuclear plants do not result from lack of experience with nuclear technology.

Some of the problems may simply prove to be without solution, critics say. Hannes Alfven, a 1970 Nobel laureate in physics, contends that one cannot claim that safety problems have been solved simply by pointing to all the efforts made to solve them.(49) "The technologists claim that if everything works according to their blueprints, atomic energy will be a safe and very attractive solution to the energy needs of the world," says Alfven. "However, the real issue is whether their blueprints will work in the real world and not only in a 'technological paradise.'"(50) Perhaps the most serious problem, and the most intractable, opponents say, is human error. Amory Lovins suggests that ensuring nuclear power plant safety may involve "not a mere engineering problem that can be solved by sufficient care, but rather a wholly new type of problem that can be solved only by infallible people."(51) Henry Kendall described nuclear power plants in 1974 as representative of "a system designed by geniuses being run by idiots."(52)

Proponents' Interpretations

The accident at Three Mile Island caused a serious split among proponents of nuclear power concerning nuclear safety issues. Before the accident, industry and government officials tended to agree that, overall, nuclear safety programs were adequate. This no longer appears to be the case. Most of the industry argues that whatever flaws existed in nuclear safety programs before the accident can be corrected, and indeed, they say, most already have been corrected. Portions of the NRC and the U.S. and international nuclear establishments, on the other hand, contend that drastic institutional changes in such fundamental areas as plant siting, plant ownership and control, utility management, and the organization of the NRC are absolutely essential to the survival of nuclear power.

Industry officials dispute critics' interpretations of the operating safety record of nuclear plants and of the NRC's regulatory role. They say that most of the concern with the operational safety of nuclear power plants comes from persons who have little technical experience with their operation. "The safety record, either on an absolute basis or in comparison with other industries, is exemplary," says Exxon Nuclear Co.(53) Industry officials also denounce critics' calls for a moratorium on future nuclear construction as irresponsible in light of the country's dependence on foreign oil. "A more appropriate response," according to Robert E. Kirby, chairman of Westinghouse, would be "an acceleration of plants under construction and a case-by-case evaluation of completed plants--an evaluation that emphasizes safety improvements as well as the welfare of the nation."(54)

The industry's commitment to safety, according to its spokesmen, is demonstrated by quality design and construction, extensive back-up systems and redundant controls, and quality assurance programs in production and operations. Plants are built with multiple barriers to contain radioactive materials--the zirconium cladding, the reactor pressure vessel, a reinforced concrete containment building--and with emergency systems in case of failure of primary systems. "We are not perfect, but we incorporate backups and conservatism all along the way so that, when failures do occur, they can be handled safely,"(55) says W.H. Arnold of Westinghouse. "Safety starts in the design." Design integrity, industry representatives say, is maintained through the most extensive quality assurance programs ever used by a commercial industry. The programs involve widespread reporting and documentation and are often administered by a separate staff. General Electric reports that it has one employee working on quality assurance for every four on production at its fuel fabrication plant. Westinghouse representatives describe their commitment to safety as personal as well as institutional: "Our own personal and professional futures are involved."(56)

Many industry representatives argue that the issue of safety is being used by nuclear critics for political purposes, in an attempt to kill the industry. Edwin Zebroski, director of NSAC, contends that one of the most important lessons not yet learned in reactor safety is the need to guard against so-called safety advice stemming from philosophical biases against energy production and nuclear power.(57) Milton Copulos, a nuclear energy analyst for the Heritage Foundation, adds that although "there's no objection to serious people questioning what they (the utilities) do ... the NRC has knuckled under to people who only want to delay everything possible and kill any nuclear efforts whatever."(58) A number of industry officials describe the campaign against nuclear power as one aimed at forcing a change in the country's political system and in people's life style. "We are in a desperate battle, with whatever you want to call them-- environmentalists, 'small is beautiful people,' consumerists," Edward Teller, a physicist credited with developing the hydrogen bomb, recently told the Atomic Industrial Forum. "If they win, the freedom of the United States, the freedom of the world is doomed," he predicts.(59)

Industry officials reserve some of their harshest criticism for the NRC. They say that the actions taken by the NRC in response to the Three Mile Island accident appear to be aimed at showing how "tough" the agency is, rather than at getting on with the safe operation of nuclear plants. Current NRC plans, says Atomic Industrial Forum president Carl Walske, have "the potential for a most ineffective use of NRC and industry resources at a time when these resources should be sharply focused in the public interest." Walske adds, "Increasing the detailed requirements and degree of current studies significantly beyond that currently under way will not improve either safety or safety attitudes. It will only drain away the productive energy that is committed to implementing the lessons of Three Mile Island through the best of our concerted efforts."(60)

Industry and utility spokesmen acknowledge that nuclear power presents some risks, but they characterize the industry's overall safety record as excellent. They accept as fair the indictment of the industry presented in the report by the Kemeny Commission, but they say that they have already corrected most of the deficiencies referred to by the report and that further steps will be taken to ensure that all nuclear utilities live up to industry safety expectations. Among the steps already taken, they say, are: individual plant safety reviews, improved equipment, additional operator training, the development of emergency response plans for each nuclear site, the establishment of the Institute of Nuclear Power Operations to establish educational and training requirements for plant operators, and the establishment of the Nuclear Safety Analysis Center to review, analyze and disseminate data relevant to the safe operation of reactors.

Finally, utility spokesmen reject that charge that utilities have bypassed safety because of commercial considerations and assert that an accident like the one at Three Mile Island could never happen at one of their plants. "We see both differences in design and in our operating procedures," says Lelan F. Sillin Jr., chairman of Northeast Utilities Co. "I don't want to minimize the seriousness of the conditions at Three Mile Island, but looking at what we know about our own plants, we are satisfied."(61) "Nothing has happened that makes us retreat from our assertions that nuclear power is economical, environmentally benign and safe," adds Bernard Trueschler, president of Baltimore Gas and Electric Co.(62)

In contrast with the widespread optimism about safety exhibited by industry representatives, many other nuclear supporters--especially government nuclear power officials--say that the Three Mile Island accident has dramatically altered their notions about nuclear safety. "Up to Three Mile Island, the perception was that we were dealing with basically a responsible industry that shared our concern about these dangerous machines and could be relied on to do what was needed," says Robert Minogue, head of the NRC's office of standards. "Now we're questioning that."(63) "My position used to be that I was for nuclear power unless somebody showed me it wasn't safe," adds Rep. Mickey Edwards (R-Okla.), who used to vote in favor of all pro-nuclear proposals. "My position now is I am for nuclear power if somebody proves it is safe."(64)

Many nuclear supporters now believe that major changes in both the industry and the way it is regulated will be necessary if safety is to be ensured. Carroll L. Wilson, the AEC's first general manager, argues that "there has been a failure to recognize that a nuclear reactor is a wholly different 'kind of animal'" (65) from fossil-fueled boilers. On safety, "a real uncertainty now exists concerning possible accidents which could have disastrous consequences," Wilson says, and "the only way to meet these objections and to resolve the current impasse is to put all new plants underground."(66) The NRC's Minogue believes that "the plants are too big," and have outrun the ability of utilities to run them properly. "Eventually you stretch beyond a line in which the thing becomes a different object altogether," Minogue comments. "I think the industry crossed that line...at about 600 megawatts," he adds.(67)

The Tennessee Valley Authority, which has more nuclear reactors under construction than any other utility, says that some utilities simply do not have the technical or financial resources to operate nuclear plants. "It may well be that the best protection the citizens of the nation have against nuclear hazards lies with restricting nuclear power development to those utilities which, like TVA, can make a major commitment of resources to provide the critical technical talent, the know-how, and the capital to make the necessary investment in safety," states a recent TVA report on its nuclear safety program.(68) Thomas Spink, a nuclear engineer on TVA's power planning staff, emphasized that financial considerations must not be allowed to influence utility safety decisions. Utilities that want to save money in the area of safety are playing a dangerous game, Spink told IRRC, and "the real attitude has got to be that you spend as much money as you possibly can on safety."(69)

A major worry of some nuclear supporters is that the government will attempt only superficial treatment of nuclear safety, assuring continued public polarization on the issue and giving nuclear critics ample opportunity to keep the safety issue in the forefront of the debate over nuclear power. "There is a grave danger that in the period immediately ahead, Congress, the NRC, the utilities and the vendors will settle for superficial, quick-fix solutions to the problem of reactor safety," says R.A. Brightsen of the NRC.(70) Such measures, Brightsen says, would likely include "additional training programs for reactor operators, more resident inspectors, hastily drawn emergency preparedness plans, and generally more money for the NRC."

If such "half-measures" constitute the country's full response to Three Mile Island, Brightsen warns, the outcome is predictable: "Few, if any, new nuclear plants will be started, and the spectre of another, more serious accident will be kept vividly alive by the anti-nuclear forces."(71) A similar argument has recently been advanced by Alvin M. Weinberg, director of the Institute for Energy Analysis and a long-time advocate of nuclear power. According to Weinberg, "technical fixes are easier to implement than are institutional fixes" but they will never be sufficient to "reforge a consensus" on nuclear power. "Therefore," says Weinberg, "far-reaching institutional and managerial changes will be needed to forestall loss of the nuclear option."(72) Among the changes Weinberg considers vital are:(73)

--*physical isolation:* "We can achieve a good deal by confining the enterprise, *forever*, to the existing sites that have few people near them."

--*separate generation and distribution:* "The operating entity must possess extraordinary strength if it is to assume the integrative role demanded by the technology.... The entity that operates a (nuclear) site might therefore, in most cases, be a consortium of utilities....(with) generation being in the hands of powerful organizations that *do nothing but generate nuclear electricity*, distribution remaining with the existing utilities."

--*professionalism:* "The responsibility borne by the nuclear operator is so great that he and his staff must be regarded as an elite--like airline pilots.... They must constitute a cadre with tradition, with competence, with confidence, with training that goes beyond what we already have."

--*heavy security:* "The nuclear enterprise will always demand far greater security than the fossil-fueled enterprise. Terrorists and saboteurs can only incapacitate a fossil plant but they can, though with difficulty, induce serious accidents in nuclear plants."

--*education about radiation hazards:* "None of the measures I propose will ensure the survival of nuclear energy unless the public, and the media, come to accept the risk of radiation as no different than the risk from other noxious agents that are products of our technology .... Without such acceptance nuclear energy cannot survive."

THE PROBABILITY OF ACCIDENTS AT NUCLEAR PLANTS

Differing interpretations of the significance of past problems with nuclear reactors and differing views about the reliability of emergency core-cooling systems have created sharp disputes over how likely it is that a loss-of-coolant accident will occur and what damages such an accident is likely to cause. Critics assert that the operating history is so replete with examples of errors and defects, and testing of emergency core-cooling systems has been so inadequate, that convincing evidence that nuclear power plants are safe should be developed before use of nuclear power is expanded further. Supporters of nuclear power respond by noting that no civilians have been killed by accidents at commercial reactors and by citing various studies that predict that the probability of a major accident at a nuclear plant is exceedingly small.

The debate over accident probability and over the adequacy of safety research is important not only because of the damages a major accident could cause, but because many observers agree that a major accident at any nuclear power plant--one involving, say, thousands of deaths--would probably evoke a sharp reaction that could include shutting down all operating plants. To appreciate this dispute, it is useful to review the history of studies that have evaluated the probable effects of a major accident and shaped the character of the debate over accident probabilities.

The 1957 Brookhaven Report

In 1957 the Brookhaven National Laboratory completed a study, financed by the AEC, estimating the "theoretical possibilities and consequences of major accidents in large nuclear power plants."(74) The study concluded that the likelihood of an accident that would result in a major release of radioactive fission products outside the reactor containment ranged from 1 in 100,000 to 1 in 1 billion per reactor year. Assuming the worst possible combination of circumstances--including a climatological inversion, the breach of all containment barriers, absence of safety systems, and inability to evacuate the population--the study estimated that a major release could result in 3,400 fatalities, 43,000 injuries, $7 billion in property damage, and 150,000 square miles of contaminated land. In the introduction to the study, its authors counseled: "It should be emphasized that these numbers have no demonstrable basis in fact and have no validity of application beyond a reflection of the degree of their confidence in the low likelihood of occurrence of such reactor accident."(75)

The 1965 Study

In 1964 and 1965 the AEC undertook to update the Brookhaven report. The commission prepared what it calls "an unfinished draft report" that concluded: "Assuming the same kind of hypothetical accidents as those in the 1957 study, the theoretically calculated damages would not be less, and under some circumstances would be substantially more, than the consequences reported in the earlier (Brookhaven) study."(76) In one extreme case, using what it called "grossly unrealistic assumptions" such as a major release of radioactivity and a simultaneous failure of all safety systems at a reactor located in the center of the city, the report estimated an accident could cause 45,000 fatalities, $17 billion in damages, and contamination of an area equal in size to the state of Pennsylvania.(77)

The 1965 study was not released until 1973, after portions of it had been obtained by nuclear power critics who threatened suit to force disclosure of the full document. The AEC maintained in 1973 that the 1965 study was never completed, that it was only released to "help the public to obtain a clearer understanding of the study undertaken some eight years ago of the probabilities and consequences of theoretical reactor accidents which have little resemblance to real situations." AEC officials said that "meaningful information will be obtained in the (then in process) Rasmussen study."(78)

The Rasmussen Study

The Rasmussen study of reactor safety, officially titled "An Assessment of Accident Risks in U.S. Commercial Nuclear Power Plants," appeared in draft form in August 1974 and was issued in final form in October 1975. The objective of the study was to provide a quantitative assessment of the risks to public health and safety from potential accidents at nuclear plants. The study was directed by Norman Rasmussen, head of the department of nuclear engineering at MIT, and it was performed by a group of experts including employees of the federal nuclear and energy agencies and laboratories, independent consultants, and employees of private companies.

The report issued by the Rasmussen group adopted a system of event-tree/fault-tree analysis, developed originally by the Defense Department and the National Aeronautics and Space Administration, to estimate the possibility of reactor accidents. The analytic system used involved identifying all sequences of events that might occur if any given piece of equipment should fail, and continuing this analysis through to describe sequences in which a major accident would occur. Then, the probability of failure of any given piece of equipment involved in such a sequence was estimated, after which the probability of a chain of failures leading to a major accident could be computed.

The Rasmussen study concluded that the possible consequences of potential reactor accidents are predicted to be no larger and in many cases much smaller than people have been led to believe by previous studies which deliberately maximized estimates of these consequences. "The likelihood of reactor accidents is much smaller than that of many non-nuclear accidents having similar consequences. All non-nuclear accidents examined in this study, including fires, explosions, toxic chemical releases, dam failures, airplane crashes, earthquakes, hurricanes, and tornadoes, are much more likely to occur and can have consequences comparable to, or larger than, those of nuclear accidents."(79)

The final version of the Rasmussen report drew several conclusions. It found that the probability of a core melt--1 in 20,000--was greater than expected, but the likelihood of a fatality from a core melt—less than 1 in 20,000--was lower than had been anticipated. The study reported that "the consequences of reactor accidents are smaller than many people had believed." A serious accident, resulting in more than 10 deaths, was likely to occur once in 3 million reactor-years of operation, the report said. A most serious accident, one likely to occur once in a billion reactor-years, would kill 3,300 people and cause latent cancers in 45,000. It would also cause an estimated $14 billion in property damage. The fatality risk to members of the public from 100 nuclear plants, the study found, was lower than that from hurricanes, tornadoes and even falling meteors.(80)

Although strongly criticized by groups such as the Union of Concerned Scientists, the Rasmussen report was widely used by the nuclear power industry and the government as an assurance of the safety of nuclear reactors. It was looked at as the final word on reactor safety by some nuclear proponents and was often used by industry representatives in regulatory hearings.

The Lewis Report

In July 1977, the NRC organized a Risk Assessment Review Group to "provide advice and information to the commission" on the Rasmussen report.(81) The review group, under the chairmanship of Harold W. Lewis of the University of California at Santa Barbara, delivered its report to the NRC in September 1978, clarifying the achievements and limitations of the Rasmussen study. The group reviewed the methodology, data base, statistical procedures and conclusions of the Rasmussen report and found that while it was "unable to define whether the overall probability of a core melt given in (the Rasmussen report) is high or low," it was "certain that the error bands are understated."(82) The report said it could not determine by how much the error bands were understated because of "an inadequate data base, a poor statistical treatment, an inconsistent propagation of uncertainties throughout the calculation" and other problems in the Rasmussen study. Nevertheless, the report said that event-tree/fault-tree analysis was "an important advance over earlier methodologies applied to reactor risks" and that it "should be developed and used more widely under circumstances in which there is an adequate data base or sufficient technical expertise to insert credible subjective probabilities into the calculations."(83)

Release of the Lewis report prompted quick action from the NRC. In a policy statement issued on Jan. 19, 1979, the NRC accepted the major criticism of the Rasmussen report found in the Lewis report. Specifically, it withdrew any explicit or implicit past endorsement of the Rasmussen report's executive summary (it was the executive summary that was most widely quoted by the nuclear industry) and said it "did not regard as reliable the Reactor Safety Study's numerical estimate of the overall risk of reactor accident."(84)

The Kemeny Commission Report

Although the Kemeny Commission's investigation of the accident at Three Mile Island did not directly examine the issue of the probability of reactor accidents, it did reach a consensus on a number of factors related to the issue. One of its major conclusions, for example, was that "the fundamental problems are people-related problems and not equipment problems."(85) This conclusion alone, according to many experts, raises serious questions about past risk-assessment studies, which tend to downplay the significance of human error. The commission also concluded that combinations of minor equipment failures coupled with human error were likely to occur "much more often" than the "large-break" accidents that the NRC has concentrated on in the past. Given the existing deficiencies in overall safety practices, the commission concluded, "we are convinced that an accident like Three Mile Island was eventually inevitable."(86)

Reaction of Nuclear Critics to the Studies

Critics believe that the NRC's repudiation of the Rasmussen report, along with the accident at Three Mile Island and the conclusions of various investigations into the cause of that accident, confirm what they have been saying all along: that the risk of nuclear plant accidents is far greater than the government has said it is. Critics note that many of the criticisms of the Rasmussen study contained in the Lewis report and many of the suggestions made by the Kemeny Commission were made back in 1974 and 1975 by safety experts from the Union of Concerned Scientists, the Sierra Club and the Rand Corp.

Many nuclear opponents remain highly skeptical about the methodology--event-tree/fault-tree analysis--used in government safety studies. Robert Augustine of the National Intervenors has described the process as one of "guesses multiplied by guesses--sheer speculation."(87) Joel Primack, professor of physics at the University of California at Santa Cruz, describes the problem of determining probabilities of accidents at a nuclear plant as "gamblers' guesses." It is a problem, he said, of trying to determine the relative probability of events that have never occurred and about which no data exist.(88)

Critics also believe that government safety studies--especially the Rasmussen study--have been misused by industry and government officials. A 1974 critique of the Rasmussen report by the Union of Concerned Scientists and the Sierra Club, for instance, accepted that event-tree/fault-tree analysis could "be very helpful in making comparisons between diverse safety systems" but concluded that the methodology could not "be employed as (Rasmussen) has done to determine absolute probability values for accident probabilities and to use these predictions as proof of the safety of nuclear plants."(89) Furthermore, the U.C.S. argued in 1979, some aspects of the Rasmussen study were so heavily relied upon by the government and the industry to "prove" that certain nuclear plants were safe that a prudent safety policy would dictate the immediate shutdown of 16 operating plants.(90) The government has "no technical basis for concluding that the actual risk is low enough to justify continued plant licensing and operation," declares Henry Kendall, an MIT physics professor and founder of the U.C.S.(91)

On the subject of the likelihood of an accident at the yet-to-operate breeder reactor plants, critics express concern that the breeder reactor involves a now-unproven technology which has safety problems that are more severe than those of the light-water reactor. They say that development of the LMFBR should not go forward until all these problems are solved. Some critics fear that safety standards may be sacrificed to make the LMFBR economically attractive. Their major areas of concern about the operational safety of the LMRBR are: (1) the use of liquid sodium as a coolant introduces serious hazards, because liquid sodium is violently reactive with air or water, becomes intensely radioactive as it circulates around the reactor core, and is susceptible to bubbles or "voids" that might lead to a chain reaction in the fuel assembly and possible explosion; and (2) the presence of "fast" neutrons in the fuel core, which is operating at higher temperatures, fuel enrichment and power densities than a light-water reactor, greatly complicates the maintenance of the integrity of the fuel core. This integrity is critically important to avoid a core meltdown and possible release of radioactivity to the atmosphere.

Reaction of Nuclear Proponents to the Studies

As on the issue of overall reactor safety, nuclear power supporters appear more divided now on the issue of the probability of nuclear accidents than they were before Three Mile Island. Many nuclear advocates say that the accident has not altered their convictions that the probability of a serious accident at a nuclear plant is exceedingly small. Others, however, acknowledge that accidents will happen, but believe that the consequences of such accidents will still be preferable to the consequences of using energy sources other than nuclear power.

Nuclear supporters who think that the chances of serious accidents at nuclear plants remain quite small tend to view the Three Mile Island accident as significant only because of its political ramifications. The accident did not show that catastrophic accidents are more likely than previously thought, they argue, and in fact, it may have showed just the opposite. Three Mile Island "may have proved meltdowns may never happen," Karl Cohen, a Stanford University physicist and a pioneer in the development of nuclear reactors, testified to the House Committee on Science and Technology.(92) According to these proponents, the Rasmussen report, despite questions about its understatement of uncertainties, remains the most authoritative study on reactor safety ever attempted and its general conclusions remain valid. Proponents believe that the Lewis report's critique of the Rasmussen study was widely misinterpreted and note that the review group's chairman, Harold W. Lewis, said he believed the Rasmussen report overstated the risk of reactor accidents.(93) Finally, these proponents say, the safety modifications and new training procedures instituted in the wake of the Three Mile Island accident make the possibility of a serious accident at a nuclear plant even more remote than it was before. According to Edwin Zebroski of the Nuclear Safety Analysis Center, when the safety measures being implemented in response to the accident are completed, the mean time for accidents as serious as Three Mile Island will have been reduced to between 3,000 and 10,000 reactor years.(94)

A second group of nuclear proponents, however, does believe that Three Mile Island showed that accidents are more likely to occur than was previously assumed. Chauncey Starr, vice chairman of the Electric Power Research Institute (EPRI), has estimated that an accident like Three Mile Island had a 50-percent chance of occurring in 400 reactor years.(95) With 74 licensed reactors, that translates into a 50-50 chance there would be an accident like Three Mile Island every 5.4 years. Even if new safety measures substantially reduce that risk estimate, it represents a substantial departure from past industry estimates of the probability of serious accidents. Morris Rosen, the International Atomic Energy Agency's top safety expert, concurs that the Three Mile Island accident has changed some experts' thinking. "The fable that accidents can be prevented in nuclear power plants has now disappeared," he says. "There is no way to ever say again that you can design a system that will not have a serious accident."(96) While these proponents agree that reactors can and should be made safer, they maintain that the public must learn to accept some risk in return for adequate energy supplies. What is significant, these proponents maintain, is not that nuclear power entails some risks but that those risks are not as great as the risks associated with alternative sources of electricity or doing without the electricity altogether.

In responding to charges that the liquid-metal fast-breeder reactor--not covered by the Rasmussen study--will pose greater risks, some officials argue to the contrary. Nobel laureate Hans Bethe maintains that not only will the breeder have all the safety features of the light-water reactor, but it will also have other aspects that increase its safety. He cites the low temperature of sodium relative to its boiling point and its high capacity to conduct heat--both features that improve response in case of an accident.(97)

THE COMPARATIVE RISKS OF ENERGY SOURCES

This chapter has examined the risks associated with the use of nuclear power, but knowledge about such risks is not really very meaningful unless they can be compared with the risks involved in alternative energy strategies. This section summarizes the views of nuclear proponents, critics and independent experts on the issue of comparative risks--recognizing that the area of the risks associated with various energy systems is one where little comprehensive research has been carried out.

Views of Nuclear Proponents

Proponents of nuclear power development generally frame the debate over energy risks with the assumption that the country will face a growing demand for energy and for electric power. They stress the need to meet this growing demand with domestic sources of energy, citing both economic and national security considerations. Proponents maintain that, for the foreseeable future, increases in the demand for electric power must be met by a combination of the two sources that are both available and economic--nuclear and coal-fired power plants. Therefore, proponents argue, the focus of any risk comparison concerning nuclear power should be a comparison of the risks of generating electric power with coal or nuclear fuel.

Proponents admit that there are adverse health and environmental effects associated with the use of nuclear power, but they say that the adverse effects associated with coal are far greater. "Nuclear reactors are not safe," states physicist Edward Teller. "But they are incomparably safer than anything else we might have to produce electric energy."(98) Proponents note that there is a growing body of scientific data which suggests that the air pollutants routinely emitted by coal plants are responsible for a far greater number of deaths and illnesses than can be associated with the radioactive emissions of nuclear plants. They cite the fact that the deaths and injuries resulting from the mining and transportation of coal are significantly higher than those resulting from the mining and transportation of uranium. They mention the serious environmental problems associated with coal strip-mining, coal plant sludge and "acid-rain." Finally, proponents note that there is increasing concern among scientists that the carbon dioxide emissions from the burning of fossil fuels--especially coal--could lead to major climatic changes.

Views of Nuclear Critics

Many critics do not accept the assumptions made by nuclear proponents concerning energy supplies and demand. Conservation could drastically reduce the growth in energy demand, critics say, yielding health, environmental and economic benefits. The inherent inefficiency of converting thermal energy to electricity, they add, makes electric power a premium form of energy that should be used sparingly. Finally, critics argue, any growth in the demand for electric power that does occur could best be met through the increased use of renewable and alternative sources of energy-- geothermal power, solar electricity, wind power and cogeneration. The health effects associated with these energy sources, critics contend, are orders of magnitude below those associated with nuclear power.

Concerning the comparison between nuclear power and coal stressed by proponents, critics do not dispute that the routine health effects associated with existing coal-fired power plants are greater than those associated with nuclear plants. But they say that proponents understate the adverse health effects of low-level radiation and virtually ignore the much greater dangers posed by the possibility of major accidents at nuclear plants. In addition, they contend that new technologies--such as stack-gas scrubbers and fluidized bed combustors--will greatly reduce the harmful effects of using coal. Furthermore, critics say, the health effects of nuclear energy and coal cannot be compared directly without taking into account the thousands of deaths that will be caused in future centuries by long-lived radioisotopes associated with the nuclear fuel cycle. Even more important, they contend, is the relationship between nuclear power development and the proliferation of nuclear weapons. If one wants to make a fair comparison of the risks involved in nuclear and coal-based energy systems, critics argue, one must account for the potential effects of nuclear weapons that were made possible by the misuse of nuclear power facilities.

Independent Analyses of Energy Risk

Energy experts say that there are very few comprehensive studies of the risks inherent in different energy systems. Those studies that have been made, they say, can be used to support the contentions of either nuclear proponents or critics depending on what assumptions one makes about the need for more utility-generated electric power.

Virtually all recent studies of the risks associated with energy systems agree that conservation--the more efficient use of existing energy supplies--is the most benign source of energy supply for the United States. The Ford Foundation's recent study, *Energy: The Next Twenty Years*, states that "the energy 'produced' by conservation has a number of advantages over energy produced in the conventional sense. It is almost always cleaner, and those disturbances to the environment and human health that are associated with it...are generally localized and easily manageable."(99) But while agreeing with nuclear critics that conservation is a much safer option than increased use of nuclear power, energy experts disagree as to the extent that conservation could substitute for increased production of electric power. Some energy experts agree with nuclear critics that energy conservation could supply most of the country's energy needs through the end of the century--when alternative sources of energy would probably be available. The majority of analysts, however, contend that nuclear proponents are correct in asserting that even if strong conservation measures are implemented there will still be some growth in energy demand that will entail the need for increased use of electricity. The real question though--and one on which experts show little agreement--is how fast will the demand for electric power grow compared with demand for other energy sources. A recent National Academy of Sciences study contained support for both critics and proponents of nuclear power when it concluded that "conservation alone cannot solve the problems facing us," but noted that its projections of electricity demand growth for the next quarter century "are considerably below industry and government projections."(100)

Assuming some growth in electricity demand, most energy analysts say that nuclear and coal-fired power plants can be expected to provide the bulk of the nation's new generating capacity for the remainder of the century. A sizable minority, however, contends that alternative sources of electric power will make a substantial contribution before the end of the century. Concerning the risks associated with these technologies, most experts agree on the following points:

1. The routine adverse health impacts associated with the use of coal are larger than those associated with nuclear power.(101)

2. Health impacts associated with nuclear power, while less likely than those associated with coal, have a greater near-term chance of being catastrophic and irreversible.(102)

3. Health impacts associated with most renewable energy systems probably would be smaller than those associated with either coal or nuclear-fueled systems.(103)

NOTES

(1) Alvin M. Weinberg, "The Nuclear Management Syndrome," *The Wharton Magazine*, Vol. 4, No. 1, Fall 1979, p. 26.

(2) Estimates of the Committee on Biological Effects of Ionizing Radiation, National Academy of Sciences, as reported in The New York *Times*, July 2, 1979, p. D6.

(3) Julia Rose, "Congress Studying Long Term Impact of Radiation Exposure," *Congressional Quarterly Weekly Report*, April 7, 1979, p. 625.

(4) U.S. Nuclear Regulatory Commission, *Final Generic Environmental Statement on the Use of Plutonium Recycle in Mixed Oxide Fuel in Light Water Cooled Reactors,* NUREG-0002, Vol. 1 (U.S. Nuclear Regulatory Commission, August 1976), p. S-24.

(5) Exxon Nuclear Co., comments to Investor Responsibility Research Center, Oct. 6, 1980.

(6) Speech at the Atomic Industrial Forum Conference on Nuclear Power, Houston, Tex., Sept. 10-13, 1978.

(7) Gail Bronson, "Cancer Cases Spark Concern About Radiation; Scientists Debate 'Safe' Limit for U.S. Workers," *The Wall Street Journal,* July 11, 1978, p. 48.

(8) Constance Holden, "Low-Level Radiation: A High-Level Concern," *Science,* Vol. 204, April 13, 1979, p. 157.

(9) Gail Bronson, op. cit.

(10) Constance Holden, op. cit.

(11) Dick Brukenfeld, "Are Nuclear Plants Unsafe--Even Without Any Mishap?" The Washington *Post,* Nov. 11, 1979, p. B4.

(12) "'Post' Story on Radiation Incorrect, NRC Staff Says," Atomic Industrial Forum INFO press release, No. 107, November 1979, p. 6.

(13) Rob Laufer, "GAO Finds Serious Questions Pervade Cancer/Radiation Debate," *Nucleonics Week,* Vol. 20, No. 50, Dec. 13, 1979, p. 3.

(14) U.S. Nuclear Regulatory Commission, *Final Generic...,* op. cit., p. S-23.

(15) Richard D. Lyons, "2 Reports See Risks in Nuclear Future," The New York *Times,* April 30, 1979, p. A1.

(16) William Ramsay, *Unpaid Costs of Electrical Energy* (Baltimore, Md., Johns Hopkins University Press for Resources for the Future, 1979), p. 39.

(17) Laurence Stern et al., "Chapter 3: A Swift Rethinking of the 'Unthinkable'," The Washington *Post,* April 8, 1979, p. A17.

(18) Westinghouse, letter to Investor Responsibility Research Center, March 18, 1976, p. 14.

(19) Estimates of the number of cancer deaths that are likely to result from the radiation releases at Three Mile Island vary widely. Official government estimates by the NRC, HEW and the Kemeny Commission all state that the accident can be expected to cause either no cancers or so few that they could never be detected. Carl Z. Morgan of the Georgia Institute of Technology says that the external dosage figures supplied by the NRC--an average of 2 millirems to a population of nearly 1 million within 50 miles of the plant--show that between 0.5 and 50 cancer deaths might be expected. On the alarmist side, Ernest Sternglass, professor of radiological physics at the University of Pittsburgh, contends that when doses received from the inhalation of fission gases are included, the fatality toll from the accident could be 300 to 2,500 cancer deaths over the next 20 years. Many experts suggest that any estimates can only be guesses because no one really knows how much radiation escaped from the plant. As a senior NRC official puts it, "We will never know with any accuracy

what radiation dose the 600,000 people living within 20 miles of the reactor were exposed to."

(20) Joanne Omang, "Nuclear Plant Shut Down for Possible Safety Risk," The Washington *Post*, Nov. 11, 1977, p. 1; also Daniel Ford and Henry Kendall, *An Assessment of Emergency Core Cooling Systems Rulemaking Hearings* (Cambridge, Union of Concerned Scientists and Friends of the Earth, 1974).

(21) Bill Curry, "Anticipating Nuclear Accidents," The Washington *Post*, Dec. 11, 1978, p. A10.

(22) "ECCS Again Performs Well in Second Live LOFT Test," Atomic Industrial Forum INFO press release, No. 101, May 1979, p. 3.

(23) "A Pump Failure, A Claxon Alert, A Nuclear Crisis," The Washington *Post*, April 8, 1979, p. A1.

(24) Carl Hocevar, "Nuclear Reactor Licensing--A Critique of the Computer Safety Prediction Methods," Union of Concerned Scientists, Aug. 14, 1975, p. 4.

(25) "What You Should Know About the Hazards of Nuclear Power," Union of Concerned Scientists (Cambridge, 1979).

(26) Bill Curry, op. cit.

(27) Quoted in "Nuclear Power Development: 1979 Analysis I," Investor Responsibility Research Center, Feb. 26, 1979, p. 13.

(28) David Comey, "Lack of Reliability of Emergency Diesel Generators at Operating Nuclear Plants," letter to L. Manning Muntzing, Sept. 10, 1974, available from Business and Professional People in the Public Interest, Chicago, Ill.

(29) A list of the generic unresolved safety issues for light-water reactors is contained in *Nuclear Proliferation and Civilian Nuclear Power*, Report of the Nonproliferation Alternative Systems Assessment Program, Volume VI: Safety and Environmental Considerations for Licensing (U.S. Department of Energy, June 1980), pp. 24-29.

(30) Jan Beyea, "Some Long-Term Consequences of Hypothetical Major Releases of Radioactivity to the Atmosphere from Three Mile Island," Draft Report to the President's Council on Environmental Quality (Princeton University, Center for Energy and Environmental Studies, Sept. 7, 1979), p. 2.

(31) Ibid., p. 3.

(32) David C. Alrich and Roger M. Blond, *Examination of the Use of Potassium Iodide as an Emergency Protective Measure for Nuclear Reactor Accidents*, Draft NUREG/CR-1433 (U.S. Nuclear Regulatory Commission, March 1980), p. 31.

(33) Jan Beyea and Frank von Hippel, "Statement on Potassium Iodide and Radiological Emergencies," June 17, 1980, p. 2.

(34) Frank von Hippel, "The NRC and Thyroid Protection--One Excuse After Another," *The Bulletin of the Atomic Scientists*, October 1980, p. 45.

(35) Exxon Nuclear Co., comments to Investor Responsibility Research Center, Oct. 6, 1980.

(36) W.H. Arnold, *Hearings on Proposition 15*, California State Assembly, Vol. IV, Oct. 22, 1975, p. 61.

(37) Philip Bray, Hearings before the Joint Committee on Atomic Energy, 1974, reprint from GE, p. 98.

(38) "Zebroski Proposes a Goal for Nuclear Regulation," *Industry Report*, Nuclear Safety Analysis Center, No. 7, July–August 1980, p. 6.

(39) Nuclear Regulatory Commission, *Report to Congress on Abnormal Occurrences*, July-September 1975, p. 1.

(40) Ibid., p. iii.

(41) "Atomic Plants Had 2,835 Incidents in '78," The New York *Times*, April 15, 1979, p. 26.

(42) Joanne Omang, "Nuclear Power Plants Around U.S. Record 2,300 Glitches in '79," The Washington *Post*, July 14, 1980, p. A20.

(43) Gregory Minor, Hearings before the Joint Committee on Atomic Energy, Feb. 18, 1976, p. 9.

(44) Ibid., pp. 494 ff.

(45) John R. Emshwiller and Walter S. Mossberg, "Plant in Pennsylvania Had Series of Problems Over 14-Month Period," *The Wall Street Journal*, April 9, 1979, p. 1.

(46) Atomic Energy Commission, *The Safety of Nuclear Power Reactors and Related Facilities*, WASH 1250 (Washington, D.C., 1973).

(47) Victor Gilinsky, speech at Brown University, Nov. 15, 1979, (reprinted in NRC news release, Vol. 5, No. 44, Dec. 6, 1979, p. 3).

(48) Dale Bridenbaugh, Richard Hubbard, Gregory Minor, Hearings before the Joint Committee on Atomic Energy, op. cit., pp. 539, 40, 41.

(49) Hannes Alfven, *Bulletin of the Atomic Scientists*, May 1972, p. 5.

(50) Quoted in "What You Should Know About the Hazards of Nuclear Power," Union of Concerned Scientists (Cambridge, 1979).

(51) Amory B. Lovins, *Non-Nuclear Futures: The Case for an Ethical Energy Strategy* (Cambridge, Friends of the Earth, 1975), p. 12.

(52) Henry Kendall, press conference to review the Rasmussen Report (Washington, D.C., Nov. 24, 1974).

(53) Exxon Nuclear Co., comments to Investor Responsibility Research Center, Oct. 6, 1980.

(54) David F. Salisbury, "Nuclear Industry Officials Talk About Comeback," *The Christian Science Monitor*, Nov. 28, 1979.

(55) W.H. Arnold, interview with Investor Responsibility Research Center, 1974.

(56) Ibid.

(57) *Nucleonics Week*, Vol. 21, No. 4, Jan. 24, 1980, p. 12.

(58) Joanne Omang, "The Politics of Atom Power," The Washington *Post*, July 10, 1979, p. A6.

(59) Salisbury, op. cit.

(60) "AIF Sees Priorities Being Disjointed by NRC Action Plan," *Nucleonics Week*, Vol. 21, No. 4, Jan. 24, 1980, p. 1.

(61) Peter Kilborn, "Utilities Fear Public Reaction Could Force Nuclear Plant Closings," The New York *Times*, April 3, 1979, p. A15.

(62) Jane Seaberry, "Baltimore Gas Reassures Shareholders on Reactors," The Washington *Post*, April 28, 1979, p. 1.

(63) Joanne Omang, "Crisis Aftermath: A-Safety Gnaws at Once-Complacent NRC," The Washington *Post*, July 9, 1979, p. A2.

(64) Ann Pelham, "Congress More Skeptical of Nuclear Power's Future," *Congressional Quarterly Weekly Report*, Nov. 24, 1979, p. 2663.

(65) Carroll L. Wilson, "Nuclear Energy: What Went Wrong," *The Bulletin of the Atomic Scientists*, June 1979, p. 16.

(66) Ibid.

(67) Joanne Omang, "The Politics of Atom Power," op. cit.

(68) Tennessee Valley Authority, "TVA Nuclear Safety Program," January 1980, p. 2.

(69) Thomas E. Spink, interview with Investor Responsibility Research Center, August 1980.

(70) R.A. Brightsen, "The Way to Save Nuclear Power," *Fortune*, Sept. 10, 1979, p. 132.

(71) Ibid.

(72) Alvin M. Weinberg, op. cit., pp. 20-26.

(73) Ibid.

(74) Atomic Energy Commission, *Theoretical Possibilities and Consequences of Major Accidents in Large Nuclear Power Plants*, WASH 740 (the Brookhaven Report), March 1957.

(75) Ibid., p. 6.

(76) David Burnham, "AEC Files Show Effort to Conceal Safety Perils," The New York *Times*, Nov. 10, 1974, p. 1.

(77) Ibid.

(78) Atomic Energy Commission, press release, June 25, 1973.

(79) Nuclear Regulatory Commission, *Reactor Safety Study, An Assessment of Accident Risks in U.S. Commercial Nuclear Power Plants*, WASH 1400 (the Rasmussen Report), October 1975.

(80) Ibid.

(81) Nuclear Regulatory Commission, "NRC Statement on Risk Assessment and the Reactor Safety Study Report in Light of the Risk Assessment Review Group Report," Jan. 18, 1979, p. 1.

(82) Harold W. Lewis et al., *Risk Assessment Review Group Report to the U.S. Nuclear Regulatory Commission*, NUREG/CR-0400 (U.S. Nuclear Regulatory Commission, September 1978), p. vi.

(83) Ibid., p. vii.

(84) Nuclear Regulatory Commission, "NRC Statement....", op. cit., p. 3.

(85) "Excerpts from Presidential Panel's Report on the Three Mile Nuclear Accident," The New York *Times*, Oct. 31, 1979, p. A22.

(86) Ibid.

(87) Robert Augustine, "AEC Finds Safety in Numbers," *Environmental Action*, Oct. 12, 1974, p. 3.

(88) Joel Primack, *Hearings on Proposition 15*, California State Assembly, Vol. V, Oct. 28, 1975, pp. 48, 67.

(89) Union of Concerned Scientists/Sierra Club, press release, Washington, D.C., Nov. 12, 1974.

(90) David Burnham, "Scientists Call for Shutdown of 16 Atomic Reactors," The New York Times, Jan. 27, 1979, p. 22.

(91) Ibid.

(92) Walter Pincus, "Reactors Safer than Alternatives, Scientists Say," The Washington Post, May 8, 1979, p. 1.

(93) "Chief Rasmussen Report Reviewer Believes Risk Lower than Projected," Energy Users Report, No. 289, Feb. 22, 1979, p. 8.

(94) Nucleonics Week, Jan. 24, 1980, p. 12.

(95) Quoted in Alvin M. Weinberg, op. cit., p. 25.

(96) Milton R. Benjamin, "World Experts Plan Secret Meeting on Nuclear Crises," The Washington Post, May 5, 1979, p. A5.

(97) Hans Bethe, "The Necessity of Fission Power," Scientific American, January 1976.

(98) Walter Pincus, op. cit.

(99) Hans H. Landsberg et al., Energy: The Next Twenty Years (Cambridge, Ballinger Publishing for Resources for the Future and the Ford Foundation, 1979), p. 31.

(100) "Academy Says Coal, Nuclear Essential, Lessened Energy Demand 'Top Priority'," Energy Users Report, No. 336, Jan. 17, 1980, p. 5.

(101) For one excellent discussion of this issue, see William Ramsay, Unpaid Costs of Electrical Energy (Baltimore, Md., Johns Hopkins University Press for Resources for the Future, 1979).

(102) Ibid.

(103) The author is aware of the study by Herbert Inhaber, Risk of Energy Production (report AECB 1119, Atomic Energy Control Board, Ottawa, Ontario, March 1978) which disputes this conclusion. However, in the author's opinion, previous studies and critiques of Inhaber's report by R. Lemberg, R. Caputo, K. Smith, J. Weyant, J. Holdren, K. Anderson, P. Gleick, G. Morris, I. Mintzer and others are more persuasive on this point than the Inhaber study.

Chapter VIII

SAFEGUARDING RADIOACTIVE
AND SENSITIVE MATERIALS

Despite increasing concern about nuclear reactor safety, many knowledgeable observers believe that safeguarding the products and by-products of nuclear power facilities--some of which are radioactive and some of which can be used to make nuclear weapons--pose problems far more serious than those raised by nuclear plant safety. They question whether safeguards can be devised that can prevent nations or terrorist groups from misusing the materials associated with nuclear fuel cycles, particularly plutonium, to manufacture bombs or to threaten to make them. They are also concerned about whether it is possible to develop safe and secure methods for permanent storage of highly dangerous radioactive wastes, some of which will need to be isolated from the environment for hundreds of thousands of years.

THE PLUTONIUM PROBLEM

In the view of some persons, the possibility that radioactive materials from the nuclear fuel cycle will be used for military or terrorist purposes represents the most significant threat to public safety posed by development of nuclear power. Amory Lovins has called the proliferation problem "the most compelling reason to reject all forms of nuclear power in favor of fission-free energy strategies."(1) A study by William Ramsay of Resources for the Future says "it is easy to imagine that the expected consequences (from weapons proliferation that results from U.S. use of nuclear power) could be of the same magnitude--or rather more than--those associated with other health impacts" of nuclear power.(2) Other nuclear experts, including many nuclear proponents, say that they are concerned whether adequate safeguards exist, or could be developed, to prevent the potential misuse of such materials. The greatest dangers now, experts say, arise in connection with plutonium.(3)

What Plutonium Is

Plutonium has been described by its discoverer, former AEC Chairman Glenn Seaborg, as one of the most toxic elements known to man. It is extremely carcinogenic; one millionth of a gram has been shown to cause cancer in animals.(4) More important, perhaps, is that physicists estimate that a crude atomic bomb could be constructed with as little as four kilograms of plutonium--about one-thirtieth of the amount of plutonium produced each year by a 1,000-megawatt light-water reactor.(5)

Each 1,000-megawatt light-water reactor produces, together with other materials in its spent fuel, about 100 to 140 kilograms of plutonium a year, depending upon the enrichment percentage of its fresh fuel.(6) Some other types of reactors, such as the CANDU heavy-water reactor in use in Canada and elsewhere, produce somewhat greater quantities of plutonium. By the year 2000, observers estimate, annual worldwide plutonium production from light-water reactors will be on the order of 100,000 kilograms. In addition, if breeder reactors come into widespread use, the production of plutonium will increase greatly. A typical breeder reactor would contain about a ton of plutonium and would produce about seven times as much plutonium as a light-water reactor of equal generating capacity. An energy economy in which breeder reactors play a major role in power generation and fuel creation will have nearly three times as much plutonium in circulation as one involving light-water reactors using recycled plutonium.(7)

THE PLUTONIUM ECONOMY

The possibility of the misuse of plutonium is an inherent characteristic of the widespread use of nuclear power systems. However, certain characteristics of the current nuclear fuel cycle--where only non-breeding reactors are used and no attempt is made to extract plutonium from the spent fuel of these reac- tors--make the threat of plutonium misuse smaller than it might otherwise be. Very little plutonium is available now in a form that would make it susceptible to theft or diversion. Plutonium is found in the spent fuel of light-water reactors, but it is mixed with other fission products that generate much more penetrating radioactivity than does plutonium. As long as plutonium is combined with these highly irradiated products, their radioactivity inhibits handling and offers some assurance that plutonium will not be stolen.

The threat of plutonium misuse, and the problems of safeguarding plutonium, could increase sharply, however, if any of the following come to pass:

--The plutonium in the spent fuel of light-water reactors is routinely recycled to produce a mixed oxide uranium/plutonium fuel for use in those reactors.

--Breeder reactors, which use plutonium as fuel but ultimately produce more than they use, are developed for commercial use.

--Conventional nuclear reactors are exported to a large number of countries around the world.

The prospects for development of breeder reactors have been discussed in Chapter VI. The prospects for plutonium recycling and of exports of nuclear reactors can be summarized as follows:

Plutonium Recycling

At this time, most of the plutonium in the spent fuel assemblies of U.S. nuclear power plants is being stored in spent fuel storage pools along with other irradiated materials. No reprocessing of these wastes is taking place on a commercial basis. However, industry support for the development of a plutonium recycling industry continues. If that industry does develop, much larger quantities of separated plutonium will be in domestic circulation, and safeguarding problems will increase. The closed nuclear fuel cycle, including reprocessing, is shown in Figure 9, p. 152.

Industry Position

Industry officials have long argued in favor of recycling nuclear plant wastes to extract uranium and plutonium for later use as a reactor fuel. Recycling, they say, is an important part of the nuclear fuel cycle. It will prolong the supply of scarce uranium resources, lower nuclear fuel costs, facilitate storage and disposal of wastes, and provide the initial fuel cores for breeder reactors. The Atomic Industrial Forum goes even farther: "The earlier reprocessing and recycle are accepted as integral steps of the nuclear fuel cycle, the earlier nuclear power will gain widespread public acceptance."(8)

Industry is greatly concerned about the lack of reprocessing capacity in the United States. The Atomic Industrial Forum says the United States needs reprocessing plants in order to "secure nuclear fuel supplies for the United States and for appropriate foreign markets." The AIF says that U.S. and foreign demand will require development of a recycling capability by the early to mid-1980s and estimates that by the year 2000 there should be some nine to 10 fuel reprocessing plants, each capable of handling 1,500 to 2,000 metric tons of spent fuel a year.(9) In addition, according to the forum, the United States will need to build shipping casks, transport systems, spent fuel storage facilities, and interim on-site waste storage and waste treatment packaging facilities. It says the total cost will be $15 billion, and adds that this level of investment will require government incentives.

FIGURE 9   Closed Nuclear Fuel Cycle

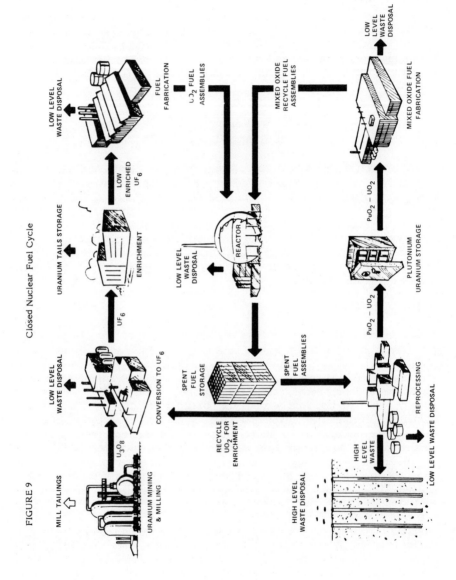

152

Industry representatives say that the costs of foregoing re-processing and recycling will be enormous. According to some sources, reprocessing would save consumers $2.5 billion a year in reduced electricity bills.(10) Perhaps more importantly, supporters say, recycling plutonium will conserve scarce uranium and fossil fuel resources. The Edison Electric Institute told the AEC that the introduction of plutonium recycling could provide a savings "in the order of 10 billion barrels of oil by 1995,"(11) an amount equal to almost three years of the country's total oil imports. Some industry officials say that recycling could reduce the demand for uranium by 13 to 14 percent. Others say it could save even more. According to John G. Haehl Jr., president of Niagara Mohawk Power Corp., "recovered uranium and plutonium would reduce both uranium and enrichment requirements by approximately 30 percent and we see nothing in a technical, economic or political sense which would preclude seeking this option as an ultimate goal."(12)

Critics' Position

In addition to objecting to plutonium recycling on the grounds that it would contribute to weapons proliferation, critics challenge both the economics of, and the need for, reprocessing. Critics note that none of industry's previous attempts to start a reprocessing industry has been a commercial success and point to various studies which conclude that reprocessing is uneconomic. A 1976 study by Pan Heuristics, a division of Science Applications Inc. in California, concludes for instance that recycling plutonium as a fuel for light-water reactors will cost 50 percent more than it would to buy fresh uranium. The study states that "the estimated costs to separate plutonium from electric power reactors have increased ten-fold in 10 years," and asserts that "recycling, in short, seems likely to lose rather than save money."(13) Critics also contend that recycling could make only a minor contribution to fuel conservation. One estimate by the Organization for Economic Cooperation and Development, critics note, says that the cumulative savings from recycling plutonium to the year 2000 might be equal to only nine months' uranium supply at that date. Pan Heuristics states that based on projections by the Edison Electric Institute, it estimates that fuel savings from uranium and plutonium recycle would amount to about 1 percent of total energy consumption between the years 1975 and 1990.(14)

Government's Position

Until 1976, the official U.S. government position on the issue of plutonium recycling was essentially the same as that taken by the industry. Government officials assumed that plutonium would be recycled because there would be compelling economic reasons for doing so. A 1976 report by the Nuclear Regulatory Commission, for instance, stated that a failure to recycle plutonium would cost the country $18 billion by the year 2000.(15) Beginning in 1976, however, the federal government's position on recycling began to swing toward that advocated by critics. The Ford administration began to place greater emphasis on nuclear nonproliferation objectives than had previous administrations. President Ford called for a reassessment of the costs and benefits of reprocessing. By 1977, President Carter had concluded that the "serious consequences of proliferation and direct implications for peace and security" of U.S. nuclear power policies required a major redirection of U.S. nuclear power programs and policies. Among the steps President Carter took were:(16)

--the indefinite deferral of commercial reprocessing and recycling of the plutonium produced in U.S. reactors;

--the restructuring of the breeder program to give greater priority to alternatives to the liquid metal fast breeder reactor, and to defer the date when breeders would be put into commercial use;

--the redirection of federal research and development programs toward alternative nuclear fuel cycles that did not involve direct access to nuclear weapons usable materials; and

--the convening of an international nuclear fuel cycle evaluation program (INFCE) to evaluate the role of nuclear power technology in an international context and to foster an increased awareness among countries of the nonproliferation, economic and other implications of different fuel cycles.

In addition to arguing against the recycling of plutonium on the grounds that it increased the risks of nuclear weapons proliferation, the government now argues that recycling and reprocessing are uneconomic. A draft report of the Nonproliferation Alternative Systems Assessment Program (NASAP), a major study funded by the Department of Energy, concludes that "the economic benefits of recycle may not be sufficient to justify the investment risks."(17) The study noted that "because a reprocessing facility has no alternative commercial application, the private sector would be unlikely to pursue this technology without strong government policy assurances" and government financial assistance. The study further stated that "the comparative costs of recycle and once-through operation would be almost equal over a wide range of U3O8 (uranium oxide) prices, ranging from $100 per pound ... to more than $200 per pound."(18) U.S. special ambassador Gerard Smith recently put forth the current U.S. view when he told the International Atomic Energy Agency's general conference that "plutonium recycle appears to us as unnecessary, marginally economic at best, and imprudent at this time from a nonproliferation standpoint."(19)

Originally, the AEC and industry had expected that by the mid-1970s two or three commercial fuel reprocessing plants would be available to separate plutonium and uranium for recycling. However, technical, regulatory and economic problems have stifled all industry attempts to start commercial reprocessing plants. General Electric has abandoned its $75-million reprocessing plant in Morris, Ill., because of technical problems. The plant is being used now to store spent fuel rods and there are indications that the government will purchase the facility for storage of spent fuel until a permanent waste repository is built. New safety standards that would have forced an investment of $800 million led Nuclear Fuel Services, a Getty Oil subsidiary, to scrap its West Valley, N.Y., reprocessing plant--saddling the federal and state government with an estimated $600 million to $1.1 billion clean-up job to stabilize and ultimately dispose of the high-level wastes at the plant. Finally, a group led by Allied Chemical Co. and General Atomic Corp. has invested $362 million in a plant at Barnwell, S.C., which was originally scheduled to begin reprocessing operations in 1976. Technical problems, escalating costs, and changes in regulatory requirements would have cost the companies another $750 million, however, and the effort was abandoned after the Carter administration announced its opposition to commercial reprocessing.(20) The 1980 Republican Party Platform said Republicans will "move toward" reprocessing. However, most analysts now predict that commercial reprocessing and plutonium recycling will not be instituted in the United States for at least a period of several decades.

Exports of Reactors

Twenty-one countries besides the United States now have operational nuclear reactors; at least another 24 have nuclear plants planned or under construction.(21) By the year 2000, according to some estimates, more than a half-million kilograms of plutonium could be flowing each year to and from more than a thousand nuclear power plants in some 50 countries.

The boom in foreign countries' interest in nuclear reactors dates from OPEC's decision in 1973 to raise oil prices. The decision forced a number of countries to recognize their dependence on foreign oil, and it dramatically increased their interest in nuclear power as a means of achieving energy independence. At the same time, oil price inflation and a recession were disrupting demand patterns in the United States and other industrial countries. Reactor vendors, seeing domestic demand for new reactors begin to fall off dramatically, began to seek new markets, particularly among the developing countries. Intense competition among vendors for foreign sales led vendors to promise the transfer of enrichment and reprocessing technology to various countries in exchange for reactor orders. Projections showed a radical increase in the sales of reactors to developing countries--and a corresponding increase in the amount of plutonium that would be produced in those countries.

Concerns about proliferation of plutonium production were aggravated by a decision on the part of the United States to cease exports of enriched uranium. In 1974, anticipating a future shortfall of enriched uranium, the United States announced that it would no longer sign new export contracts. Thus, countries interested in purchasing reactors took a greater interest in acquiring reprocessing or enrichment technology as well in order to assure themselves of an adequate fuel supply in the future. A study by the International

Atomic Energy Agency predicted that 46 countries would need to use reprocessing facilities by 1990.

The prospect of a rapid proliferation in nuclear technology led the U.S. government to reexamine its policy governing the export of nuclear plants and materials. Since the launching of its Atoms for Peace program in the mid-1950s, the United States had been an active proponent of international trade in nuclear technology for civilian uses. The aim was to demonstrate that the atom could be harnessed for peaceful uses. Through more than $4.5 billion in loans and guarantees from the Export-Import Bank, the United States has subsidized the sale of reactors to buyers in 11 countries.(22) Between 1970 and 1975 it trained 1,478 scientists from 41 countries in nuclear engineering--at least seven of them in plutonium technology.(23) Both industry and the government developed a heavy financial stake in nuclear trade.

During the mid-1970s, concern about U.S. export policy began to grow. Congress, the administration and a variety of independent groups began to debate the wisdom of pushing nuclear exports. A consensus developed that some kind of controls should be placed on foreign sales of nuclear materials. In 1976, more than a dozen bills relating to proliferation were introduced in Congress and, for the first time in the NRC's short history, an NRC commissioner dissented from a commission regulatory opinion--one that granted an export license for sale of a nuclear reactor to Spain. The commissioner, Victor Gilinsky, said the agreement with Spain "contains a vital flaw involving the controls over the plutonium--a nuclear explosive--which will be produced in the operation of the reactor." Gilinsky criticized past U.S. policy and commented, "I think it's just unfortunate that we didn't think through some of these problems (control of plutonium) earlier."(24)

President Ford lent support for Gilinsky's position by urging Congress to tighten U.S. policy governing the export of nuclear materials and calling for a moratorium on the export of reprocessing and enrichment technology. "Given the choice between economic benefits and progress toward our nonproliferation goals," said President Ford, "we have given, and will continue to give, priority to nonproliferation."(25) During his 1976 election campaign, President Carter called for even tougher measures concerning nuclear exports. In April 1977, he announced his decisions about deferring the re-processing of domestic spent fuel, delaying commercialization of the breeder, and advocating greater controls over the nuclear materials produced as a result of U.S. reactor exports. One year later, the basic elements of Carter's policy became law in the U.S. Nuclear Non-Proliferation Act of 1978. That act, in general, seeks to deny non-nuclear weapons countries access to nuclear fuels and equipment that could be readily used to make nuclear weapons. Among other provisions, the act requires the renegotiation of all existing U.S. fuel contracts, and the cutoff of fuel supplies to countries that have not placed all their atomic facilities under international safeguards by March 1980. "Our policy takes a responsible course between foregoing the energy benefits of nuclear power, and becoming committed to commercialized use of plutonium before we know that we can deal safely with its risks," stated President Carter in 1978.(26)

THE DEBATE OVER PROLIFERATION
AND THE PLUTONIUM ECONOMY

At the heart of all concerns about the proliferation of nuclear power plants, both domestic and foreign, is the fear that plutonium or other weapons-usable materials in the spent fuel will be misused. "Unfortunately," President Ford said in 1976, "and this is the root of the problem, the same plutonium produced in nuclear plants can, when chemically separated, also be used to make explosives."(27) Few nuclear experts, including proponents of nuclear power, deny that a relationship exists between the use of nuclear energy systems and the potential for the misuse of nuclear materials. But critics and proponents of nuclear power tend to disagree on what steps, if any, should be taken to stop the proliferation of nuclear technology or sever the link between nuclear power systems and the ability to make nuclear weapons. The general arguments of nuclear proponents and critics on the issue of proliferation can be summarized as follows:(28)

Proponents

Proponents of nuclear power stress that weapons proliferation has never resulted as a consequence of facilities associated with a purely civilian nuclear power program. They admit that nuclear power facilities could hypothetically be used to gain a weapons capability, but they contend that there are other paths to a weapons capability that are less difficult in a technical sense, less expensive, and less time-consuming. "A simple analysis of well-known facts shows that there are today no fewer than eight different ways available to produce weapons materials," says Chauncey Starr of the Electric Power Research Institute. Among them, Starr says, the commercial nuclear power fuel cycle "is the most expensive route, requires the highest level of support technology, the broadest base of industry support, and takes the longest to install and to yield mate-rial ...."(29) Thus, proponents continue, countries that really want nuclear weapons will be able to attain them regardless of the status of their nuclear power programs. The proliferation threat, then, is real, but it is best countered through influencing the incentives and disincentives for the acquisition of weapons, not through futile attempts to place embargoes on technology. Even if some countries did wish to pursue a weapons program through the use of nuclear power facilities, proponents argue, unilateral actions by the United States to stop the export of nuclear technology will be ineffective because other nuclear supplier nations will be more than willing to pick up U.S. business. Current U.S. policy is misguided and counterproductive, proponents say, because it creates uncertainties among nuclear importers about the adequacy of U.S. fuel supply contracts, giving them a greater incentive to acquire their own reprocessing or enrichment facilities. Finally, proponents say, the risks of a global nuclear war resulting from a worldwide shortage of energy are greater than any risks associated with the widespread use of properly safeguarded nuclear power facilities.

Critics

"Atoms for peace and atoms for war are Siamese twins," says Swedish physicist Hannes Alfven, summing up the feeling of many nuclear critics.(30) Nuclear power may not be the quickest or cheapest direct route to nuclear weapons, critics say, but it provides a convenient means of acquiring a weapons capability. This is particularly true if a closed nuclear fuel cycle is adopted through the introduction of plutonium recycling or breeder reactors. Moreover, critics say, the operation of nuclear power facilities carries with it significant technology transfers, making it far easier and less expensive for nations to develop a weapons capability once they have a nuclear power industry. Nations without an existing nuclear power industry would require quadruple the amount of time and 50 to 100 times as much money to build and test a nuclear device as would nations with a nuclear power industry, according to one study.(31) Nuclear proponents are correct in their assertion that there is no "technical fix" for the nuclear fuel cycle, critics assert, but the implication of that finding is not that nuclear technology should be available to all countries, but rather that nuclear power should not be utilized by any countries. Rapid development of alternative energy sources that are more economic and safer than nuclear power, along with a concerted effort on nuclear disarmament issues, could radically reduce the incentives for other countries to develop nuclear weapons, critics conclude. And only the United States, because of the importance of its nuclear industry in the international nuclear market and its technological dominance in both nuclear and alternative energy fields, can initiate a major international change away from nuclear energy systems and toward renewable energy sources, critics say. "From the perspective of one living in Europe it is obvious," argues physicist Amory Lovins, "that no country outside the United States could sustain a significant nuclear program without America's technical support, technical services, materials, and most important, *political support*."(32)

Potential Threats

Irrespective of their position on the best way to deal with the problems posed by nuclear proliferation, nuclear analysts agree that there are serious potential threats associated with the widespread use of plutonium. Concerns over these threats can be described as follows:

Nuclear Bomb

Terrorist groups or foreign governments, with the necessary knowledge, could build a nuclear bomb. Terrorist groups, the argument runs, could steal a relatively small quantity of special nuclear materials--10 kilograms of plutonium or uranium 233 or 25 kilograms of highly enriched uranium--and build a crude, transportable nuclear fission bomb. Proponents of this theory believe such a bomb could have an explosive force of 20 kilotons--equal to the Nagasaki bomb, and enough to kill tens of thousands of people and destroy property worth millions of dollars. "The acquisition of special nuclear materials," a special AEC task force on safeguards reported in April 1974, "remains the only substantial problem facing groups which desire to have such weapons."(33)

The AEC task force commented that lack of knowledge was not a problem inhibiting the development of nuclear weapons. "Widespread and increasing dissemination of precise and accurate instructions on how to make a nuclear weapon in your basement,...a slow but continuing movement of personnel into and out of the areas of weapons design and manufacturing (creating) larger and larger numbers of people with experience in processing special nuclear materials," have increased the possibility that terrorist groups "are likely to have available to them the sort of technical knowledge needed to use the now widely disseminated instructions for processing fissile materials and for building a nuclear weapon."(34)

With the necessary knowledge, most experts argue, the task of building a bomb is not particularly difficult. Theodore Taylor, who once helped design atomic bombs for the U.S. weapons program, has written with Mason Willrich that "under conceivable circumstances, a few persons, possibly even one person working alone, who possessed about 10 kilograms of plutonium oxide and a substantial amount of chemical explosive, could within several weeks design and build a crude fission bomb.... This could be done using materials and equipment that could be purchased at a hardware store and from commercial suppliers of scientific equipment for student laboratories."(35) Moreover, according to Taylor, if an explosive device was built ahead of time and required only the insertion of fissile material, the time between the diversion of the material and the explosion of the first bomb "conceivably could be a few days or hours."(36)

Most observers now agree that the greater the number of countries with nuclear reactors, the larger the likelihood that nations will divert plutonium produced by the reactors to manufacture a weapon. The difficulty of reprocessing spent fuel to separate the plutonium from other irradiated elements acts as a temporary restraint on plutonium use for weapons development. For a number of years some observers hoped that this restraint, together with international safeguards agreements, would provide an effective disincentive to diversion. India's nuclear explosion in 1974, using plutonium produced by a reactor given by Canada and fueled with "heavy water" from the United States, destroyed that hope. According to Joseph S. Nye Jr., a former State Department official who is an expert on proliferation issues, "The idea that damaging uses of nuclear energy need not follow from benign ones was publicly discredited" by the Indian explosion.(37)

Many experts consider it relatively easy for countries to develop a small-scale reprocessing capacity. Experts estimate that many countries already have such capabilities. In addition to the five original nuclear powers (United States, Britain, Soviet Union, France and China), they include Japan, India, Canada, Taiwan, Argentina, Spain, Sweden, Switzerland, Israel, South Africa, Poland, Czechoslovakia, East Germany and the Euratom countries (West Germany, Belgium, Italy and the Netherlands). In the heat of competing for the nuclear export market, France and West Germany also included reprocessing technology as a "sweetener" in a package sale of reactors for several years. France originally agreed to include a reprocessing plant in its sales of reactors to Pakistan, Iran and South Korea--although U.S. pressure succeeded in getting reprocessing removed from these agreements--and West Germany has agreed to supply Brazil with a reprocessing plant in connection with reactor sales to that country. In 1978, at the instigation of the United States, an agreement was signed by the United States, the Soviet Union and 13 major nuclear supplier nations placing greater restrictions on future sales of reprocessing and other sensitive technology, but the agreement specifically excluded the plants to be built in Pakistan and Brazil.(38) Perhaps more ominously, it has been reported that Iraq is using its leverage as Brazil's largest oil supplier to extract a long-term nuclear pact that would eventually give Iraq access to the nuclear technology Brazil is acquiring from West Germany.(39)

Less threatening than diversion of nuclear materials by a national government, but still of concern to many critics of the plutonium economy, is the possibility that terrorist groups will steal enough plutonium to construct a bomb. Brian Jenkins, manager of the Rand Corp.'s study project on terrorism, says the prospect of terrorists using nuclear weapons cannot be ruled out, but making an accurate assessment of the probability that a specific kind of event will occur is impossible. It is important, he says, to put terrorists' objectives into proper perspective. Terrorists generally have made limited efforts to seek support, to attract public attention, or to use fear in order to obtain specific objectives. They have had access to materials--poisons or conventional explosives--which in certain situations could have produced large numbers of casualties. Thus far, he notes, apparently they have concluded that their objectives would not be advanced if they used these potent weapons to create incidents of mass destruction.

But Jenkins says it is possible that, under certain circumstances, the level of violence employed in acts of terrorism will change. If terrorists think that governments and populations are growing inured to lower levels of violence, he says, they may decide that more dramatic actions are required to attract attention to their cause. It also is possible, he says, that because of inbred fears of atomic devices, nuclear weapons would prove more attractive to terrorists than other esoteric forms of destruction. For example, he suggests, a theft of plutonium is likely to receive more publicity than a theft of chemical poisons, and the threat of an atomic bomb would cause greater concern to the general population than a threat of fire in a petroleum tank farm.(40)

Radiological Weapons

Smaller quantities of plutonium could be used to build dispersal weapons that would lethally contaminate very large volumes of air. Plutonium emits alpha particles that have very little penetrating power in comparison with gamma or X-rays, and hence it can be handled with minimal shielding for hours without hazard. If taken into the bloodstream, however, plutonium becomes one of the most carcinogenic agents to be found. It is particularly dangerous if inhaled. Particles weighing some 10 millionths of a gram, if inhaled, can cause death from fibrosis of the lungs within a few weeks.(41) According to Ralph Nader, "an amount of the lethal plutonium-239 not exceeding 20 pounds, if efficiently dispersed, could give lung cancer to everyone on earth."

The possibility of dispersal this efficient is surely remote. Nevertheless, Nader's example serves to emphasize that very small quantities of plutonium can cause tremendous harm. It is estimated that even a few grams dispersed through the air-conditioning system in an aerosol suspension could pose a serious threat to the occupants of a large office building or enclosed industrial facility. Effective dispersal in open areas would be more difficult, but experts calculate that a few dozen grams of plutonium could contaminate several square kilometers sufficiently to require the evacuation of people in the area and necessitate a very difficult and expensive decontamination operation.(42)

Nuclear Blackmail

Some experts believe that an expanding nuclear industry will make the theft and misuse of nuclear materials seem so plausible that criminal groups might be able to extract huge ransoms from threats of nuclear explosion or radiation without actually having possession of any lethal materials or without constructing a bomb. An incident that occurred in Orlando, Fla., in 1970 is frequently cited in support of this view. The mayor of Orlando received a note threatening destruction of the city by a nuclear bomb and demanding $1 million and safe passage to Cuba. Accompanying the note was a diagram of a crude bomb that some experts thought should be taken seriously. Both federal and municipal authorities took the threat seriously, until a local high school student explained it was a hoax he had perpetrated. More recently, a worker at GE's Wilmington plant attempted to extort $100,000 from the company in return for 150 pounds of low enriched uranium that he stole from the company's plant. The worker, who was arrested by the FBI, had threatened to mail samples of the uranium to prominent government officials and to disperse the uranium powder in a large city in an attempt to cause a panic if the company failed to deliver the money.(43)

Some experts say that such incidents demonstrate not only that a credible threat can occur, but that a bomb is not necessary in order for the threat to be effective. The potential effectiveness of such a threat may encourage a black market in plutonium. Taylor and Willrich estimate that the commercial value of nuclear weapons materials will be between $3,000 and $15,000 per kilogram--roughly equal to the price of heroin on the black market. "The same material might be hundreds of times more valuable to some group wanting a powerful means of destruction," or as a means of seeking a ransom.(44)

Nuclear Sabotage

Some observers also believe that the proliferation of nuclear power plants and fuel reprocessing and fabrication facilities will greatly increase the likelihood that attempted acts of sabotage will occur, with potentially catastrophic effects. Some fear that trained saboteurs using explosive devices could cause the dispersal of highly irradiated nuclear fuel that is in transit or in facilities where spent fuel assemblies are stored or reprocessed. Others are concerned that a skyjacked aircraft might be used to crash into a nuclear reactor, causing a core meltdown and consequent release of intense radioactivity. They say power plants are designed to sustain the impact of a 200,000-pound aircraft, and a Boeing 747, for example, weighs 365,000 pounds. Still others see a danger in the possible takeover of a nuclear power plant by a band of highly trained, sophisticated terrorists who might destroy it in such a way as to kill thousands, perhaps tens of thousands, of people. A former official in the U.S. Navy underwater demolition program has testified to Congress that he "could pick three to five ex-underwater demolition Marine reconnaissance or Green Beret men at random and sabotage virtually any nuclear reactor in the country...."(45) And a former guard at the Trojan nuclear plant in Oregon, where 11 security guards were recently arrested on drug charges, contends that "80 percent of the guards out there would throw down their weapons rather than use them in an attack."(46) Rand's Brian Jenkins cites nine cases in which acts or threats of sabotage involving radioactive materials occurred between 1970 and 1975. "The rapid growth of the nuclear industry, increasing traffic in plutonium, enriched uranium, and radioactive waste material, the spread of nuclear technology both in the United States and abroad--all increase the opportunities for terrorists to engage in some type of nuclear action," Jenkins concludes.(47) Recently, the prospect of insider sabotage has been raised by several incidents. In 1979, for instance, two operator-trainees at Virginia Electric & Power Co.'s Surry nuclear plant were convicted of pouring a corrosive chemical on new fuel rods that were scheduled to be placed in the reactor. And in 1980, an FBI investigation determined that it was insider sabotage that caused a number of unscheduled shutdowns at TVA's Browns Ferry plant in February 1980.(48)

THE SAFEGUARDS CONTROVERSY

No one denies the need for safeguards against the misuse of plutonium, and most observers admit that current safeguards are inadequate. But there are points of serious disagreement on how great the threat of misuse of plutonium is; whether effective international safeguards can be established; whether adequate domestic safeguards can be instituted; how expensive effective safeguards will be and who will cover the costs; and whether safeguards measures will endanger individuals' civil liberties.

Proponents and opponents of nuclear power agree that safeguards questions present the industry with particular and important problems, but opponents in general feel that nuclear power should be slowed down--or even brought to a halt--until the problems are resolved, and supporters generally are more confident that institutions, systems, and technology can meet the concerns that have been raised. Many critics assert that proponents do not comprehend the dimensions of the problem; proponents say that critics have exaggerated the problem. Almost universally, proponents of nuclear power maintain that it would be a mistake to slow the momentum of nuclear power development because of safeguards problems. On specific questions, these are the stands of both sides:

Threat of Misuse

The strongest critics of nuclear power contend that the dangers of plutonium misuse are so severe that further development of nuclear power should be abandoned. If it is not, they say, pressure from utilities and manufacturers almost certainly will lead to development of a nuclear fuel recycling industry and increased exports, and it may lead to development of breeder reactors (if the technical and economic problems in the breeder program can be solved). Moreover, if the United States continues to pursue domestic expansion of nuclear power, it will not be able to sponsor with credibility any slowing of development of nuclear power abroad.

Some persons concerned with safeguards focus their attention on stopping recycling, the breeder reactors, or exports of nuclear power plants. Others who do not oppose development of a domestic or an international plutonium economy say nonetheless that much more attention must be devoted to strengthening safeguards if development is to proceed.

Critics of the export program say that one aspect of the problem is the difficulty of assuring long-term security. A study by Pan Heuristics states that "the most immediate prospects for acquiring nuclear explosives tend to be small or less-developed countries, especially those outside the Soviet orbit, not--as once expected--the most advanced industrial powers." The authors say that "some of the countries that may soon acquire nuclear weapons ... are politically unstable and much more liable to sudden threats of mass destruction from dissident factions."(49) South Korea, Taiwan, Pakistan, South Africa, Iran, Brazil, Nigeria, Argentina, Spain, Yugoslavia and Rumania are among those most frequently cited as having taken or being close to a decision to develop a nuclear weapons capability.

Even if a country is stable at the moment, in a secure relationship, and is apparently able to offer assurance of adequate safeguards, it is possible that the situation may change in the future. As the number of countries with nuclear plants and a capability for reprocessing the spent fuel increases, so does the likelihood that one of these countries will decide to divert plutonium from the spent fuel to develop a weapon. Former AEC Commissioner Henry Smyth comments that a stockpile of plutonium may build up under a stable government. "Now suppose there's a revolution. A totally new and crazy government comes in, and there's the plutonium just sitting there asking to be made into a bomb."(50)

In general, industry and government officials agree that the threat of diversion by foreign governments in order to make nuclear weapons is real and serious, and they support efforts to tighten international safeguards to prevent misuse. But they are not so concerned, as are many critics, about the possibility that terrorists will succeed in stealing enough material to build a bomb. Government officials, for instance, disagree with the statements by Taylor and others about the ease with which a nuclear bomb can be constructed. They say it would take a half-dozen or dozen "quite competent, very skilled scientists, engineers, electronic people to fabricate such a device." The need for extremely tight security during the entire undertaking, they say, would further reduce the chances for a successful outcome. They do not rule out the possibility that a theft might occur, but they consider it less likely than do many critics.

Industry officials also argue that the nuclear industry has been singled out unfairly by critics as a potential target for sabotage or theft. There are other, more attractive targets, they say, involving materials that are easier to obtain than plutonium. For example, one industry representative said, nonnuclear bombs could be placed in large population centers; germs or LSD could be used to contaminate water supply systems; or an oil tank farm, natural gas storage area, or ship filled with propane gas could be attacked with explosives. The efforts being made to protect against thefts of nuclear materials, proponents say, are more extensive than the security measures being taken against more conventional man-made disasters, and the risk of blackmail or sabotage from nuclear materials should be no greater.

International Safeguards

Those who oppose export of nuclear materials do so for three specific reasons: (1) foreign governments, particularly in countries with weak law-enforcement capabilities, extreme political ideologies, or active terrorist organizations, may not be capable of protecting nuclear materials; (2) the government of a country with a civilian nuclear power program may choose to divert some of the materials to develop nuclear weapons, as India did in 1974; and, perhaps most important, (3) the International Atomic Energy Agency (IAEA), the multicountry agency working to monitor the use of nuclear materials, is not capable of regulating international nuclear activity.

As mentioned earlier, when the United States launched its Atoms for Peace program in the mid-1950s, the hope was that the sharing of nuclear power for peaceful purposes would help to mitigate against its being used for war. Access to the new technology, which was then virtually a U.S. and Soviet monopoly, would be tied to international controls that would protect against its misuse.

In 1958 the International Atomic Energy Agency was established to carry out the inspection of nuclear facilities. Its role was broadened a decade later by the negotiation of the treaty on the nonproliferation of nuclear weapons. Under the terms of the treaty, the 97 signers, in states without nuclear weapons, agreed to allow the IAEA to monitor all nuclear activities. In exchange, it was understood that they would receive preferential access to nuclear power-- including the technology for enriching uranium and for recycling plutonium. For a time, there was faith that this agreement would be the basis for workable international safeguards.

The Indian explosion seriously shook that faith. Observers pointed out that there are major loopholes in the nonproliferation treaty. The signer has the right to conduct any nuclear activity short of producing a nuclear weapon, and any signer can withdraw from the treaty after giving 90 days' notice. A country may go a long way toward development of a weapons capacity but stop just short of the final step which would result in violation of the nonproliferation treaty. It is conceivable that the country could then withdraw from the pact and proceed with the last actions required to manufacture a weapon. The problem is accentuated by what some experts call the "shrinking critical time" required to make a nuclear explosive. "The fundamental problem," Albert Wohlstetter wrote in a Pan Heuristics report on proliferation, "is that, for an increasing number of 'non-weapons' states, the critical time to make an explosive has been diminishing and will continue to diminish without any necessary violation of the clearly agreed-on rules--without any 'diversion' needed--and therefore without any prospect of being curbed by safeguards that have been elaborated for the purpose of verifying whether the mutually agreed-on rules have or have not been broken."(51)

There is also a problem with the enforcement capacity of the International Atomic Energy Agency. The agency does not have the capacity to enforce agreed-upon international safeguards. Less than 10 percent of the IAEA's staff of 1,500 employees are involved in inspecting safeguarded reactors, and these manage to visit most facilities no more than several times a year. "You can't actually stop a country from doing something it shouldn't this way," one IAEA official has noted. "Our function is to sound the warning when something has been done."(52) In addition to lacking the capacity to rigorously inspect nuclear facilities, the IAEA has no sanctions authority to call into play in the event that it finds wrongdoing. "Perhaps the most that can be expected from the IAEA system is a yellow warning light as a result of frustration of its inspection process," states Mason Willrich.(53) But some critics are skeptical that the IAEA is even capable of providing an early warning system. Unsafeguarded reprocessing facilities are already operating in several countries, critics note, and the IAEA does not even consider enforcing safeguards to be its primary function. Rather, most of the agency's staff is engaged in what the IAEA describes as its principal objective: "To accelerate and enlarge the contribution of atomic energy to peace, health and prosperity throughout the world."(54) As Jose Goldemberg, chairman of the Brazilian Society of Physicists, puts it: "The IAEA is basically a company for promoting the sale of reactors."(55)

Proponents tend to have somewhat more faith in the ability of the IAEA to carry out its mission, although many proponents are in favor of strengthening existing safeguards. But proponents stress that the need to strengthen institutional arrangements for monitoring nuclear materials does not imply a need for stricter controls on nuclear technology. Any attempt by the United States or a group of countries to prevent the export of nuclear technology, proponents say, is likely to damage nonproliferation efforts. "The best policy for the U.S. appears to be to support international cooperation in the development of reprocessing, waste disposal and safeguard procedures for spent fuel," says C.A. Orem, Babcock & Wilcox's director of corporate planning and development. "Strengthening the IAEA or some other inspection agency would provide assurances that power reactors are not used as a source of weapons material," Orem states, but the United States "would have more impact by becoming a major participant in this worldwide control system than by controlling the export of our technology."(56)

Domestic Safeguards

Although domestic safeguard systems have been upgraded in recent years, critics on this issue contend that the conclusions of a 1973 AEC safeguard study group remain valid. The study group found that existing safeguard systems were "entirely inadequate to meet the threat" and that the development of adequate safeguards would be a most difficult task.(57) Current safeguard systems, Theodore Taylor has commented, "simply do not go anywhere far enough to prevent thefts by groups of people with at least the skills and resources that have been used for major thefts in the past."(58) The development of adequate safeguards, critics contend, is likely to be one of the greatest challenges the country has ever faced.

One major problem will be to develop technical devices that will allow accurate and continuous accounting of plutonium inventories. In the past, critics point out, large amounts of weapons-usable materials have "disappeared" from inventories and have not been found. The U.S. General Accounting Office reported in July 1976 that tens of tons of nuclear material, much of it weapons-grade, was missing from 34 uranium and plutonium processing plants around the country.(59) And determining whether weapons-grade material has already been stolen is likely to prove impossible. According to Charles Thornton, former director of nuclear materials safeguards for the AEC: "The aggregate MUF (materials unaccounted for) from the three U.S. diffusion plants alone is expressible in tons. No one knows where it is. None of it may have been stolen, but the balances don't close. You could divert from any plant in the world, in substantial amounts, and never be detected .... The statistical thief learns the sensitivity of the system and operates within it and is never detected."(60) A former NRC safeguards official characterizes the commission's procedure for investigating inventory disparities as follows:

> The NRC shows the flag and sends a task force to investigate, they have one or two reinventories, they find or lose 3 or 4 kilograms and arrive at a final figure. They then look at the whole operation and say the material unaccounted for could have disappeared into the river or hung up in the pipes or whatever, but say they find no direct evidence of theft or diversion. It's just a ritual with a lot of thrashing around, with letters from congressional oversight committees demanding to know what's going on .... It's a ho-hum thing for everybody in the system. The fact of the matter is they are playing a game and nobody really believes in the accounting system.(61)

Many government and industry officials agree that safeguards have not always received the attention they deserve, but most contend that times have changed. "We really only started upgrading our security in 1972, after the terrorist attacks on the Munich Olympic games," former ERDA official James Liverman has said.(62) In the beginning, industry officials say, keeping track of nuclear materials was viewed mainly as an accounting problem. But over the years, they continue, the NRC has constantly improved the safeguards in response to changing perceptions of levels of threat. Romano Salvatori of Westinghouse commented in 1974 that "regulations currently being implemented by the nuclear industry provide more than adequate assurance that this material will not be readily susceptible to theft or diversion .... The material accountability requirements provide protection against the undetected diversion of special nuclear materials.

Protection against actual theft is provided by physical protection systems .... The risks of theft of special nuclear materials have been identified, and appropriate accounting and security systems have been developed to reduce these risks."(63)

Nevertheless, many critics say, any conceivable safeguards system will suffer from the same basic weakness--the fallibility of man. Alvin Weinberg--a strong supporter of nuclear power--has noted that a "continuing tradition of meticulous attention to detail" will be required to protect nuclear facilities and materials. He has suggested that the establishment of an elite "scientific priesthood" may be required.(64) Others argue that no "priesthood" made up of as many people as might have access to special nuclear materials can be trusted completely. The Natural Resources Defense Council, for example, has written that "the New York Police Department has proven incapable of maintaining security over confiscated heroin. Are similar losses of plutonium acceptable?"(65) Critics further charge that despite all of the NRC's attempts to improve safeguards, losses of nuclear materials continue. They cite the NRC's temporary shutdown of Nuclear Fuel Services Corp.'s Erwin plant in 1979 as an example of the continuing problems in this area. The latest inventory at that plant, which fabricates fuel assemblies for the nuclear submarine program, indicated that at least 20 pounds of high-enriched uranium could not be accounted for, bringing accumulated inventory losses at the plant to 409 pounds since 1968. After a widely publicized investigation, the NRC concluded that there was no evidence that the missing material had been stolen and allowed the plant to reopen. In addition, the NRC relaxed existing inventory performance standards for the plant.(66) In response, the Natural Resources Defense Council has filed a lawsuit against the NRC. Problems such as those at the Erwin plant, contends one government expert on arms control, have "important implications for proliferation policy. There has been a lot of talk recently about multinational plants to make plutonium processing facilities (in nonnuclear weapons states) safer," he says. "Here we have an example of a plant in a very sophisticated country having inventory problems. It reemphasizes the problem of whether anyone can make facilities with weapons-grade nuclear materials safe."(67)

Costs of Safeguards

Another problem, critics say, may be the costs of safeguards technology and the manpower required to form federal or private security forces. Although they make no estimates of the costs of a safeguards program that they would consider adequate, critics say the costs could be significant. Safeguards, like safety research and storage, have been subsidized, critics contend, and the subsidy must be counted as a cost, which may affect the competitiveness of the nuclear option.

Industry officials also are concerned over how the increasing costs of safeguards programs will be allocated. General Atomic Corp. has asserted that the "cost of maintaining a federal protective service should be borne by the taxpayer as a special type of police arrangement which the national security interest requires. The security needed is clearly in excess of that required to protect the property interests of the owner of the material and, in fact, is directed at protecting the security interests of the body politic."(68)

In any event, proponents maintain that safeguards costs will not seriously affect the competitiveness of nuclear power. Taylor and Willrich argue that even if total costs for safeguards were to rise to $800 million a year for the entire industry, which they believe is most unlikely, "this would hardly be sufficient by itself to affect substantially the overall economics of nuclear power."(69) An official of the Atomic Industrial Forum has asserted that it is "possible to protect special nuclear material sufficiently so that reasonable people agree that any risk from diversion or sabotage is negligible...at a cost which, although high, need not be so high as to cripple the economics of nuclear power."(70)

One way to reduce safeguards costs would be to combine some or all of the facilities involved in the nuclear fuel cycle--fuel fabrication, reprocessing, and power reactors--in "nuclear parks." These would eliminate some vulnerable transit stages and enable a consolidation of physical protection requirements. Alvin Weinberg, among others, has argued in favor of nuclear parks as a means of reducing some of the problems and costs associated with nuclear power. Unlike many proponents, however, Weinberg concedes that "it is not impossible that what one must pay for an acceptable nuclear system--with its better technology, its higher-paid care, its tighter security--conceivably could price nuclear out of the market."(71)

Civil Liberties

Some critics believe that if a safeguards system were to be implemented, it would infringe unacceptably on many persons' civil liberties. The Natural Resources Defense Council maintains: "An adequate safeguards (system) would not be acceptable in prac- tice...due to the tremendous cost of such a system in terms of human freedom and privacy."(72)

Government officials do not discount the possibility that there will be serious civil liberties questions connected with a growing use of nuclear energy. "If someone runs off with a substantial amount of this stuff (weapons-grade material) from one of these plants," says a top NRC official, "you are probably going to go out and break down all the doors in America to get it back."(73) John H. Barton, a Stanford University law professor who studied the problem for the NRC, adds: "I have a strong fear that in the event of an actual incident civil liberties could end up being ignored."(74) In a lengthy treatment of the civil liberties impact of plutonium recycling, in the *Harvard Civil Liberties Law Review*, Russell W. Ayres, a lawyer, concludes that "the challenge to the legal system's competence to adjust social interests in public policy with individual interests in civil liberties may be the most significant social cost of plutonium."(75)

Industry representatives acknowledge that some of the security measures that will be required for a large nuclear industry raise a threat to civil liberties. They agree with Carl Walske of the Atomic Industrial Forum that it is up to the industry "to guard vigilantly against any such abuse." Moreover, industry sources say they do not expect that any extensive monitoring of citizens will be required, and they see any minimal loss of privacy as a small price to pay for an assured supply of electric power.

DISPOSAL OF RADIOACTIVE WASTES

Critics of nuclear power development are also extremely concerned over provisions for handling and safely disposing of the radioactive wastes associated with the use of nuclear power--some of which must be isolated from the environment for hundreds of thousands of years. "We consider radioactive waste to be one of the grave issues posed by this nation's large nuclear program," writes Daniel Ford, executive director of the Union of Concerned Scientists. "It's deadly. And nobody knows exactly what to do with it."(76)

The Scope of the Nuclear Waste Problem

The United States would have a nuclear waste problem even if it had never embarked on a nuclear power program because of wastes associated with its nuclear weapons program. In fact, a large percentage of the most highly radioactive wastes currently stored at various sites around the country are directly attributable to nuclear weapons programs. But although defense-related activities are responsible for a large proportion of existing wastes, the nuclear power industry is currently generating radioactive wastes at a much greater rate than are weapons programs. Consequently, although the waste problem was not created by the nuclear power industry, the future magnitude of the problem may be largely dependent on the rate at which nuclear power develops. A recent report by the Interagency Review Group on Nuclear Waste described the situation as follows:

During the last 30 years defense-related nuclear activities produced most of the radioactive wastes in terms of volume and radioactivity. Today, and as projected for the future, the radioactive waste generation rate of the defense-related programs is about constant and small in relation to the future generation of the nuclear power industry. The commercial nuclear power industry has grown...and, as a result, has now generated more radioactive waste (measured in terms of cumulative radioactivity) than the past defense-related activities.(77)

Nuclear power plant wastes can be divided into three general categories: high-level wastes, transuranic wastes, and low-level wastes. Each poses different kinds of problems.

High-Level Wastes

Fission products in high-level wastes emit gamma rays, which have a highly penetrating radiation and require massive shielding in transit or in storage. The longest-lived of the fission products, cesium 137 and strontium 90, have a half-life of 30 years and become harmless after 800 to 1,000 years.

High-level wastes also include transuranic elements, the most dangerous of which is plutonium. Transuranic elements emit alpha particles, which have little penetrating power and, consequently, require little shielding. But some, like plutonium, have a high specific radio-toxicity and an extremely long half-life. Plutonium has a half life of 24,000 years and is considered to present a potential hazard for at least 250,000 years, and possibly as long as a million years.

Most of the high-level wastes in the United States have been produced by the nation's weapons program. Since the 1940s, the nuclear weapons program has produced 215 million gallons of high-level nuclear wastes. Of this amount, 80 percent has been solidified, and in January 1976 the military's high-level waste inventory was "about 75 million gallons, half of which was in solid form," according to a report by Mason Willrich.(78)

Commercial nuclear reactors have produced only about 612,000 gallons of liquid high-level wastes, all resulting from the operation for several years of a commercial reprocessing plant at West Valley, N.Y. In addition to these liquid wastes, however, commercial reactors have generated about 2,300 tons of spent fuel assemblies which the government defines as high-level waste.(79) These are currently stored in utility spent-fuel storage ponds around the country.

Most experts agree that the problems of dealing with high-level wastes result not so much from quantity, but from the difficulty of devising a suitable method of long-term isolation and confinement. A 1,000-megawatt nuclear plant will produce only about 60 cubic feet of solidified high-level waste annually.(80) William Ramsay has noted that "if all the uranium thought to be available in the United States were to be used up as fuel, the total amount of spent fuel would probably be less than 95,000 cubic meters,...a volume (that) could easily be contained, for example, in the extensive, but not gargantuan, space occupied by the offices of the Department of Energy at Germantown, Md."(81) But although the quantities of high-level waste being generated are not enormous, many questions remain about exactly how to dispose of these wastes safely. In general, experts agree that the wastes should be buried in deep geologic repositories, but major uncertainties remain concerning the specific methods and materials that should be used. A technical study by Science Applications Inc. for the Department of Energy summed up some of the uncertainties:

> Of all the issues associated with deep geologic repositories, hydrogeology and waste containment is understood least, particularly for non-salt rocks. Information is lacking on as basic an issue as whether the rock mass permeability and porosity of such rocks as granite, shale and basalt will increase or decrease in the elevated temperatures of a repository environment. Uncertainty exists in the leach rate and nuclide migration data, especially at elevated temperatures. Data on the duration of canister materials in geologic repository environments is almost non-existent.(82)

In addition to uncertainties about the permanent disposal of high-level wastes, temporary storage of these wastes--particularly those in liquid form--has proved troublesome. Many of the steel tanks and bins in which these wastes are stored have begun to leak, in some cases releasing radioactivity into the environment. At the government facilities in Hanford, Wash., alone, 18 tank leaks have resulted in the leakage into the soil of 430,000 gallons of high-level wastes from the U.S. weapons program.(83)

Transuranic Wastes

Transuranic wastes contain many of the same elements as high-level wastes, but in smaller quantities and without such highly penetrating radiation. These wastes result primarily from spent fuel reprocessing, the fabrication of plutonium to produce nuclear weapons, and, if it should occur, the fabrication of plutonium for recycling in nuclear reactors. Transuranic waste is currently defined as material containing more than 10 nanocuries of transuranic activity per gram of material.(84)

Before 1970, no distinction was made between transuranic wastes and low-level wastes--wastes that have little or no transuranic content but that have been contaminated by radioactive materials--and both were buried at a number of sites. Since then, however, transuranic wastes have been stored above ground in a retrievable fashion, as it is now believed that these wastes should be disposed of in the same manner as high-level wastes. As was the case with high-level wastes, most of the country's existing transuranic wastes were produced in the nuclear weapons program. Of these commercial wastes, more than half are buried at Maxey Flats, Ky., and the remainder at Hanford, Wash., Sheffield, Ill., Beatty, Nev., and West Valley, N.Y.(85)

The permanent disposal of transuranic wastes is expected to be less difficult than the disposal of high-level wastes because transuranic wastes generate much less heat. Burial of transuranic wastes in shallow trenches in the past, however, may pose problems in the future. A General Accounting Office report notes that "some radioactive migration has occurred at several of these burial sites. If the situation worsens, it may entail exhuming the waste. If this is required, it can be quite expensive, running into hundreds of millions of dollars."(86)

Low-Level Wastes

Two major types of low-level waste are generated by the nuclear power industry. In addition to contaminated clothing and reactor equipment--which are buried along with transuranic wastes at a number of commercial and government-operated sites--vast quantities of uranium mine and mill tailings are piled in various western states. As of January 1977, 51 million cubic feet of transuranic and low-level wastes generated by military programs and 16 million cubic feet from commercial activities had been buried at six commercial and 14 DOE-operated sites.(87) In addition, about 500 million cubic feet of uranium mill tailings, weighing about 140 million tons, have accumulated at 22 locations where uranium mills have shut down.(88)

The major problems seen resulting from low-level wastes tend to be related to the great volumes in which they are produced rather than to their levels of radioactivity. Some experts, for example, are predicting a shortage of low-level waste storage sites as more and more states pass laws forbidding the dumping of nuclear wastes. Furthermore, demand for burial space is expected to grow rapidly, especially as utilities begin to decommission old reactors. According to the Interagency Review Group report, "Projections indicate that commercial generation of LLW (low-level waste) and thus demand for burial ground capacity will increase dramatically in the decades ahead. Currently, over 2 million cubic feet of LLW are disposed of each year at commercial sites and over 1 million cubic feet at DOE-operated sites."(89)

Far more serious than any shortage of low-level waste storage sites, in the opinion of many experts, are the problems associated with uranium mill and mine tailings. As discussed in Chapter VII, these tailings will continuously emit radon gas for thousands of years. Because of the large volumes of tailings generated--approximately 10 to 15 million tons of mill tailings per year and even larger quantities of less dangerous mine tailings--it is unclear whether these wastes will ever be stabilized in a manner sufficient to prevent them from being a health hazard. The Interagency Review Group report states:

> By virtue of their presence at the surface, the actinide elements in mill tailings may constitute a greater potential problem than those in deeply buried HLW and TRU wastes. Past control of mill sites has been poor, with little or no attention to the problem of proper disposal of tailings upon completion of milling operations. Tailings have been removed from disposal sites for use in construction of homes and commercial buildings.(90)

The General Accounting Office further contends that "even at sites where tailings have been stabilized through adequate ground cover and restricting water movement through the sites, none of the tailings can be considered adequately stabilized for long-term storage."(91) It concludes that radiation from the five worst tailings sites can be expected to cause as many as 1,000 cases of cancer in the next century.(92)

The Waste Management Program

The responsibility for development of a comprehensive nuclear waste management program has been divided among several government agencies, each of which is responsible for particular aspects of the program. In general, the Environmental Protection Agency is responsible for the promulgation of environmental protection criteria for all types of radioactive waste; the NRC will adopt procedures and technical requirements for the licensing of geologic repositories and interim storage facilities, update regulations on uranium mill tailings, and assist in the operation of disposal facilities; and the Department of Energy has prime responsibility for the development of waste management technology, selection of repository sites, and construction and management of federal waste repositories.(93)

The government's nuclear waste management program has been in flux for a number of years. Rep. Morris K. Udall (D-Ariz.), chairman of the House Interior Committee, has observed that the dates for operation of a full-scale commercial waste respository have been postponed from 1970 to 1985 to the 1990s "like a receding mirage in the Arizona desert." As recently as March 1978, the government said it would demonstrate by 1983 that spent nuclear fuel could be stored safely and by 1988 that high-level radioactive wastes could be permanently buried without harm to the environment.(94) In order to meet that timetable, the Department of Energy was placing most of its hopes on the Waste Isolation Pilot Plant (WIPP), a controversial plan to demonstrate the storage of spent nuclear fuel and defense wastes in salt beds near Carlsbad, N.M. But heated opposition from local citizens, some scientists, state officials and Congress first forced DOE to drop the idea of demonstrating spent fuel storage at the site.(95) Then, in February 1980, the Carter administration announced that it was deferring the WIPP project in favor of accelerated research on a broad variety of possible host rocks and repository sites.(96) The move was broadly interpreted as a blow to the nuclear power industry because it effectively postponed the opening of any permanent disposal site until at least the mid-1990s. "We should be ready to select the site for the first full-scale repository by about 1985 and have it operational by the mid-1990s," President Carter stated. "This effort must proceed regardless of future developments within the nuclear industry--its future size and resolution of specific fuel cycle and reactor design issues," he said.(97) Eleven possible locations for a final repository are under consideration by the Energy Department, and more will be examined. The sites now being studied include underground salt domes in Mississippi, Louisiana and Texas; bedded salt formations in Texas, New Mexico and Utah; a compacted volcanic ash formation in Nevada; and a deep basalt formation in Washington.

The Carter administration's deferral of the WIPP project and decision to emphasize further research appear to have resulted from a major split among scientists on the question of which kind of underground formation is safest for permanent burial. The Energy Department and its predecessors have operated for the last 20 years on the assumption that the best way to dispose of waste would be to encapsulate it in glass and bury it in salt formations. There is no longer a consensus among scientists, however, that this is an acceptable disposal method. In fact, a number of scientists believe it might be one of the worst possible options. "Glass is soluble and it's leachable--it's what you would do if you wanted to maximize activity in the geologic environment," says William Luth, a geochemist at Stanford University.(98) "The mystique has built up that salt is dry and it's okay," adds David Stewart of the U.S. Geological Survey. "Salt is not dry and it's not okay. Dense brines are corrosive environments, more corrosive than anything nuclear engineers have ever coped with," he says.(99)

Regardless of the outcome of the scientific debate over alternative waste disposal methods, the issue of waste disposal will be the subject of a major political controversy in the years ahead. In addition to the problems raised by the siting of a permanent repository--which no state seems eager to accept--the recent postponement of the earliest date when a repository might be available ensures that the government will need to begin building at least one, but more likely several, away-from-reactor spent fuel storage facilities. In 1980, the Carter administration asked Congress for $300 million to begin building the first such facility.(100) Although Congress was unable to agree on a nuclear waste bill in 1980, these facilities are likely to be pushed by the Reagan administration because utilities will begin running out of spent fuel storage space within the next few years. The 1980 Republican Platform set the goal of implementing plans for regional away-from-reactor storage of spent fuel no later than 1984.

The building of new temporary storage facilities is likely to add fuel to the debate over nuclear waste disposal as critics have already begun to lambaste the government plan as a political and economic bailout for the nuclear industry. In the opinion of many observers, the nuclear waste issue could seriously jeopardize the public's acceptance of further nuclear power development unless the government can establish a consensus on its waste management policy. Robert Stobaugh and Daniel Yergin, co-editors of a major energy study by the Harvard Business School, sum up the situation as follows:

Unless government and industry leaders start to work now with nuclear critics, existing plants will begin to run out of spent-fuel storage within four years. The federal government will then face a very difficult choice: shutting down the plants or riding roughshod over the nuclear critics. And without a consensus on waste policy, including the certainty of a satisfactory method for ultimate disposal, there can be no end to the nuclear power stalemate.(101)

THE WASTES CONTROVERSY

Persons on all sides of the nuclear power question agree that the development of a safe, permanent waste disposal system is vital. The current method of storage--by utilities in ponds--is inadequate. But opponents and critics differ over the difficulty of implementing safe, permanent storage and over the question of what should be done with the wastes in the interim.

Views of Nuclear Opponents

Critics of nuclear power argue that until a technology for safe, permanent containment of radioactive wastes has been developed and tested, it is irresponsible to continue producing them. Their concern is heightened by two factors: the extremely long periods during which some wastes remain dangerous and must be safeguarded, and what they view as the unsatisfactory and careless record of the government in handling waste and planning for its disposal.

The most persistent concerns regarding nuclear wastes stem from the need to isolate these wastes for extraordinarily long periods of time. Many feel that a span of even 800 years transcends man's ability to predict events. Hannes Alfven says: "The problem is how to keep radioactive waste in storage until it decays after hundreds of thousands of years. The deposit must be absolutely reliable as the quantities of poison are tremendous. It is very difficult to satisfy these requirements for the simple reason that we have had no practical experience with such a long-term project."(102)

Others point out that virtually none of man's political or social institutions has remained stable and free of revolution for as long as 1,000 years. Alfven sees the need for a society "with unprecedented stability." The Center for Science in the Public Interest states that "no society in history has lasted an instant compared to the long times involved in the nuclear waste problem."(103) The Union of Concerned Scientists declares that "institutional arrangements do not exist and never have existed to guarantee the monitoring of or attendance upon storage facilities over a millennium."(104)

Does man have the right, these critics ask, to create a danger of potentially cosmic proportions which will, in effect, last forever?

Some feel strongly that the answer is no. The National Council of Churches has condemned the use of plutonium and has said that the problem of waste storage creates a "fundamental ethical question" of one generation's right to burden another with "an element of risk comparable to that of our vast store of nuclear arms."(105) The Center for Science in the Public Interest alleges that a policy of promoting nuclear power "follows the principle of eating, drinking and being merry for the earth has no tomorrow. It takes the chance of compromising the earth as the home for succeeding generations."(106)

Significantly, many nuclear critics are not so much concerned with the technological difficulties posed by the waste issue as with political and social concerns. "I think there is a high technical probability that wastes can be relatively safely and satisfactorily disposed of," comments Terry Lash of the National Resources Defense Council. But, he adds, "I am not sure that technically competent people will be working on it or that our political processes will let us implement it before the end of the century."(107) James M. Cubie, a nuclear expert on the staff of Sen. Edward M. Kennedy (D-Mass.), agrees. "The question is not whether a feasible site may exist someplace. It may exist," writes Cubie. "The question is whether we will be prescient enough to find it, and intelligent enough to implement the disposal in that situation, and further, put into operation a method that will protect the waste for hundreds of thousands of years to come."(108)

Critics are unanimous in saying that past efforts to deal with the problem of waste disposal have been inadequate. Moreover, they say, by attempting to find a speedy solution to the problem on several occasions, the Energy Department and its predecessors have alienated many states and the public. They cite the AEC's aborted effort to store wastes in salt mines near Lyons, Kan., as an example of the government's eagerness to find a solution outdistancing its technical capacity. In 1970, after years of work on the Lyons project, the AEC announced that it was going to open a demonstration repository at that site. Scientific and political opposition forced a delay in the implementation of the project until it could be certified as safe by an independent panel of experts. Before this certification process could proceed, however, the AEC's efforts lost public acceptability when the American Salt Mining Co. informed the AEC that it was carrying on hydraulic mining operations less than two miles from the proposed repository and William Hambleton, director of the Kansas Geological Survey, revealed that on one occasion the company had "lost" about 180,000 gallons of water down a mine.(109) If wastes had been deposited in the salt mine before these problems had been discovered, critics say, they might have quickly reached the environment and recovery or removal of them might have been impossible.

Critics applaud the Carter administration's recent decision to defer the WIPP project and concentrate government resources on a broader research and siting effort. But many still do not trust the Energy Department, which has prime responsibility for implementing waste policy. "The jury's still out," says Thomas Cochran of the

Natural Resources Defense Council. "The policies adopted are basically sound ones, but they'll depend on implementation by the Energy Department, which was pushing for a faster timetable."(110)

Views of Nuclear Proponents

Supporters of nuclear power development generally maintain that, when viewed in context, disposal of high-level wastes does not pose a danger substantially different from any that man already lives with. They cite, as examples, the many hazardous materials (such as poisonous gases) already stored in the earth that are subject to natural disasters of one kind or another and the many man-made structures, such as large dams, that might one day suffer damage causing untold tragedy. Society has accepted such hazards in the belief that the benefits derived far outweigh the risks, they say. So it is with nuclear power; what society gains more than compensates for the risks. Weinberg summed up this attitude when, after describing the risks of nuclear power, he concluded: "What we offer in return, an all but infinite source of relatively cheap and clean energy, seems to me well worth the price."(111)

Those in favor of nuclear power also contend that critics have greatly exaggerated the potential risks of nuclear waste disposal. They say that a 1,000-megawatt power plant using coal produces 50,000 tons of bottom ash and 250,000 tons of fly ash per year; a similar plant using oil produces 1,400 tons of ash; and an equivalent-size nuclear reactor generates 1.4 to 2.3 tons of solidified high-level wastes. Supporters of nuclear power are confident that finding a method for permanent disposal of such a relatively small quantity of material presents no major technological problems. The major problem, they say, is political. "It is our belief that effective solutions to the entire question are available and would have already been demonstrated were it not for the political-institutional decision delays that have prevented the development work from proceeding...," writes Chauncey Starr, president of the Electric Power Research Institute.(112) "It is our opinion that technological options exist for both interim storage and permanent or retrievable permanent disposal of nuclear wastes," states T.J. Feehan, president of Brown & Root Inc., an engineering company that is involved in a number of nuclear projects. "We believe that these options have been studied, tested and implemented to the point that practicality has been clearly established, that these options will assure little if any risk from nuclear waste to the public now and in the future, that these options can be implemented on whatever schedule is required to meet the needs of a vigorous development of nuclear power plants....."(113)

Some nuclear supporters express concern about the motives of nuclear critics who call for a slow, cautious approach to the waste problem. "The anti-nuclear forces will continually present arguments in the guise of public concern to delay the effective resolution of the issues because it is to their advantage not to resolve the waste management issue," says W. Donham Crawford, former president of the Edison Electric Institute.(114) "Action, not more study, is required," he says.

Nuclear proponents are generally critical of the Carter administration's decision to defer the WIPP project and postpone the opening of a permanent respository. Tom Kuhn of the American Nuclear Energy Council, for instance, calls the deferral of WIPP "just another nondecision."(115) But proponents hold out some hope that the recent delays will be the last, and that the government is now on track toward a permanent solution to the issue. "I would vote for a faster program," GE's Bertram Wolfe recently told *Business Week*. "But I would go for anything that looked like an honest-to-God effort to get a repository going in any meaningful time frame."(116)

NOTES

(1) Amory B. Lovins, "Thorium Cycles and Proliferation," *The Bulletin of the Atomic Scientists*, February 1979, p. 21.

(2) William Ramsay, *Unpaid Costs of Electrical Energy* (Baltimore, Johns Hopkins University Press for Resources for the Future, 1979), p. 85.

(3) Plutonium is currently the source of greatest concern both because of its extreme toxicity and because it is an excellent bomb-making material. Other materials used in the nuclear fuel cycle, including uranium-235 and uranium-233, are also excellent for bomb-making purposes but isolation of them would require isotopic enrichment techniques of some sophistication. Isolation of plutonium from spent fuel, on the other hand, requires only chemical separation techniques and is currently considered the easiest and most likely path toward a weapons capability. Advances in uranium enrichment technology, however, could change this situation.

(4) J. Gustave Speth, Arthur R. Tamplin, and Thomas B. Cochran, "Plutonium Recycle: The Fateful Step," *The Bulletin of the Atomic Scientists*, November 1974, p. 15.

(5) Nuclear Regulatory Commission, "Final Generic Environmental Statement on the Use of Recycle Plutonium in Mixed Oxide Fuel in Light-Water Reactors," NUREG-0002, Vol. 2, August 1976, p. II-31; also, Theodore B. Taylor and Mason Willrich, *Nuclear Theft: Risks and Safeguards* (Cambridge, Mass., Ballinger Publishers, 1974), p. 64.

(6) Harold A. Feiveson, Frank von Hippel, and Robert H. Williams, "Fission Power: An Evolutionary Strategy," *Science*, Vol. 203, Jan. 26, 1979, p. 332.

(7) Taylor and Willrich, op. cit., pp. 60ff.

(8) Atomic Industrial Forum, "The Importance of Closing the Nuclear Fuel Cycle," Oct. 1, 1976.

(9) Ibid.

(10) "Article Says Reprocessing Benefits Exceed Risks 7-1," Atomic Industrial Forum INFO press release, January 1979, p. 7.

(11) W. Donham Crawford, Edison Electric Institute, letter to S.H. Smiley, AEC, Oct. 25, 1974.

(12) John G. Haehl Jr., letter to the Senate Subcommittee on Science, Technology and Space, Feb. 13, 1978 (reprinted in Hearings on Nuclear Waste Disposal before the Subcommittee on Science, Technology and Space, Senate Committee on Commerce, Science and Transportation, No. 95-136, part 2, p. 838).

(13) Pan Heuristics, *Moving Toward Life in a Nuclear Armed Crowd*, prepared for the Arms Control and Disarmament Agency, ACDA/PAB 263, April 22, 1976, p. 5.

(14) Ibid.

(15) Nuclear Regulatory Commission, op. cit., Vol. IV, p. XI-1.

(16) Jimmy Carter, "Statement on Nuclear Power Policy," April 7, 1977.

(17) Department of Energy, *Nuclear Proliferation and Civilian Nuclear Power*, Report of the Nonproliferation Alternative Systems Assessment Program, DOE/NE-0001, Vol. 1, December 1979, p. 93.

(18) Ibid.

(19) *Nucleonics Week*, Dec. 13, 1979, p. 10.

(20) Jeffrey A. Tannenbaum, "Big Plant to Recycle Nuclear Fuel is Hit by Delays, Cost Rises," *The Wall Street Journal*, Feb. 17, 1976, p. 1; Steven R. Weisman, "U.S. and New York Agree on Disposing of Nuclear Wastes," The New York *Times*, March 21, 1979, p. A1; also, Edmund Faltermayer, "Keeping the Peaceful Atom from Raising the Risk of War," *Fortune*, April 9, 1979, pp. 91, 92.

(21) *Nucleonics Week*, Jan. 24, 1980, pp. 15, 16; also, Atomic Industrial Forum, INFO news release, Feb. 6, 1980.

(22) Clarence D. Long, "Nuclear Proliferation: Can Congress Act in Time," contained in *Reader on Nuclear Proliferation*, prepared for the Senate Subcommittee on Energy, Nuclear Proliferation and Federal Services by the Congressional Research Service (Washington, Government Printing Office, 1978), p. 275; Energy Research and Development Administration, "U.S. Nuclear Export Activities," Vol. 1, April 1976, pp. 1-20; and Gloria C. Duffy and Gordon Adams, *Power Politics: The Nuclear Industry and Nuclear Exports* (New York, N.Y., Council on Economic Priorities, 1978), p. 57.

(23) David Burnham and David Binder, "U.S. Dilemma: World Energy Need Encourages Spread of Atomic Arms," The New York *Times*, Oct. 11, 1976, p. 1.

(24) Murray Marder, "Curb on Atom Plant for Spain Rejected," The Washington *Post*, June 22, 1976, p. 1.

(25) Gerald Ford, "Statement by the President on Nuclear Policy," Oct. 28, 1976.

(26) Joseph S. Nye Jr., "Balancing Nonproliferation and Energy Security," *Technology Review*, December/January 1979, p. 52.

(27) Gerald Ford, op. cit.

(28) These arguments are summarized from various sources, especially Marvin Miller, "The Nuclear Dilemma: Power Proliferation

and Development," *Technology Review*, May 1979, pp. 18-20.

(29) Chauncey Starr, "Nuclear Power and Weapons Proliferation--The Thin Link," in *Reader on Nuclear Proliferation*, op. cit., p. 418.

(30) Quoted in Marvin Miller, op. cit., p. 20.

(31) Pan Heuristics, op. cit.

(32) Amory B. Lovins, comments on *The Economic and Social Costs of Coal and Nuclear Electric Generation* (Washington, D.C., Stanford Research Institute for the National Science Foundation, 1976), p. 114.

(33) Atomic Energy Commission, "Special Safeguards Study" (Rosenblum Study), April 29, 1974.

(34) Ibid.

(35) Taylor and Willrich, op. cit., p. 20.

(36) Quoted in Edmund Faltermayer, op. cit., p. 91.

(37) Joseph S. Nye Jr., op. cit., p. 50.

(38) "U.S., Soviet Union, 13 Others Agree on Nuclear Export Restrictions," *Energy Users Report*, No. 232, Jan. 19, 1978, p. 21.

(39) Ernest McCrary, "Iraq's Oil Ploy to Gain Nuclear Know-how," *Business Week*, Dec. 3, 1979, p. 62.

(40) Telephone interview with IRRC, 1974; also see Brian Jenkins, *Hearings on Propositon 15*, California State Assembly, Vol. X, Nov. 19, 1975, p. 61.

(41) Taylor and Willrich, op. cit., p. 13.

(42) See John McPhee, Profiles: "Theodore B. Taylor," *The New Yorker*, Dec. 3, 10, 17, 1973; also Taylor and Willrich, op. cit., p. 25.

(43) Thomas O'Toole, "Uranium Theft, Extortion Plot Laid to Worker at GE Plant," The Washington *Post*, Feb. 2, 1979, p. A1.

(44) Taylor and Willrich, op. cit., pp. 107, 108.

(45) David M. Krieger, "Terrorists and Nuclear Technology," *The Bulletin of the Atomic Scientists*, June 1975.

(46) "Low Pay and Poor Morale Loosen Security," *Not Man Apart*, Vol. 10, No. 1, January 1980, p. 8.

(47) Brian Jenkins, "Will Terrorists Go Nuclear?" California Seminar on Arms and Foreign Policy, November 1975, p. 3.

(48) John R. Emshwiller, "Sabotage by Insiders: How Serious Is Threat to Atomic Facilities?" *The Wall Street Journal*, Sept. 3, 1980, p. 1.

(49) Pan Heuristics, op. cit., pp. 3, 4.

(50) Henry Smyth, Hearings before the House Committee on Foreign Affairs, July 9, 1974.

(51) Pan Heuristics, op. cit., p. 19.

(52) Milton R. Benjamin, "The Atomic Energy Agency: The Pusher Is the Policeman," The Washington *Post*, Dec. 3, 1978, p. A2.

(53) Mason Willrich, "A Workable International Nuclear Energy Regime," *The Washington Quarterly*, Vol. 2, No. 2, Spring 1979, p. 19.

(54) Benjamin, op. cit.

(55) Ibid.

(56) Quoted in Gloria C. Duffy and Gordon Adams, op. cit., p. 70.

(57) Atomic Energy Commission, "Special Safeguards Study," op. cit.

(58) Taylor and Willrich, op. cit.

(59) Tom Zito, "Report Faults Accounting of A-Materials," The Washington *Post*, July 28, 1976, p. A1.

(60) Quoted in Denis Hayes, *Nuclear Power: The Fifth Horseman* (Washington, D.C.; Worldwatch Institute, 1976), p. 52.

(61) Constance Holden, "NRC Shuts Down Submarine Fuel Plant," *Science*, Vol. 206, October 1979, p. 30.

(62) Zito, op. cit.

(63) Romano Salvatori, testimony before the Michigan House of Representatives, Oct. 24, 1974.

(64) Alvin Weinberg, "Social Institutions and Nuclear Energy," *Science*, July 7, 1972, p. 27; also, Alvin Weinberg, "The Nuclear Management Syndrome," *The Wharton Magazine*, Vol. 4, No. 1, Fall 1979, pp. 20-27.

(65) National Resources Defense Council, *The Plutonium Decision* (Washington, D.C., September 1974), p. 19.

(66) Nuclear Regulatory Commission, news release, Vol. 6, No. 3, Jan. 22, 1980, p. 1.

(67) Constance Holden, op. cit., p. 32.

(68) General Atomic Corp., "Safeguards," *Public Affairs*, 1974.

(69) Taylor and Willrich, op. cit.

(70) Atomic Industrial Forum, "The Importance of Closing the Nuclear Fuel Cycle," op. cit.

(71) Alvin M. Weinberg, "The Nuclear Management Syndrome," op. cit., p. 25.

(72) Natural Resources Defense Council, op. cit., p. 23.

(73) Bill Richards, "Nuclear Plant Security Poses Civil Liberties Dilemma," The Washington *Post*, Nov. 21, 1977, p. A2.

(74) Ibid.

(75) Russell W. Ayres, "Plutonium Policy: The Civil Liberties Fallout," *Harvard Civil Liberties Law Review*, 1975.

(76) Daniel Ford, Union of Concerned Scientists funding appeal letter, n.d.

(77) Department of Energy, *Report to the President by the Interagency Review Group on Nuclear Waste Management* (Washington, D.C., Department of Energy, 1979), p. 8.

(78) Mason Willrich, "Radioactive Waste Management and Regulation," report to ERDA, Sept. 1, 1976, pp. 2-12.

(79) Department of Energy (IRG report), op. cit., p. 11.

(80) Frank Pittman, testimony before the House Committee on Interior and Insular Affairs, April 29, 1975, p. 580.

(81) Williams Ramsay, op. cit., p. 62.

(82) Science Applications Inc., for the DOE, "Technical Support for GEIS: Radioactive Waste Isolation in Geologic Formations," Vol. 1, April 1978, p. 3-16.

(83) Willrich, "Radioactive Waste Management and Regulation," op. cit., pp. 2-16.

(84)   Department of Energy (IRG report), op. cit., p. 9.

(85)   Ibid., pp. D-16, D-17.

(86)   U.S. General Accounting Office, "Cleaning Up the Remains of Nuclear Facilities--A Multibillion Dollar Problem," EMD-77-46, June 16, 1977, p. 8.

(87)   Department of Energy (IRG report), op. cit., pp. D-12, D-14.

(88)   U.S. General Accounting Office, "Major Unresolved Issues Preventing a Timely Resolution to Radioactive Waste Disposal," EMD-78-94, July 1978, p. 8.

(89)   Department of Energy (IRG report), op. cit., p. 77.

(90)   Ibid., p. 81.

(91)   U.S. General Accounting Office, "Major Unresolved Issues . . . ," op. cit., p. 9.

(92)   Hearings before the Subcommittee on Energy Production and Supply of the Senate Committee on Energy and Natural Resources, *Uranium Mill Site Restoration Act and Residual Radioactive Materials Act*, 95-146, July 24, 1978, p. 38.

(93)   Department of Energy (IRG report), op. cit., pp. H-20, H-21.

(94)   Thomas O'Toole, "U.S. Sets Timetable for Storing Spent A-Fuel, Burying Wastes," The Washington *Post*, March 16, 1978, p. A6.

(95)   Peter Melnick, "Opposition to Nuclear Dump Grows," *In These Times*, April 11-17, 1979, p. 19; Molly Ivins, "'Nuclear Dump' Debate Heats Up in Carlsbad, N.M.," The New York *Times*, Jan. 22, 1978; and "DOE Officials Say WIPP, If Built, Would Be Unlicensed Defense Waste Site," *Inside D.O.E.*, May 25, 1979, p. 3.

(96)   "Carter Wants to Wait on Nuclear Waste," *Business Week*, Feb. 4, 1980, p. 36.

(97)   "Carter Outlines Costly Plan for Burying Nuclear Waste Permanently by Mid-'90s," *The Wall Street Journal*, Feb. 13, 1980, p. 4.

(98)   Thomas O'Toole, "Glass, Salt Challenged as Radioactive Waste Disposal Methods," The Washington *Post*, Dec. 24, 1978.

(99)   Ibid.

(100) Thomas O'Toole, "U.S. Official Tells Panel of Nuclear Waste Needs," The Washington *Post*, Feb. 14, 1980.

(101) Robert Stobaugh and Daniel Yergin, "After the Second Shock: Pragmatic Energy Strategies," *Foreign Affairs*, Spring 1979, p. 855.

(102) Hannes Alfven, speech before Ralph Nader's Critical Mass, Nov. 18, 1975.

(103) Center for Science in the Public Interest, "Nuclear Energy: The Morality of our National Policy," Washington, D.C., 1974.

(104) Union of Concerned Scientists, "The Nuclear Power Issue: An Overview," n.d.

(105) Philip M. Boffey, "Plutonium: Its Morality Questioned by the National Council of Churches," *Science*, April 23, 1976, p. 358; see also, *Energy and Ethics* (National Council of Churches, 1979).

(106) Center for Science in the Public Interest, op. cit.

(107) Edmund Faltermayer, "Burying Nuclear Trash Where It Will Stay Put," *Fortune*, March 26, 1979, p. 99.

(108) James M. Cubie, letter to the Senate Subcommittee on Science Technology and Space, Jan. 23, 1978 (reprinted in *Hearings*, op. cit., p. 771).

(109) Katherine Seelman and David Gray, *Energy and the New Poverty* (New York, National Council of Churches, 1979) pp. 13-17; also John Abbotts, "Radioactive Waste: A Technical Solution?" *The Bulletin of the Atomic Scientists*, October 1979, p. 14.

(110) "Carter Outlines Costly Plan for Burying Nuclear Wastes Permanently by Mid-'90s," op. cit.

(111) Weinberg, "Social Institutions and Nuclear Energy," op. cit.

(112) Chauncey Starr, letter to the Senate Subcommittee on Science, Technology and Space, Jan. 25, 1979 (reprinted in *Hearings*, op. cit., p. 773).

(113) T.J. Feehan, letter to the Senate Subcommittee on Science, Technology and Space, Jan. 27, 1978 (reprinted in *Hearings*, op. cit., p. 804).

(114) W. Donham Crawford, letter to the Senate Subcommittee on Science, Technology and Space, Feb. 16, 1978 (reprinted in *Hearings*, op. cit., p. 851).

(115) Joanne Omang, "Carter's A-Waste Site Policy Takes Time, Benefits States," The Washington *Post*, Jan. 10, 1980.

(116) "Carter Wants to Wait on Nuclear Waste," op. cit.

Chapter IX

ANALYSIS AND CONCLUSIONS

In attempting to analyze the impact of moral, technical, economic and political questions on the future of nuclear power development, one is immediately struck by the enormous number of uncertainties involved. In many areas the facts are in dispute, in most areas the interpretation to be given to existing data is bitterly contested.

Persons interested in determining what the prospects for nuclear power development are, or whether continued development of nuclear power is socially responsible, face the task of attempting to determine the probability that certain events will (or will not) occur. They must also determine the implications of their vision of the future. On several issues, such as whether it is appropriate to generate long-lived nuclear wastes before a permanent solution to the problem of waste disposal is found, or whether it is more responsible to deplete scarce fossil fuel resources, the final decision may be influenced by moral principles. On others, such as how effectively nuclear power can compete with coal, a more objective appraisal is possible. On almost all of the issues that comprise the debate over nuclear power, however, the complexities involved dictate that one attempt to look beyond the simplistic rhetoric frequently used on both sides of the issue.

This final chapter assesses, to the extent possible, the significance of the issues, the data, and the arguments of the interested parties.

DEMAND FOR ENERGY

During the coming decades, one factor that will continue to exert a very strong influence over the development of nuclear power is the rate at which the demand for energy--and, in particular, for electricity--increases. For the near term at least, and probably through the 1980s, this influence is likely to be a strongly negative one. Over the last six years, the demand for electricity has grown at a rate considerably below industry and government projections. Many utilities have sizable reserves of excess generating capacity. Although some electric utilities, particularly those in several western states, will need additions to generating capacity in the near future, the industry as a whole had excess capacity of about 38 percent in 1979.(1) Moreover, this reserve margin could increase over the next several years.

Although a slowdown of growth in demand appears certain to lessen pressures to expand development of nuclear power in the near term--making it very unlikely that nuclear power will expand at anything close to past projections by government and industry--the prognosis for growth in electric power demand farther out in the future remains less predictable. Certain developments in either the international or the domestic scene could significantly alter the United States' current energy situation and policy-makers' perceptions of it. On the international front, continued instability in oil supplies from the Middle East could encourage increased reliance on domestic sources of energy--including nuclear power. Domestically, the return of truly vigorous economic growth to the U.S. economy or the widespread introduction of electric cars--if either were to occur --could significantly increase the demand for electric power. In addition, if actual energy shortages were to occur, the public's perception of the risks of further nuclear power development could change dramatically. On the other hand, it seems very likely that further measures will be taken by government and industry to stimulate increased energy efficiency. The cost of generating electricity is rising rapidly and will continue to rise over the next several years. The combination of past and future legislative efforts, increased public consciousness of the possibilities of energy conservation, and rising electricity prices will undoubtedly mitigate against any dramatic increases in the demand for electricity.

FINANCIAL CONDITION OF ELECTRIC UTILITIES

A second factor that could greatly affect future nuclear power development is the financial situation of the electric utility industry. Currently, the financial condition of the industry is so poor that many large utilities could not finance a new nuclear plant even if they desperately needed the new capacity and concluded that nuclear power was the best option for meeting their requirements. Of those few utilities that could afford to finance a new nuclear plant, most could do so only by selling stock below its book value--an action that dilutes the value of existing shareholders' stock. In addition to inhibiting future ordering, utilities' financial problems could lead to further cancellations of nuclear plants already on order.

Thus, the question of whether the current financial condition of the electric utility industry will persist appears to be of great importance to the future of nuclear power in the United States. Although the utility industry has undergone, and recovered from, periods of financial hardship in the past--usually during periods of high inflation--many utility analysts are now suggesting that the problems faced by the industry are structural rather than temporary. If these analysts are correct, and electric utilities continue to encounter financial difficulties, nuclear power will not be able to expand at anywhere near the rate that government and industry analysts are predicting regardless of how fast electricity demand grows. As a recent study by Mans Lonnroth and William Walker of the International Consultative Group on Nuclear Energy notes:

> Quite apart from the political problems that beset nuclear power in the USA, it therefore looks unlikely at this moment that the utility sector will be able to make substantial headway with nuclear expansion unless the federal government intervenes to give financial relief, whether by providing direct loans and guarantees, or by changing the system whereby rates are regulated.... Some have even gone as far as to recommend the restructuring of the U.S. utility industry into a limited number of large generating boards as a necessary condition for the continued expansion of nuclear power in that country.(2)

The poor financial condition of the electric utility industry in the United States illustrates the need to question many of the simplistic assumptions that tend to dominate the debate over nuclear power. Many nuclear proponents, for example, view rapidly rising world oil prices as a positive development for the nuclear power industry. Rising oil prices, they say, will make nuclear plants even more economic and will help the public recognize the need to build more nuclear plants. But this logic fails to take into account the effects of rapidly rising oil prices on the *ability* of utilities to build new generating capacity. Rising oil prices perpetuate inflation, drive up electricity prices--thereby encouraging conservation, and tend to worsen the financial condition of electric utilities. Thus, while such price rises may create a need for more nuclear plants, they also tend to ensure the continuation of an economic environment in which the construction of new nuclear power plants will not be feasible for most utilities.(3)

COMPETITION WITH ALTERNATIVE SOURCES

Another extremely important factor affecting the rate at which nuclear power will develop is how effectively new nuclear power plants can compete with alternative sources of electric power. Over the next decade, this competition will continue to be predominantly between nuclear and coal-fired power plants. By the 1990s, however, several other sources of electricity--probably including wind power, geothermal electricity and, perhaps most importantly, the cogeneration of power by industry--are likely to be competing effectively for any increases in electric power demand. All of these sources are already more economic in some parts of the country than new nuclear or coal-fired generating capacity.

The costs of both nuclear and coal fuel cycles are subject to numerous uncertainties. Analysis of the available data, however, indicates that three factors are likely to be critical to this equation: (1) the comparative capital costs of nuclear and coal-fired power plants; (2) the comparative capacity factors at which large nuclear and coal-fired plants will operate; and (3) the prices of uranium and coal.

The capital costs of nuclear and coal plants are likely to continue to rise in the future and will be substantially affected by regulatory decisions. Air quality standards and the cost of equipment to meet them will play an important role in the total capital costs of new coal plants. Experts estimate that stack-gas scrubbers, which will be required on all new conventional coal plants, will cost between $75 million and $150 million. Moreover, industry representatives say that scrubber systems may have to be rebuilt every seven to 10 years because of corrosion problems. Similarly, new government safety requirements resulting from the accident at Three Mile Island will increase capital costs at nuclear plants.

During the last decade, for various reasons, the capital costs of nuclear plants have significantly outpaced those of coal plants. A continuation of this trend during the 1980s would almost certainly make nuclear plants started today uneconomic before they could be completed. Currently, more than half the cost of a nuclear plant is the interest paid on funds borrowed during construction and on cost escalation during the construction phase. If the time now required between the initial application to build and the operation of a nuclear plant could be cut substantially, the capital costs of nuclear plants could be significantly reduced. But if licensing and construction delays continue to plague nuclear plants as they have in the past--and if inflation and interest rates remain high--the economic position of nuclear power probably will continue to erode relative to that of coal-fired power plants, even though capital costs at coal-fired plants will be increasing rapidly.

Fuel costs, too, may affect the relative positions of coal and nuclear plants--although for the moment at least they appear to be less critical than do rapidly rising capital costs. A rapid rise in the price of uranium or coal could affect the competitiveness of nuclear power. The competitiveness of coal plants will probably continue to suffer from escalating costs of equipment required to meet environmental and safety standards for coal mining and, more importantly, from rapidly rising railroad rates. But there will also be substantial new costs associated with the nuclear fuel cycle, including costs associated with the permanent disposal of nuclear wastes and the decommissioning of old reactors.

Overall, the total average costs of nuclear and coal-fired electric power remain quite close--with nuclear cheaper in some sections of the country and coal cheaper in others. But a number of factors--the most important of which appear to be skyrocketing capital costs and the nation's general inflationary environment--are adversely affecting the competitive position of new nuclear plants relative to coal plants. Nuclear power is being priced out of the U.S. market. For big government-owned utility systems like the Tennessee Valley Authority, nuclear power development may remain a viable option. But unless dramatic changes occur in some of the factors underlying present cost trends, it is unlikely that nuclear power will capture anything near the share of the electricity market that government and industry planners have predicted it will. Moreover, new nuclear and coal-fired plants are *both* likely to face greatly increased competition from industrial cogeneration arrangements, alternative sources of electric power supply, and other forms of energy.

It is important to note that these conclusions--which some will regard as overly pessimistic--are directed toward *additions* to existing generating capacity, not toward the existing plants themselves. Nuclear critics tend to note the fact that alternative sources of electricity supply are becoming economic at the margin and leap to the conclusion that these sources could replace existing nuclear plants. In reality, the widespread introduction and use of many clean, renewable energy technologies--such as solar hot water heaters and pumped storage hydroelectric facilities--appear most compatible with the cheap off-peak power available from existing nuclear plants. Ironically, closing those plants would probably delay the time when many renewable technologies could compete economically.

DECISION-MAKING ISSUES

The controversy over nuclear power development embraces institutional as well as substantive issues. Three basic conclusions can be drawn about the roles that have been played by utilities, manufacturers, the Joint Committee on Atomic Energy, the Congress, the AEC, the NRC and the Department of Energy:

First, the people involved have tended to operate on the basis of good intentions and their past experiences. There is very little evidence of bad faith.

Second, impelled by a desire to accomplish their objectives, the supporters of nuclear power have tended to disregard opportunities to reexamine the implications of the nuclear power program and have devoted inadequate attention to the unique problems involved in, and alternatives to, nuclear power development.

Third, major institutional changes are occurring, particularly on the part of government authorities, which are likely to lead to marked shifts in the roles being played by various institutions.

Private Sector

Within the private sector, the electric utilities will continue to play a critical role in the development of nuclear power because of their role in deciding whether or not to build nuclear plants. For some utilities, the decision to build a nuclear plant has proven to be a wise investment. For others--including many of the utilities that now have one or more nuclear plants under construction--the decision to go nuclear has meant nothing but headaches. For a few, including the owners of the Three Mile Island plants, the decision has proven to be a financial disaster. For all of them, however, it has brought fundamental changes in the way they must do business and in the magnitude of their responsibilities. As described by James E. Connor, a former AEC planning officer:

> The move into the nuclear age has perhaps had its greatest institutional impact on the nation's utilities. For decades, the utilities have operated as rather simple, straightforward business enterprises, ordering equipment and technical services from other firms wholly responsible for their products. Seldom was any technical capability retained by the utility itself. If a piece of equipment did not perform satisfactorily and corrective action was not taken expeditiously, the vendor could be taken to court. Utilities expected delivery of reliable, bug-free equipment and passed the safely predictable costs on to their customers. The utilities could operate in this fashion because there were few uncertainties about the costs or reliability of coal- or oil-fired plants.(4)

It has been charged, with some validity, that the utilities' commitment to nuclear power--particularly in its extensiveness--was premature. Many utilities made an enormous financial commitment to nuclear power on the basis of relatively scanty performance data. Ironically, however, it is quite likely that those utilities that managed to build nuclear plants early in the game, when capital costs (even in real terms) were much lower than they are today, will reap the greatest benefits from the use of nuclear power. Utilities with plants currently under construction or commitments to build future plants stand to be hurt the worst.

Since 1973, a number of events--the Arab oil embargo, the recession, rising energy prices, lower demand, and the accident at the Three Mile Island plant--have greatly slowed utilities' plans to build nuclear plants. Utilities with nuclear plants in advanced phases of construction are fighting to complete work on them and have them licensed and brought into their rate bases. But utilities that have ordered nuclear plants but not started construction on them are canceling them outright or deferring work on them in order to monitor future economic and regulatory developments. Finally, no utility appears willing to order a new nuclear plant in the existing political, economic and regulatory environment.

This self-imposed moratorium on nuclear plant orders has allowed many utilities to develop and study nuclear plant performance data more extensively than they have in the past. It has also allowed them to consider the growing uncertainties--rising capital costs, the Carter administration's decision to defer recycling, new safety and environmental requirements, and waste disposal problems--that are likely to affect nuclear power in the future. As a result, utilities will not be as dependent upon manufacturers' recommendations in the future as they were in the past, and any renewed commitment to a second generation of nuclear plants is likely to be more qualified.

As concerns the manufacturers, it appears that they have been and will continue to be relatively hard-nosed in their dealings with utilities and that their behavior is based on legitimate business considerations. All the major manufacturers lost considerable sums of money building early nuclear plants. They have since moved to develop relationships with utilities and parts suppliers where there is a shared responsibility for the reliability of nuclear plants. This development indicates a maturing of the nuclear industry. It also shows a recognition that nuclear plants may have problems and that manufacturers' control over nuclear plant reliability is not as complete as they once had indicated.

It is true, too, that industry representations about the economic advantages, safety, and reliability of nuclear power often have been unduly optimistic. In part, this may have stemmed from an initial desire by the manufacturers to overcome the public's fears of nuclear energy. The public image of nuclear power was negative; atomic energy meant weapons. But the industry appears to have overcompensated for its fears about the public by making claims for the technology that could not be delivered. The industry became tied to descriptions of superhuman perfection, flawless systems, 80 percent capacity factors, perfect safety, and electricity "too cheap to meter" that range from unrealistic to impossible. In the words of one state energy commissioner, the industry has taken "such an uncompromising position of advocacy for nuclear power that they've undermined their best arguments by overstating the attractiveness of the fuel form and refusing to concede any of the liabilities." This has given critics endless opportunities to point out the discrepancies between the industry's claims for nuclear power and its actual performance. A continual need within the industry to explain these problems has led the industry to become defensive, in some cases where there is little need for it. The defensiveness, in turn, has engendered public mistrust.

Another factor affecting the flow of information from both utilities and manufacturers has been the technical nature of nuclear power. Industry has had some difficulty in deciding which audience to address. Much of the industry's material is directed at others in the industry. Most of the remainder has been designed to explain nuclear technology in very simple terms to the layman. Very little has been directed at dealing seriously with those questions raised in good faith by critics.

To some extent, until 1975, industry refused to take the concerns of the critics seriously; it seems to have been more worried about what the concerns might do to the industry than about the substance of the concerns themselves. This led some persons in industry to write off critics as obstructionists, to speak of nuclear blackmail, and to concentrate more on personalities than on issues. Others, however, acknowledged the critics' questions but considered them answered. "This is a responsible and well-researched industry," one industry representative said. "We have spent a great deal of time thinking about these issues and have resolved most of them to our satisfaction. The critics are rediscovering the wheel."

Developments in recent years have brought some change to the level of discussion between nuclear proponents and their critics. The embracing of the anti-nuclear position by some influential members of Congress and the accident at Three Mile Island and its aftermath appear to have had a sobering effect on many persons within the industry. Some continue to question the qualifications of persons opposed to nuclear development and argue that their concerns have already been resolved. But others have recognized the depth and extent of public concern over the issues raised by nuclear power development and have begun to respond to these concerns in greater depth than they had earlier. Among critics, there has been a growing realization of the need to suggest viable alternatives to nuclear power if its development is to be slowed or halted and a growing recognition of the problems inherent in one major alternative to nuclear power --increased use of coal.

Still, in spite of the changes, the debate over nuclear power development grows more polarized by the day. The polarization, it seems fair to say, is as much the fault of the critics of the industry as it is of the industry itself. Many of the industry's reactions, for instance, have been stimulated by the nature of critics' presentations. And while some critics have been careful and judicious in their pronouncements, others have relied on rhetoric, outdated studies, and discredited data. But regardless of the reasons behind the increasing polarization of the nuclear power debate--or the "Vietnamization" of nuclear power as one prominent nuclear supporter has characterized the situation--it seems clear that its effect will be to slow further the rate at which nuclear power develops.

Public Sector

The institutional changes that have occurred in the public sector in recent years appear to be even more dramatic than those that have taken place in the private sector. Among the most important of these changes are: the emergence of nuclear power as a major issue in the national political forum, the greatly increased intervention of state and local authorities into the nuclear decision-making process, changes within Congress that have facilitated discussion about and questioning of the implications of nuclear power, and changes within the NRC and other federal agencies involved in the regulation of the nuclear power program.

Until the mid-1970s, most government bodies with jurisdiction over nuclear matters operated in a manner that lent credence to the arguments of critics. The Joint Committee on Atomic Energy and the AEC, for instance, provided little opportunity for a discussion of the implications of nuclear development and were inclined to ignore skeptics and get on with the job of development. The same was true of most state public service commissions. In addition, because of a lack of expertise in this area, persons in Congress and the Executive Branch tended to follow the advice of the regulators rather than asking questions or examining the questions that critics were raising.

Changes over the last decade, however, have fundamentally altered both the function and the effect of government involvement in the oversight and regulation of the nuclear industry. The joint committee has been abolished, its responsibilities taken over by a number of congressional committees that are more skeptical about the merits of nuclear power. The AEC has been superseded by the NRC--an agency which, despite continued strong support for nuclear power among much of its staff, appears increasingly willing to make decisions that have an adverse impact on the economic viability and political acceptability of nuclear power. Many state energy agencies and public service commissions are imposing restrictions on nuclear development citing unresolved economic, technical and political issues.

Overall, these changes do not mean that the public sector is actively opposing continued nuclear power development. Rather, they suggest that there is no longer a consensus among government institutions concerning further nuclear development. Various government agencies and institutions are now taking different positions on the issues raised by the use of nuclear power. On many issues, government institutions are struggling against one another for public policy dominance. NRC chairman John F. Ahearne recently described the disarray among government institutions as follows:

> U.S. policy development is fragmented. In the Congress, some people are definitely pro-nuclear, and want to accelerate the licensing process .... Some people are very strongly against proliferation of nuclear weapons, believe proliferation risks are great, and that the risk of proliferation is perhaps the most hazardous risk facing the world .... And others in Congress are anti-nuclear. In the Executive Branch, the Council on Environmental Quality is trying to move the world away from nuclear power, while the Department of Energy is trying to market enrichment services around the world and, under congressional pressure, is providing about one half billion dollars per year for breeder reactor development. The Arms Control and Disarmament Agency argues heatedly against the sale of some items of technology while the Commerce Department, albeit inadvertently, allows the export of inverters to assist

Pakistan in its nuclear weapons program. The State Department focuses primarily on today's problems--they will worry about tomorrow when it comes, if it does. And the NRC is a multi-schizophrenic organization.(5)

Although many public sector institutions seem less tied to a specific position on the nuclear power debate than their private sector counterparts, the prognosis for an early end to the government stalemate on nuclear power is not good. The election of the Reagan administration in 1980, together with Republican control of the Senate, is certain to lead to increased support for nuclear power development from the federal government. The Reagan administration is expected to push for accelerated construction and licensing of nuclear power plants, increased funding for nuclear research and development projects and the breeder reactor, and new policies on reprocessing and other issues relating to international nonproliferation efforts. But whether the Reagan administration will be able to translate its ideas about nuclear power into legislation, and whether such legislation would be sufficient to overcome the many obstacles to continued nuclear power development, remains to be seen. The issues involved do not seem especially amenable to compromise. Moreover, the decentralized nature of the political system in the United States leaves many of the federal government's decisions concerning nuclear power subject to approval by state and local authorities.

SAFETY CONCERNS

The debate over the safety of nuclear power focuses primarily on concerns about dangers associated with nuclear power plants and the nuclear fuel cycle. The major issue as posed by opponents of nuclear power is whether the electric utilities, with the support of industry and government, should make a commitment to a form of technology that may pose unprecedented threats not only to the present generation but also to future generations. The threats arise from the highly radioactive character of the materials in the nuclear fuel cycle, which remain hazardous for extremely long periods.

The commitment to nuclear energy has been described by Alvin Weinberg, director of the Institute for Energy Analysis, as a "Faustian bargain": "On the one hand, we offer--in the catalytic nuclear burner --an inexhaustible source of energy .... But the price we demand of society for this magical energy source is both a vigilance and a longevity of our social institutions that we are quite unaccustomed to." Weinberg said that the issues to be resolved are "transcientific," to be "adjudicated by a legal or political process rather than by scientific exchange."(6) He concluded that the benefits of developing nuclear power outweighed the risks. Others, however, are more concerned with what they see as the irreversible consequences of nuclear power development and urge that it be halted.

Nuclear Plant Safety

The dispute over the safety of nuclear power plants was fundamentally affected by the accident in 1979 at the Three Mile Island plant in Pennsylvania. Before that accident, the prevailing view within the industry and the NRC was that a serious reactor accident could not happen. Critics' complaints about safety problems at nuclear plants were often brushed aside, and the burden of proof seemed to lie with those who claimed that nuclear plants were not safe. Today, the NRC is busy writing new safety regulations, the industry is setting up several new organizations to monitor utilities' safety programs, and the burden of proof--in the minds of the regulators, the Congress and the public--seems to have passed from those who claim that nuclear plants are not safe to those who claim that they are safe.

Perhaps the most important conclusion resulting from the accident and the various investigations into it is that no one really knows the probability of serious nuclear plant accidents. Even before the accident, the NRC had withdrawn its support from the Rasmussen report--a controversial government safety study that concluded that the probability of a serious nuclear plant accident was exceedingly remote. But the NRC's primary objections to the Rasmussen study were based on inaccuracies in the calculations and statistics used in that study, not on the methodology it used. The accident at Three Mile Island, in the opinion of many safety experts, has brought into question even the most basic assumptions that have been made in past safety studies. Individually, each of the events that made up the accident at Three Mile Island had happened many times at other nuclear plants. But the specific chain of events that resulted in core damage to the Three Mile Island plant had never been analyzed by industry or government safety experts. The implications of that fact are that the safety experts know less about the probabilities of nuclear accidents than they once thought. "I have always been very confident about nuclear power," noted one NRC safety official. "But this accident has been a real shock because it has shown there are an awful lot of things we just don't know about reactors."

In addition to increased uncertainty about the probability of serious nuclear plant accidents, there appears to be a growing acknowledgement among scientists that we know less about the harmful effects of low-level radiation than was previously thought. Many scientists believe that past assurances that low-level radiation does not represent a serious health threat are valid. Bernard Cohen, for instance, professor of physics at the University of Pittsburgh, says that "if all our power were nuclear, and if you considered the whole nuclear fuel cycle--making the fuel, using it, and reprocessing it--then the total effect of all such radiation would be equal to the risk of smoking one cigarette every 20 years, or of an overweight person's adding 1/100th of an ounce of his weight."(7) But a growing number of scientists, including some prominent experts in the field, challenge this assumption and contend that past government studies have systematically understated the adverse health effects associated with the nuclear fuel cycle. "The risk of nuclear power is not worth the economic benefits," states Herbert Abrams, professor of radiology at the Harvard Medical School.(8)

In spite of increased uncertainty about the overall safety of nuclear plants, it is by no means clear that nuclear power involves health and safety risks that are greater than those associated with coal-fired power plants. Although there are many uncertainties involved in comparing the risks of alternative energy systems, there is increasing evidence that the routine health effects associated with the coal fuel cycle are significantly greater than those associated with the nuclear fuel cycle. Nuclear power, on the other hand, appears more likely to be associated with catastrophic or irreversible consequences, especially in the near term. Finally, it is likely that the adverse health impacts of many of the alternatives to nuclear or coal-fired power--including conservation and some renewable energy technologies--would be smaller than those of either nuclear or coal technologies.

Safeguards and Proliferation

Many knowledgeable observers contend that nuclear power's single greatest drawback is its connection, however tenuous, to the worldwide proliferation of nuclear weapons. On questions involving the safeguarding of nuclear materials and weapons proliferation, however, many of the decisions required relate more to human and national behavior than to technology. Because of the difficulties posed by the prediction of human behavior, the decision-maker is again confronted with the problem of uncertainty. Agreement now exists among the major nuclear exporting countries that the risks of proliferation are real and that there is a need to develop institutional mechanisms to safeguard plutonium and other special nuclear materials. But this consensus breaks down when it comes to assessing how great the risks are when compared with the alternatives and what policies should be implemented to guard against them.

The risk that appears the greatest is the prospect that other countries will reprocess reactor wastes to acquire plutonium for construction of nuclear weapons. India has demonstrated that diversion of wastes is possible, although the plutonium for India's bomb came from an experimental, not a power, reactor. The International Atomic Energy Agency cannot prevent diversion; it has authority only to keep track of special nuclear materials, and some observers question how effectively it does the job. Moreover, it is now generally agreed, among experts on both sides of the nuclear power debate, that there is no technical means by which nuclear power can be completely divorced from the ability to make weapons. The recent report by the International Nuclear Fuel Cycle Evaluation Conference(INFCE), for instance, concluded that as many as 1,000 nuclear plants may be in operation around the world by the year 2000 and that there is no technical means of preventing this from increasing the risk of nuclear weapons proliferation. Thus, it seems probable that the international development of nuclear power will facilitate proliferation of nuclear weapons--a trend that is inconsistent with current U.S. government policy.

The United States has come to recognize this likelihood and for the last several years has been exploring methods of limiting it. Unilaterally, the United States decided in 1977 not to export either reprocessing or enrichment technology. Later, most other major exporters of nuclear technology agreed to reexamine their own export policies. Under pressure from the United States, France withdrew from offers to supply South Korea, Pakistan and Iran with reprocessing facilities. It remains unclear, however, exactly what effect a halt in the export of sophisticated nuclear technologies will have on countries interested in pushing ahead with nuclear development. In the short run, most countries will no doubt rely on enriched fuel supplied by the exporting countries. But in the long run, some countries are likely to attempt to develop their own reprocessing and enrichment capabilities.

Although it is clear that the U.S. government still carries a great deal of influence when it comes to world nuclear affairs, the INFCE report also shows that most of the world does not agree with the U.S. government's current policy of attempting to deny sensitive nuclear materials from developing countries that do not yet have a nuclear weapons capability. (The INFCE report basically endorsed the concept of breeder reactors and plutonium reprocessing, acknowledging that they would lead to a rapid increase in the worldwide availability of weapons-usable plutonium.) The United States, therefore, will continue to be faced with a decision about whether to continue to embargo the export of sensitive nuclear facilities and technology in the hope that other countries will eventually adopt a similar position, or give up on the idea that it is possible to control the spread of sensitive nuclear technology. This decision could have important implications for the international energy economy.

The prospect that terrorist groups--foreign or domestic--will obtain plutonium and construct nuclear weapons seems a lesser threat than that posed by foreign governments, although it is by no means nonexistent. One line of defense would be to require more stringent protection measures for nuclear facilities and materials. A second--which so far no country has endorsed--would be to abandon plans for recycling plutonium and for development of breeder reactors.

The principal argument in support of breeder reactors and recycling is that supplies of uranium are limited. While concern about the adequacy of uranium supplies remains strong--especially in nations that do not have large uranium reserves--recent setbacks in the domestic and world nuclear power industry appear to have lessened the chances of a near-term uranium shortage. In addition, many observers suggest that the uranium supply situation is not anywhere near as pessimistic as some persons contend it is.

In the United States, the prospects for early development of the breeder appear to be diminishing as a consequence of both economic and political concerns. A number of other countries, however, particularly France and the Soviet Union, are pushing ahead with attempts to build commercial breeder reactors. The economics of these programs may well turn out to be a major factor in world energy and nonproliferation policies. If breeders turn out to be an economical source of electric power supply, as the INFCE report contends they will be, the United States could face both increased economic competition and a defeat of its nonproliferation objectives. If the economics of the breeder turn out to be an absolute disaster, on the other hand, as Henry Rowen of Stanford University, Albert Wohlstetter of the University of Chicago, and Thomas Cochran of the Natural Resource Defense Council have suggested, France may find itself, in the words of a *Business Week* editorial, with "a monopoly on a dangerous and uneconomic energy strategy."(9)

Waste Disposal Issues

In many ways, the questions raised about the disposal of nuclear power plant wastes parallel those raised about safeguards. The greatest uncertainty lies in predicting human behavior over an extended period of time. The technical problems posed by the permanent disposal of radioactive wastes appear--at least in principle--to be solvable. But the technical problems have not yet been solved in spite of nearly two decades of work on the issue by the federal government. The government's latest estimates suggest that the United States will not have a permanent repository in operation until at least the mid-1990s. The inability of the federal government to provide for safe, permanent storage of lethal reactor wastes, in turn, will continue to create enormous political problems for the domestic nuclear power industry. A number of states have already declared moratoriums on future reactor construction until the waste issue has been solved. More are likely to do so in the future. In addition, no state seems eager to become a dumping ground for the rest of the nation's nuclear wastes.

CONCLUSIONS

Economic, political and technological uncertainties continue to plague the nuclear power industry. A renewed commitment to a second generation of light-water reactors is not likely to come soon, and in the absence of dramatic changes in the current political, economic and regulatory environment, it may never come at all. Nuclear plant cancellations are likely to continue over the next several years as utility companies confront lowered demand forecasts, financial difficulties and stricter nuclear safety regulations. Re-cycling of plutonium may be postponed indefinitely, or at least until an economic justification for it becomes apparent. Without reprocessing, the breeder reactor program will continue to face great scepticism and commercial use of breeders in the United States is likely to be dependent upon their economic success abroad.

Assessments of nuclear power's role in meeting future energy demand have fallen dramatically in the last several years and further downward revisions are likely. What was viewed several years ago as a primary energy source is viewed increasingly as an energy source of last resort. Increasingly, energy planners, politicians, investors and consumers are emphasizing energy conservation before energy growth, coal and renewables before nuclear. The development of nuclear power will be limited to that which is necessary, and vast efforts are underway to limit that necessity.

NOTES

(1) Alden Meyer, "Peak Growth Collapses," *The Power Line* (Environmental Action Foundation), Vol. 5, No. 5, December 1979, p. 7.

(2) Mans Lonnroth and William Walker, "The Viability of the Civil Nuclear Industry," working paper for the International Consultative Group on Nuclear Energy (New York, The Rockefeller Foundation, 1979), p. 34.

(3) For further discussion on this point, see Ibid., p. 38.

(4) James E. Connor, "Prospects for Nuclear Power," reprinted from "The National Energy Problem," *Proceedings of the Academy of Political Science*, Dec. 31, 1973, p. 67.

(5) John F. Ahearne, speech before the American Nuclear Society Executive Conference, New Orleans, La., Sept. 11, 1979. (Reprinted in NRC news release, Vol. 5, No. 33, Sept. 18, 1979.)

(6) Alvin Weinberg, "Social Institutions and Nuclear Energy," *Science*, July 7, 1972, p. 33.

(7) Richard Brookhiser and Bernard Cohen, "Understanding a Trillion-Dollar Question," *National Review*, Feb. 2, 1979, p. 147.

(8) Stacy Jolna, "Physicians Urge Halt in Reactors," The Washington *Post*, March 30, 1979.

(9) Don Ediger, "A Threat to the U.S. Lead in Atomic Power," *Business Week*, Aug. 27, 1979, p. 58.

ABOUT THE AUTHOR

Scott A. Fenn is research analyst and treasurer with the Investor Responsibility Research Center in Washington, D.C., where the major focus of his work has been on energy issues. He earned his BA degree in economics from Williams College in 1978. He has written a number of reports on nuclear power development, energy conservation, energy pricing and nuclear weapons production, and is the principal author of *Energy Conservation by Industry,* an IRRC study published in 1979.